A chance for every child?

A chance for every child?

ACCESS AND RESPONSE TO PRE-SCHOOL
PROVISION

SHEILA M. SHINMAN

TAVISTOCK PUBLICATIONS
LONDON AND NEW YORK

First published in 1981 by
Tavistock Publications Ltd
11 New Fetter Lane, London EC4P 4EE
Published in the USA by
Tavistock Publications
in association with Methuen, Inc.
733 Third Avenue, New York, NY 10017
© 1981 Sheila M. Shinman
Typeset in Great Britain by
Scarborough Typesetting Services

Printed in Great Britain at the
University Press, Cambridge

British Library Cataloguing in Publication Data
Shinman, Sheila M.
  A chance for every child?
  1. Education, Preschool — Great Britain
  I. Title
  372.21'0941   LB1140.25.G7   80-41101

ISBN 0-422-77420-0

To my parents

Contents

Acknowledgements

Many people have helped, either directly or indirectly, to make this book possible. In particular, I wish to thank Dr A. H. Halsey for his generous advice, guidance, and encouragement in its publication.

Professor W. D. Furneaux of Brunel University supervised the Ph.D thesis which provided the source material. In preparing a less technical version for the general reader, his wise and illuminating comment has been invaluable.

The 'Hillcroft' study began in collaboration with Mr Willem van der Eyken who was then Senior Research Fellow in the Department of Education at Brunel. I am greatly indebted to him for advice regarding early instrumentation and methodology and for considerable help and encouragement in the initial stages of drafting the material. This part of the investigation was supported by a grant from the Social Science Research Council.

I am grateful to the very many people who have given help and advice — as colleagues, as private persons, or as representatives of public bodies or voluntary agencies. Dr Wendy Keys, formerly in the Education Department, and the staff within the computer services at Brunel, gave a great deal of assistance. I would also like to record my particular thanks to the Directors of Social Services of the London Borough of Hillingdon and of the London Boroughs referred to as 'Kingswell' and 'Higham', and to the members of their staff for their active support and co-operation.

For permission to illustrate from their projects thanks are due to Mrs Anne Yarwood, formerly Area Voluntary Organizer for Bracknell, Berks; to the Rev. Barritt of the National Childrens' Home; to Dr John Bowlby and Mrs Nathan Isaacs of the Bunbury Trust; to Mrs Margaret Harrison of 'Homestart' and to Dr Nehama Nir-Janiv, Director of Early Childhood Education for Israel.

x *Acknowledgements*

All the studies owe much to the co-operation and goodwill shown by many members of the Pre-school Playgroups Association, both at national and branch levels. I should particularly like to mention the helpful comment and advice on the manuscript offered by Mrs Brenda Crowe, former National Adviser. Especial thanks are due also to members of the Inner London PPA, who were involved in the fieldwork, and to its officers and staff for their support.

To avoid breach of confidence, individuals cannot be named, but I am above all aware of my debt to the project workers and to all the mothers and minders who gave so generously and so unstintingly of their time.

Finally, I would like to thank Mrs Ann Kerrison and Mrs Christa Steele of Brunel who typed the manuscript so efficiently. Their good humour and forbearance were matched only by that of my family, without whose patience, tolerance, and forthright comment, this book would never have been finished.

Foreword

Two great issues of policy have been drawn together in the past decade — the repeatedly documented inequalities of childhood and the emerging, less well-documented change in the position and outlook for women. In combination these two issues are nowhere more sharply expressed than over the question of pre-schooling, or to put it more broadly, the up-bringing of children before the age of five. Against the background of demographic change towards smaller and less stable families, the increasing incorporation of women into paid employment outside the home, and the continuing concern for ensuring 'a fair start' for children whatever their circumstances, answers are urgently sought to the question of what public provision for pre-schooling ought to be made. The answers have to take into account not only the two great issues of class and sex but also the subtleties of the relation between 'supply', 'demand', and 'need' for such services.

Dr Shinman has set out in this book to discover the answers. What she has to say is soundly based both theoretically in a superbly commonsensical refusal to accept either simplified or fashionable doctrines as to the causes of things, and practically in a determination to translate academic study of mothers, minders, and children into proposals that are usable by professionals and volunteers in the pre-school field. Her three studies of 'Hillcroft', 'Kingswell', and 'Higham' are themselves a meticulously collected array of evidence (more generalizable than she so cautiously allows), but she has supplemented them by a careful review of all the available evidence from other recent studies.

Benevolent intentions towards childhood inequality have characteristically foundered on the inaccessibility of the 'child furthest down'. Those whose need is greatest are those also hardest to reach. This is where Dr Shinman begins. But the end is further advanced. She brings out clearly that the mother, her conditions, capacities, and attitudes, is the key to access. The analysis is sophisticated. She does not, for example, erroneously assume that today's trend is tomorrow's universal establishment, and so avoids the simplification that all mothers need a standard, if varied, pre-school provision, while they join the labour market. Indeed many, if not the majority of women with children under five, prefer to be at home with them. She does not, to take another example, crudely equate inaccessibility with class, nor assume that non-use or desire for pre-school facilities derives from a single cause. On the other hand she does (with her Index of Maternal Alienation) try to give to the professionals a method of predicting those who are most likely to run into difficulties with their young children and therefore be most likely to need help, as well as those least likely to seek it or to be able to use it effectively.

The outcome is a realistic picture of the relation between the public and the private aspects of child rearing, including that blend of the two which is childminding. Whatever view the reader may take of the social priorities of public policy, he or she may learn from Dr Shinman of the complexities of successful partnership between mothers and the educational services for young children and despite the complexities find a practical guide to economical and effective action.

A. H. HALSEY
Professor of Social and
Administrative Studies
University of Oxford
April 1980

PART ONE

THE PROBLEM AND
ITS BACKGROUND

CHAPTER ONE

Take-up of pre-school provision

It is an established fact, recognized amongst those providing welfare services such as clinics, dental, and family advice centres, that many families never make use of them. Moreover, as the Court Committee on Child Health Services (1976) made clear, many families who do not come forward to use facilities are those in most urgent need of care. This phenomenon has been identified as a major problem and a challenge for practitioners and administrators alike (Brimblecombe, 1975).

Whether a similar problem exists in the field of pre-school provision is a crucial question largely masked by the constant clamour for more facilities and, except in a few areas, the manifest lack of nursery and day-care places sufficient to meet demand. The resulting impression is that the only difficulty is one of expansion. Nevertheless, it is a commonly held view of teachers, playleaders, and social workers that a significant proportion of those who do not bring their children to nursery class or playgroup, even when places are available, are socially and educationally disadvantaged.

Government views are clearly set out in a policy document, the Education White Paper: Framework for Expansion (1972). A ten-year programme envisaged free nursery education for all three and four-year-old children whose parents wish for it. Demand was estimated, according to the Plowden Report (1967: para. 328) at a maximum of 90 per cent of four year olds and not more than 50 per cent of three-year-old children. Responsibility lies with local authorities to plan their provision so that nursery classes, schools, voluntary playgroups, day nurseries, and other forms of day care all play their part (para. 23 of the White Paper). It makes clear, however, that most of this provision is expected to be part-time and in the form of nursery classes in primary schools (paras. 24 and 26).

3

Intentions and ethos underlying these proposals are plain:

The value of nursery education in promoting the social
development of young children has long been acknowledged.
In addition, we know that, given sympathetic and skilled
supervision, children may also make great educational progress before the age of five . . . The opportunities . . . for
families living in deprived areas — both urban and rural —
in bringing up their children will be particularly important.
Priority will be given in the early stages of the programme to
areas of disadvantage. (paras. 19 and 20)

Some far-reaching assumptions are implicit in the White Paper
and the Plowden Report. They suggest that part-time provision
is best and that few mothers require or should be encouraged to
seek day care for their children. Further, it is inferred that pre-
schooling, in general, will act in an interventionist way in
deprived areas, and that provision on demand means virtually
universal demand and thus encompasses the disadvantaged.

Yet the view that part-time provision is necessarily best is by no
means general. Pressure of public opinion for extended facilities
is currently focused not so much on part-time nursery education
as on the needs of working mothers for day care. A recent Gallup
poll (February 1979) of 4,000 people, a representative sample of
the population, suggested that more than half the mothers with
school-age children and more than a quarter of the mothers with
under-fives now go out to work, but holiday play-schemes, after
school care and nursery places, cater for only 3 per cent of their
children. The poll heralds a campaign to encourage self-help
among mothers as well as to press government to provide
adequate day-care facilities. Government recognition that the
proportion of parents wanting day care was underestimated in
the White Paper came at the Sunningdale Conference on low-
cost day care (1976), but there has been little progress towards
provision for other than priority cases.

Even the hope that pre-schooling, in general, will act in an
interventionist way may also be mistaken. American experience
in Headstart initially indicated that although some pre-school
intervention programmes resulted in gains amongst disadvantaged children, it was the precise content and approach of
these programmes that was important in compensatory education, rather than generalized pre-school activity such as one
might find in day nurseries, playgroups, and nursery classes in

England. Subsequently, it seemed that although, in the beginning, highly structured programmes appeared more effective,
gains were not maintained. The more successful programmes,
in both America and England, in the long term have been those
that involved mothers and were community based, like some of
the Educational Priority Area projects, notably those in Liverpool and West Yorkshire (Halsey, 1972; Midwinter, 1972).
Indeed, some of the most recent evidence (Moore, 1978) suggests that a key element in success might be a new relationship
between the child and its parents generated by participation in
a programme that focuses special attention on the child. As
Professor Halsey (1980) concludes, from the evidence of
combined studies of long-term effects from the most notable
American Compensatory Education Programmes started in the
sixties, there *are* ways in which education can compensate for
society. The striking feature of these latest findings from the
Consortium of research groups led by Irving Lazar and Richard
Darlington is that while individual projects varied considerably,
the common denominators were enthusiasm and support underlying careful organization.

Enthusiasm and support are the necessary precursors of
playgroups. It may be relevant, therefore, that a recent study
(Turner, 1977) of random samples of all children not physically
or mentally handicapped, from forty-eight Belfast playgroups
and from control groups of children who did not attend,
emphasized the value of playgroup experience. Over a period of
six months, playgroup children showed significantly greater
gains in measures of general, intellectual, social, and motor
development (particularly balancing, jumping, and ball control) than children who did not attend. Overall, atttendance at
a playgroup appeared more important than either a child's
individual level or that of his playgroup.

There have been sufficiently encouraging results from some
programmes, notably the West Riding E.P.A. Scheme, for
some teachers and researchers to stress 'the importance of 100
per cent cover, so that all children entering the reception classes
had been to a nursery group' (Halsey, 1972 : 115). A similar
conclusion was drawn from a study of children aged between
three and four in a nursery school from both relatively
advantaged and disadvantaged homes and a similar group of
non-nursery children (Cohen and Bagshaw, 1973). Results
suggested that

where there is provision for some and not for others; non-nursery working class children already performing linguistically at a lower level than middle class children will find the differential even greater when they attain primary school age and enter into competition with children who already have two years of nursery schooling behind them. For disadvantaged children this gap is likely to be correspondingly greater. (p. 740)

Yet there is persistent anecdotal evidence that many disadvantaged children tend not to take advantage of pre-school facilities. Even if they did, there is little reassurance from research studies that the gap between children of different social strata would be closed. Under circumstances where parents are free to choose whether they take up compensatory education, it is not likely to be effective for those groups who need it most.

Two inter-related areas of concern are therefore discernible. One is the need to know more about effective strategies for pre-school intervention – about curriculum and methods of approach; the other, and the focus of this book, centres on factors that influence take-up of provision and, in particular, the characteristics of unresponsive families, with a view to understanding their needs and finding ways of meeting them. This does not imply favour of compulsory attendance or a belief that those parents who are unconvinced of the value of pre-school education and who are happy and confident in keeping their under-fives at home should be under social compulsion to make use of nursery facilities; it is rather to suggest that given institutionalized provision 'on demand', it is sensible to probe any evidence that even quite small groups of people, although expressing a desire for pre-schooling, may be unable to avail themselves of it. This may be especially important if such groups are found to predominate among the disadvantaged.

'DEMAND' AND 'NEED'

It is not easy to disentangle the facts regarding major influences in failure to take up services and the characteristics of unresponsive families. These are issues with political overtones and evidence is often presented in a biased way to promote individual viewpoints. The concepts of 'demand' and 'need' inherent in 'take-up' of any service are confused and defined in varying ways. 'Demand', for example, may be judged by the length of waiting lists at existing institutions, the weight of pressure groups, letters to the press and other media, the emergence of self-help groups, and also surveys which 'express parental opinion'. But how are they to be evaluated and interpreted? In most areas parental choice of facilities is very limited and whatever is available is almost certainly over-subscribed; parents may therefore put their children's names on more than one list. Those who are most vociferous and articulate may not be as representative as they imagine; many of the small surveys which have been carried out are insufficiently thorough.

Simple appraisals of 'demand' are usually based on estimates of 'need'; but this can be interpreted in a variety of ways (Bradshaw, 1972). Is it a desirable standard laid down by some informed, probably professional body, such as the Plowden view that young children should, except in exceptional circumstances, be at home with their mothers (1967 : para. 330)? Is it simply a need that is felt by individuals for some form of provision which is not available, as reflected in current pressure for day care? Is it such need turned into action, as in waiting lists, which for reasons already given, may offer a poor indication of the true situation? Or is it found by studying those receiving a service, so that if some people within a homogeneous group are not benefiting from it, they are deemed to be 'in need'? Understood in this way, all pregnant women need antenatal care and children of all working mothers should enjoy state-run day-care facilities. The same interpretation could support the case for all children having the stimulus of a good nursery school. 'Need' is sometimes equated with 'disadvantage' and a variety of indicators are used by researchers. Some emphasize the known association between class and educational achievement; they refer to parental income, occupation, family size, and housing. Disadvantage is seen as class linked.

Yet there may also be other reasons for observed social differences, which originate in the early parent–child relationships and influence the child's educational opportunity long before he gets to school. A study that attempted to probe these differences (Miller, 1971) suggested that some parents, not necessarily because they do not care about their children, but in spite of it, through habits and attitudes that militate against development of skills, inhibit their children's positive responses to education.

The Plowden Report (1967) typified another interpretation; it defined disadvantage through area. This approach, although a convenient administrative tool, has drawbacks; it limits the interpretation of disadvantage to lack of amenity, especially schools, and to particular districts of high social and physical deficiencies. It is difficult to quarrel with the conclusion (Joseph and Parfit, 1972) that unless careful analyses are made both of need and of existing provision, pockets of greatest need, even within an educational priority area, may not be identified.

While such criteria may cover some of the most extreme types of deprivation, it is clear that there are other sources of disadvantage which are not limited to specific areas and which cut across all strata of society. Children in high-rise flats or in areas of high lead contamination, handicapped children, those who lose one or both parents, or who suffer deficiency in diet or from excessive noise, are obvious examples.

The problem may not be a small one. A study of 10,500 children, representative of all in the National Child Development Study of children born in the first week of March, 1958 (Wedge and Prosser, 1973) found that one in every sixteen children (on average, two children in every British classroom) will be seriously 'disadvantaged'. Such children will come from a one-parent family or have at least four brothers or sisters *and* live in poor housing on a low income. It is surely vital to know the extent to which provision is likely to achieve its objective and reach such children. Findings in that study were unequivocally pessimistic.

EVIDENCE OF SUPPORT FOR PRE-SCHOOL PROVISION

One thing is clear. Since the Campaign for Nursery Education began as long ago as 1965, pressure of public opinion has moved dramatically in favour of pre-schooling. In 1968 only eighteen out of 153 local education authorities gave support to the so-called 'Lollipop Lobby'. Four years later, seventy-two sent encouraging messages in support of a Petition for Nursery Education; a further forty expressed sympathy. By 1980 local authority support for pre-school provision in principle is commonplace. Nor has response to the needs of under-fives been limited to professionals. The Campaign has had the support of ordinary mothers throughout the country. It was also the determination of mothers, in the absence of government action, to do something for their children that was instrumental in the phenomenal growth of the Pre-school Playgroups Association. Membership increased from 550 in 1965 to 8,300 in 1973. By the end of 1975 national playgroup membership stood at about 10,000 with possibly another 4,000 attached at branch level only. By 1978 membership in England and Wales had risen to 14,000, of which 3,500 were individual members and 10,500 were at group level. These playgroups were attended by 400,000 children, mainly aged three and four years (PPA, 1979). Unfortunately no reliable figures are available of mothers who attended courses during this period.

There is also increased public pressure for other forms of provision, notably day care; thus there can be little disagreement regarding active desire for pre-schooling by a significant proportion of local authorities and parents.

MIDDLE-CLASS DEMAND?

How respresentative these parents are of the whole population and whether they include the 'disadvantaged' is another matter. One view is that provision 'on demand' really means 'middle-class demand'. Although not synonymous in educational terms, disadvantage and working class are often linked together. Given the known association between class and educational achievement and the Government's expressed intention that provision should be of special benefit to the disadvantaged, there is a curious paradox in the fact that provision seems to be biased towards the middle class.

Such a paradox is perhaps reflected in the coverage accorded the White Paper proposals by the national press. *The Times* made it front page news and stated that the White Paper 'had the potentiality of a major social advance' and the *Guardian*, also on its front page, described it as the 'first systematic step since 1870 when compulsory education at the age of five was introduced'. The proposals were also welcome by the *Daily Telegraph*, although the leader recorded disappointment that there was no provision for fee paying in nursery schools — 'these could be made the subject of a means test, and would probably be of greater help to poorer children than the present blockbuster discrimination in favour of the deprived areas'. Both the *Daily Mail*, which has vigorously backed the campaign for Nursery Education, and the *Daily Express*, commented favourably, but on their inside pages; in the more popular newspapers, comment was harder to find, negligible, and more grudging in its approval. 'Take 100 lines, Mrs Thatcher' wrote the *Sun*. 'I must get my priorities right . . . it doesn't make sense to talk about spending £96,000 on education so soon after stopping free milk for seven and eleven year olds.' A similar pattern emerged in the coverage by the Sunday papers; although *The Times* and the *Telegraph* had devoted a considerable number of column inches to the subject in Thursday's papers when the Report was published, an average of some forty column inches was given to a review of the White Paper proposals on Sunday; but there was no mention made of them in the *Sunday Express* or the *News of the World*. Yet there is marked bias on the part of the upper and middle classes towards *The Times*, the *Telegraph*, and the *Guardian*, while the working classes tend to favour the *Sun*, the *Mirror*, *Mail*, and *Express*.

It is indeed paradoxical that those papers read mainly by parents whose children might be thought to be most 'in need', gave least publicity and showed least interest in the proposals.

The likelihood of predominantly middle-class take-up of pre-school provision is not a universally held view. During the past decade a number of surveys of working-class areas have consistently reported desire for nursery provision or day care. A small survey of attitudes to nursery schools was undertaken by the East Newcastle Action Group in an intensive study of about one square mile of working-class housing in Newcastle where two schools opened nursery classes under the Urban Aid Programme in 1971. The researchers concluded that 'nursery education was an issue on which the vocal middle-class pressure groups had working class support all the way' (ENAG, 1972 : 1). At the time of their survey, however, maintained nursery schools and classes catered for about 10 per cent of the three-to-five age group; 'for the vast majority of under fours and a high proportion of the four pluses, no places were available' (ENAG 1972 : 2).

In Kirkby, near Liverpool, a team under the late Professor Jack Tizard obtained further evidence for working-class support for pre-school provision. It carried out door-to-door interviews in working-class districts where the majority of families were council tenants. They found that eight or nine out of every ten in their sample of 460 families with children of pre-school age wanted some form of pre-schooling (Moss, Tizard, Crook,

1973). Similar surveys by the Thomas Coram Research Unit in three areas of Inner London in 1974/5 also found up to 90 per cent of mothers saying they wanted some form of pre-school care for their three- and four-year-old children; about one in five families expressed a desire for day care. No class differences in demand emerged (Tizard, Moss, Perry, 1976).

Strikingly similar results were claimed for a study of demand in rural areas of the south west, part of the Bristol 'Child Health and Education in the Seventies' project in conjunction with Somerset Pre-school Playgroups Association (Osborn, 1975). While the patterns of usage of provision showed much in common with the Liverpool and Inner London surveys in that playgroups provided places for a much larger proportion of children than local authority nursery classes and schools, the nature of the demand was rather less clear. Overall, of the 978 mothers with children aged three and a half who were interviewed, 44 per cent (434) had children who were not attending any form of provision; of these, two thirds (290) were taking no active steps to find a place. What is not known, of course, is whether this was due to mothers' wish to keep their children at home, to lack of facilities, to local characteristics, or to the inaccuracy of waiting lists as measures of intent. It was manifest, however, that a large proportion of unskilled and semi-skilled workers' children were attending no form of pre-school provision at all (57 per cent compared with 48 per cent of skilled manual workers and 31 per cent of professional and white-collar workers).

A more comprehensive survey (Bone, 1977) based on interviews with some 2,000 mothers and 2,500 children showed that whilst 32 per cent of children used facilities, 63 per cent of mothers desired them. The picture that emerges from this plethora of statistics is not so much of overwhelming demand for state-run provision for children of women working full time, but for progressively more part-time provision as the child grows older. The majority of mothers (81 per cent) required no provision for the first year; those who did were equally split between day-nursery provision and childminders (6 per cent each). It is not until children reach three and four years of age that the demand, mainly for playgroups and nursery classes, reaches appreciable proportions, with a clear indication that playgroups are seen as a stepping stone to nursery school (Bone, 1977 : 15, Table 3.6). Yet confidence in the value of the figures is somewhat undermined by noting that 5 per cent of mothers preferred playgroup or nursery class for babies up to one year old, 23 per cent for one-year-old children, and 55 per cent for children up to two years old. As these forms of provision are not available for very young children, how much did mothers really understand about what they were opting for? How far do such large surveys blur differences between localities and how far are attitudes conditioned by lack of real choice in the type of facility or by lack of job opportunities?

That these unanswered questions are relevant is suggested by findings in a study carried out by a voluntary agency, 'Priority', in four contrasting areas of Liverpool in 1976/7. Among the 1,400 families in the sample the general level of husband's unemployment was one in four, considerably higher than the national average of 6.4 per cent. Yet only one mother in five had a full or part-time job. The breakdown of reasons for not working outside the home suggested that a third of mothers wanted to be at home with their children (33.5 per cent). Other important reasons for not going out to work were a lack of suitable facilities (19 per cent) and mothers' feeling that their children were too young (16 per cent). A further 13 per cent would have liked to work, but could not get a job. A thought provoking comment was that the survey had 'shown up a genuine confusion and ignorance about pre-school provision among families' (van der Eyken, 1978a : 16).

UTILIZATION OF PRE-SCHOOL PROVISION

There are grounds, then, for thinking that assessment of demand may not be as straightforward as it seems. 'Demand' for a service may be a function of supply; expression of demand may be influenced by availability and knowledge of services. It is also difficult to judge opinion on a complicated issue like pre-school provision from questionnaires and doorstep interviews; people do not always understand the differences between forms of provision and may tend to give the answer they think is required of them or one that will get rid of the interviewer quickly.

A better test might be to provide the facility and to study who actually makes use of it. In 1972 Inner London Pre-school Playgroups Association monitored the inception of a new play-group in a high-need area of Lambeth (P.P.A., 1972). This different approach to assessment of demand shows the situation in another light, although as a pilot study it had certain limitations and shortcomings.

Once it was known that premises were available, mothers in the immediate area (about half a square mile) were circularized and visited by the playgroup organizer. In a sample of 100 mothers with children under five, when only those of playgroup/nursery school age were considered, it was found that 29 per cent of mothers had children who already went to playgroup, the offspring of 36 per cent attended a nursery class, and 35 per cent said their children made no use of any form of pre-school provision. This latter group comprised 20 per cent who said they did not want any type of provision and 15 per cent who, although expressing great enthusiasm and determination to join the playgroup, did not avail themselves of the opportunity. This suggests that at least in this working-class area, the majority of mothers used some form of provision, but there was a discrepancy between what some people said they wanted and what they actually did when they had the opportunity.

One particularly revealing point was that one-parent families (where the mother was on social security and did not work) and young mothers without close family ties predominated amongst those who made no use of pre-school provision for their children. Most mothers had left school at fifteen, feeling failures; they did not wish their children to start school before the statutory age. Emotional difficulties can combine with low living standards to affect not only diet but aspirations for the children of such 'mothers alone'. They may become so vulnerable that normal social life becomes an ordeal (Marsden, 1969).

A more detailed study of the use made of pre-school playgroups in an Urban Aid area (Joseph and Parfit, 1972) was particularly concerned to gauge the extent to which disadvantaged families were reached. Playgroups were successfully established in a high need area, but in terms of the particular indicators of need used in the research, they did not attract the children it was most hoped would come. It seemed that many of the children with the most disadvantaged parents were not coming forward and that a proportion were making a conscious decision not to do so.

Thus there is conflicting and inconclusive evidence as to demand and utilization of services. The danger is that parents who recognize the value of pre-school education are those who will actually make use of it, whilst some of those who are already at a disadvantage for a variety of reasons, may not. The gap between the haves and the have nots will be widened and a fundamental aim of national pre-school policy undermined. There is clearly a need to examine any relevent factors; do they lie in the nature of the provision itself, its location or structure and organization, or do the roots lie in the family situation, in social or economic pressures, or even in the type of relationship and interaction between mother and child or the child and its family *vis à vis* the outside world?

FACTORS AFFECTING TAKE-UP

i. Siting

Speculation focuses on a number of reasons that may interact to tip the balance between take-up and non take-up of provision. Some basic considerations (Joseph and Parfit, 1972) are the pinpointing of high-need areas and the convenient siting of facilities within them. The type of accommodation in which a family lives may also affect attitudes towards pre-schooling.

It is conceivable, especially in high-rise flats, that the business of getting an under-five ready to go out at a fixed time may become a chore and 'not worth the bother', particularly where education is not a high priority. While the plight of families in such accommodation is now widely recognized, a more recent realization (Gittus, 1976) is that families with young children living only one or two storeys up are also vulnerable to loneliness, problems of safety, and lack of play facilities. One would imagine that mothers and children in such environments would welcome the friendship and stimulus of a nursery class or playgroup.

Some undoubtedly do. Others feel they cannot allow their child out to play because the ground and safe areas are out of sight and hearing; they are constantly worried about the dangers of windows and balconies. Any outside contacts are practically dependent on shopping expeditions; children are isolated in their own homes, with a striking lack of stimulation and opportunities for mixing with other children (Maizels, 1961 : 11). The possibility of resultant behavioural difficulty is supported by Pearl Jephcott (1971) who in a study of 'Homes in High Flats' found that the pre-school age child failed to develop a sense of security and that its curiosity was stultified.

It would be understandable, particularly where there are several younger children, if a mother felt that the strains of humping pram or pushchair up and down even one or two flights of stairs and coping with a fractious baby who needed to be bathed and fed, just to get a four year old to a nursery or playgroup, were not worth the effort.

Even more inhibiting may be the practical problems that face mothers in rural areas when the nearest provision may be miles away and there may be no public transport. Mothers in middle-class families, backed by the resources which their educational and material advantages afford, can cope with such a situation with comparative ease. Yet when use of transport was monitored over five months in a study of thirty playgroups for children in high need (Ferri, 1977), surprisingly, such support made very little difference to attendance. It was even thought a possible disadvantage as mothers did not come to the play-groups and they had no opportunity to observe or get involved in activities there. Anecdotal evidence from other groups who provide transport for mothers as well as children, however, suggests a contrary view, notably several of the schemes discussed in chapter 3.

ii. Mobility

New urban development, whether high-rise flats or new-town estates, has meant the break-up of traditional family networks; stresses are aggravated where young mothers no longer have their own mothers and relatives to turn to for help. This removal of considerable sections of the population to new districts and the consequent period of uncertainty could be another factor in feeling that attendance at a nursery or play-group is 'not worth the bother'.

Mobility emerges as a striking feature in an unpublished survey carried out in 1972 as part of a course for Senior Social Workers in the Southwark Community Project. This survey covered Save the Children Fund Playgroups and aimed to obtain the views of parents regarding the adequacy and appropriate-ness of the facilities, if used, together with any reasons for non-use.

The researchers hoped to interview fifty families. The SCF provided names and addresses of families who were regular attenders at the playgroup as well as those who had registered but only came sporadically. Contact with mothers who did not use any form of provision was through health visitors. Letters were sent out at the beginning of January and followed up within two weeks. Nevertheless eighteen families had already moved and a further three were expecting to move. This was clearly not a case of a long time lag between initial contact and follow-up; in this small study population mobility was judged an important inhibiting factor in non take-up of provision.

Similar instability is likely wherever there is housing re-development. It can also result from some housing policies. One example is the practice of rehousing families in two-bedroomed accommodation if they have two children of differing sex. The period of change can be expected when the younger child is one year plus (the second child is often not counted until it is one year of age) and the older one between three and four − that is playgroup or nursery school age. In the upheaval of an impending move, regular attendance or even beginning some form of pre-schooling could be more than a mother can cope with. This suggestion is reinforced by the conclusion by researchers in the Red House Scheme that stability in school and community was an important factor in achieving results. They quote the experience of operating a home visiting scheme during a national pit strike to demonstrate how fluidity could fundamentally change a situation (Smith and James, 1975).

iii. Failures in communication

In the period prior to moving, it is understandably inadvisable to settle a child into one group, only to uproot him or her in the near future. After a move, the period of adjustment can be a long one; new friends have to be made and for many people this is a slow process − especially in new towns and overspill 'communities'. The gap caused by removal of close family and friends is not always immediately compensated for by improved accommodation. Some newcomers may just not talk to their neighbours or feel like getting involved with local activities.

In such circumstances the usual 'grapevine' type of communi-cation, which is often relied on for passing information about pre-school provision, cannot operate. But it is not only in mobile communities that communication seems to be a problem. One of the aims of the East Newcastle Action Group (ENAG, 1972) was to find out how well mothers had been informed about existing nursery opportunities. They discovered 'a remarkable and apparently unnecessary lack of information' (p. 1). Schools confirmed that parents were expected to inform themselves through older children, neighbours, and welfare workers, except where substantial new provision was made: parents were then informed in writing. Although schools were confident that everyone knew of the existence of their nursery classes – only thirty-eight out of eight-four mothers, when asked to name a local state nursery, were able to do so; 95 per cent of parents stated they had received no written communication about nursery provision. It seems likely that such information is mislaid or misunderstood by parents.

Many other small studies have reported similar findings; the Brent Campaign for Under Fives carried out a survey, typical of most, of forty-three mothers living in Kilburn (1972); one in five mothers had not heard of the existing provision. It was concluded that ignorance kept demand at a low level.

There are, however, communities where lack of knowledge cannot be put forward as the reason for disregarding facilities. In the National Bureau's study (Joseph and Parfit, 1972), for example, possible users were alerted by local advertisement, the distribution of leaflets, personal canvassing, and, in a few cases, through health visitors. Nevertheless, as had already been pointed out, response in terms of those it was most hoped to reach, fell short of expectation. The Save the Children Fund supports many playgroups in areas of special need; supervisors go out of their way to publicize playgroups and to contact mothers, but often with disappointing results. It could be that in claiming ignorance of the facilities, mothers are masking other reasons for non-attendance.

iv. Expense

Expense would seem to be one such likely factor preventing mothers from making use of provision. This is the view of many social workers, health visitors, and playleaders. Where fees are high, this is probably so. Nevertheless in an analysis of housegroups (PPA, 1972b), a nationwide survey, it appeared common practice for organizers to accept payment in whatever way suited the mother or to waive it altogether, but still 'those who needed the playgroup most did not come forward' (p. 16). In the National Bureau's study (Joseph and Parfit, 1972), most playgroups charged 5p a session; Save the Children Fund also makes only a nominal charge. Yet in spite of considerable individual efforts to do so, these playgroups do not attract the mothers they most want. The more recent NCB study (Ferri and Niblett, 1977), while recognizing that prior payment of fees could alienate some mothers, found that advance payment of fees — with no refunds — tended to encourage a relatively high rate of attendance.

There is a further point that serious anomalies exist in a system of pre-school education where nursery schools and classes are free, but playgroups may charge anything from a purely nominal sum to 60p or 70p a session (PPA, 1978/9) and attendance at a day nursery can depend on a means test. In addition, parental choice is limited since there is varying acceptance of differing forms of provision between local authorities; playgroups are a welcome facility in some areas, but not others (PPA in press). Childminders are a resource valued by certain authorities but others prefer a fully professional service for under fives.

v. Parental participation

The National Bureau's study (Joseph and Parfit, 1972) also raised the question of the part played by parental participation in attracting or discouraging use of facilities. It is sometimes felt that parents should not be asked to participate — simply that they should be offered the services of a first-class nursery or even that 'mother participation and the bringing of a service to children in greatest need are incompatible goals' (p. 36).

Nevertheless, there is manifestly increasing awareness of the potential value of involving parents, whether in nursery school or playgroup. The White Paper certainly underlines the importance attached by government to the 'lessons that can be learnt from experience of playgroups' (para. 29) and parent participation is now encouraged in many nursery schools and other forms of provision.

Research findings are not easy to evaluate in this respect. Even in American projects of compensatory education from Headstart onwards, research designs do not usually permit assessment of just how far gains were due to highly structured programmes, to parental involvement, to a combination of both, or to some unspecified factors. Some of the more successful projects in terms of specific skills (Bereiter and Englemann, 1966; Karnes, 1968), tended to ignore the mother's possible contribution to her child's education and to remove him or her to a planned environment and professional teaching.

Recognition that children spend the greater part of the day within the family led in other projects, notably the Early Education Program at Ipsilanti, Michigan, to mothers being given an active role. In reviewing the major American programs, Bronfenbrenner (1973 and 1976) has drawn attention to the extent of parental and community involvement as the two factors that seemed associated with persistence of any gains. Particularly effective were home visiting programs which focused on the mother as the main agent of change.

The Red House Experiment (Poulton and James, 1975) included parent involvement and a home visiting scheme with a structured approach to learning. Unfortunately, due to differences in ages between the twenty boys and girls taking part in the home visiting scheme and those who went to nursery school, comparison was not possible. Results were again inconclusive, but tended to confirm American findings that parental involvement results in improved play equipment in the home and changes in attitudes towards discipline.

In common with small projects proliferating throughout the country which aim to increase parental involvement, the focus of attention was the testing of methods of intervention on self-selected or pre-selected samples. Families who, even if such facilities were freely available, might not come forward to benefit from them, were left out of account. The assumption seems to be that they would naturally respond to provision which was successful among self-selected groups.

But again, how far are the 'disadvantaged' likely to be involved? Elsewhere in the NCB Report (Joseph and Parfit, 1972) it was made clear that mother-involved groups *could* work well. The more systematic attempt to evaluate mother-involvement among the disadvantaged (Ferri and Niblett, 1977) concluded that different types of involvement were appropriate according to the nature and origins of mothers' disadvantage. Four broad categories of mother involvement were identified:

1. through serving on committees and participating in the management and administration of a group;
2. through assisting in the day-to-day running of the group by

taking part in a rota system and helping playleaders during
playgroup sessions;
3. through fund raising, through outings, and helping set up
equipment;
4. accepting the offer of some positive form of welcome — a
mothers' club or language class or, more probably, simply
the opportunity to relax over a cup of tea with other mothers
and the playleaders.

Clearly, for overburdened mothers, first priority was often relief
from the responsibility of children. What the research does not
bring out, however, and as the fieldwork lasted only five
months, this is hardly surprising, is the possibility of changes
and developments that may occur among such mothers passing
from the stage of relief from what is felt the burden of child-
care, through stage four to other levels of participation.

vi. Inappropriate provision

One important group to whom this discussion cannot apply is
working mothers — for them any provision that intrudes on
working hours is inappropriate. The Plowden Report (1967),
acknowledging the difficulty in estimating demand, recommended full-time provision for 5 per cent of mothers with
children between three and five who work full-time and for the
10 per cent of mothers identified as unable to care for their own
children. Yet the previous year the National Labour Women's
Survey (1966 : para. 331) found that two thirds of parents would
have liked their children to have started full-time school before
the age of three. This raises problems not only of interpreting
surveys of opinion but also of how far professional assessments of
'need' should take precedence over the 'felt needs' of mothers.
The Plowden Committee (1967) was quite unequivocal in its
judgement:

> We do not believe that full-time nursery places should be
> provided even for children who might tolerate separation
> without harm, except with exceptionally good reasons . . .
> Some mothers who are not obliged to work, may work full-
> time regardless of their children's welfare. It is no business of
> educational service to encourage these mothers to do so.
> (para. 330)

As long ago as 1968, however, warning was given in the Seebolm Report on the Social Services that nursery education would not be of use to working mothers unless more day care was provided. Another warning of the way attitudes and customs might change (Hunt, 1968) drew attention to the number of working mothers whose children were cared for by other members of the family, notably 'granny' and the danger of assuming that when the present generation of children had grown up, their mothers would be as willing to accept responsibility for their grand-children.

We now have cogent evidence from recent census data and experience in other European countries which shows a wide-spread trend towards more women working once their children have reached the statutory school age. The proportion of mothers with children under five working full-time has re-mained reasonably stable; recent analysis put the number of children under five who should be given high priority for a place in a day nursery at 6 per cent, the same figure for mothers with under-fives who work full-time (Bone, 1977).

Whilst there are likely to be wide regional variations, there is increasing pressure on mothers, including one-parent families, to work because of financial problems due to the inflationary spiral. Only a minority get their under-fives into day nurseries or crèches. Others still prefer to leave their children with someone they know and trust, a relative or childminder. But where relatives are themselves working, where there are not enough childminders, the needs of neither child nor mother will be met.

Awareness of problems that are likely to result from such a situation has led to suggestions of offering adequate benefits to mothers who wished to stay at home and for comprehensive units of pre-school provision (Kellmer-Pringle, 1973, 1979). A major recommendation of the Halsey Report (1972) was also the setting up of nursery centres linking all forms of pre-school provision. One example of such a scheme, the Coram Children's Centre, opened in 1974. It provides an integrated service in-cluding a nursery school, one o'clock club, day nursery, clinic, and activities for parents under one roof. It brings together health and social services, education, and parents in a quite unique way, based explicitly on providing flexible services to respond to parental demand instead of identifying and servicing priority groups or promulgating certain types of provision because 'experts' consider them desirable. But even this progressive concept leaves out of account mothers who may not have the information or confidence to come forward and the problems of people who work irregular hours — nurses, long-distance lorry drivers, some shift workers — whose problems become that much more acute if they are one-parent families.

In the last analysis, whether any form of pre-school provision reaches those in greatest need depends on parental response to what is available. While it is no longer believed that short-term intervention will bring about long-term gains (Tizard, B., 1975), there is clear evidence from studies both in this country and in America (Woodhead, 1976) of the benefits of certain types of experience for all children, and in particular, for the disadvantaged. Is the assumption justified that simple extension of pre-school facilities will ensure that those who need those experiences most, will benefit? There is a distinct possibility that a small but important section of the population will not avail itself of facilities. It is these unresponsive families who need to be better understood.

CHAPTER TWO

Theoretical framework

Several broad themes recur in discussion of pre-school policy
and help to explain the virtually worldwide focus of attention on
the pre-school years in the last decade. This increased valuation
of early childhood education, initially enhanced by economic
expansion, has led to calls for effective teaching and reduction
of failure rates. Current economic uncertainty may temporarily
halt the trend, but cannot negate the foremost theme emphasized by research; educationalists, sociologists, and psycholo-
gists have documented the formative influence of the first five
years of life. By virtue of coming first, these early years set in
motion a train of events that are the basis for later development.
Consequently it is vital to ensure that opportunities are not
missed during this period when children develop new skills at an
extraordinary rate. So far, there is agreement. Yet considerable
differences emerge as to how these skills should be fostered and
in the understanding of how cultural and environmental effects
operate. A vast body of accumulated knowledge supports and
explains the various attitudes, strategies, and policies.

STIMULUS-ORIENTATED STUDIES

One view of development sees it as a series of steps promoted by
appropriate stimuli which can work completely independently
of the child's background. Animal studies have suggested a
crucial role for an unrestricted and varied environment in
encouraging cognitive development. Casler (1961, 1968) is
amongst those who have taken an extreme position, maintaining that the range of stimuli offered the child is of paramount importance. He grants that the mother is frequently the
intermediary of such experience but considers her dispensable
in this capacity. A common assumption, for example, might be
that a mother has an important role in comforting a crying
baby; but according to Casler's view, the mother's presence is

unnecessary. Thus, babies stop crying when automatically rocked at sixty cycles a minute; rocking at fifty cycles a minute is ineffective, while a few babies require rocking at seventy cycles a minute (Ambrose, 1969).

This highly automated concept of rearing children has little relevance to contemporary practice, but many highly structured programmes of compensatory education derive their theory from such observations and studies. Demonstration that cognitive changes can be brought about by appropriate stimuli, together with evidence that the results of early deprivation can be reversed (Skeels, 1966; Clarke and Clarke, 1976) has encouraged the belief that structured, professionally administered, and comparatively short enrichment programmes can compensate for inadequacies in the home environment. Findings in some projects in the American Headstart and Follow Through Programs support this view. The positive reinforcement of systematically organized sets of stimuli or learning programs produced consistent gains, but it was subsequently reported (Bronfenbrenner, 1973) that such gains tended to decline one or two years after the end of the program. It is now widely recognized that continued intervention is necessary; as with nutrition, no one would assume that a brief period on a first-class diet would ensure good health if the regime were discontinued.

In addition to these difficulties, it now appears that achievement in such schemes was normally measured by IQ tests, which because of their verbal and cultural bias may have been quite inappropriate for use with some under-privileged groups. The chief preoccupation was with scholastic achievement; but this is only one aspect of human development. Many practising nursery school teachers and playleaders rate social and emotional development of at least equal importance.

MOTHER-ORIENTATED STUDIES

A point of view that does not negate the importance of adequate stimulation but takes account of culture, social conditions, and life-styles, emphasizes the central role of the mother or mother-substitute. It also draws much supporting evidence from animal studies, which are thought to suggest the need for human companionship; they focus on the role of the mother. One well-known series of experiments with monkeys showed that, offered the choice, young monkeys will seek the comfort of a cloth model mother, even though it does not lactate, rather than a lactating wire one (Harlow and Zimmerman, 1959). Another of Harlow's studies (1961) was concerned with the effects of early isolation. One group of monkeys was reared in partial isolation, which meant they could see and hear people and other monkeys, but during their early months they had no close interaction with them. This condition closely resembled children deprived of human company and interest. The monkeys subsequently manifested severe emotional disturbance related to the length of time they had been isolated.

Numerous studies of birds and animals have shown that there seem to be particularly sensitive periods when the young attach themselves to a 'mother' figure, and that the attachment is vital for subsequent healthy development. This process of 'imprinting' is seen in humans as the bond or attachment that develops between a young child and its mother usually at about six months or at least within the first two years. There is a gradual and natural growth in independence in the child from three years upwards. Dr John Bowlby, whose report to the World Health Organisation in 1951 deeply influenced professional attitudes to child care, stressed the overwhelming importance of the mother in behaviour attachment; a more recent re-assessment of maternal deprivation (Rutter, 1972) confirms the importance of early relationships for later development, but moves away from a view that restricts bonding to the mother.

THE ISSUE OF DAY CARE

The way bonding is viewed has substantial implications for pre-school provision, not so much where children of three and four years old are concerned, as attachment normally assumes diminishing importance by then, but in relation to day care for very young children.

This, the second major theme that permeates discussion of early childhood education, is becoming more insistent. Patterns of family life have changed dramatically in the last twenty years; fewer children, a blurring of the roles of husband and wife, the struggle for equality between the sexes, the need and/or desire of more women to work — and consequent pressures for day-care facilities — are well documented trends.

Yet in 1951 the World Health Organisation Expert Committee on Mental Health stated that the use of day-nurseries and crèches, which included children under three, resulted in permanent damage because of the effects of early separation on the bond. A growing number of studies cast doubt on this assertion, however, as well as on the irreversible influence of early experience and the critical nature of the first few years. Re-assessments (Clarke and Clarke, 1976 and Kagan, 1979) of the available evidence give a more hopeful prognosis for children with unfortunate early experiences; attention is directed to studies that show the influence of later life experience.

But the crux of the matter lies in whether a young child may be at risk of damage by being looked after for the greater part of the day by one or more caretakers and not his mother. English studies of working mothers do not suggest that their children are likely to show behavioural disorders or to suffer as a result of having more than one mother figure, provided they receive warm, consistent care from each. American research also fails to support the view that children of working mothers are adversely affected. Again, it is the quality of care that emerges as the crucial factor and the quality of the relationships within the family or institution.

Anthropological studies (Mead, 1954, 1962) cast doubt on the biological origin of the bond and experience in other social settings is superficially re-assuring. Since the 1920s, for example, Israeli Kibbutzim have been carefully studied. In these collective communities both parents work during the day; they have their own sleeping quarters but eat in a communal dining room. Children are cared for collectively in their own 'houses' from babyhood by nurses and teachers. They see their parents regularly, but for comparatively short periods; that these periods are brief and spaced serves to highlight the importance attached to them by both children and parents. Such patterns of child care have raised a group-oriented generation which shows 'considerably less emotional disturbance, both in number of cases and in severity, than would a comparable group in the USA' (Bettelheim, 1971:172). Multiple caretaking seemed to have some positive advantages.

In Russia too Bronfenbrenner (1972) has indicated that many children are brought up from the first year of life in a collective setting. In the USSR 48 per cent of 'age-eligible' women work;

as a result, nurseries which cater for their children aim to provide all the necessary physical, psychological, and social conditions from the age of three months. In the first stage, babies are put in play pens which are raised off the ground so that staff are face to face with their charges. There are six to eight infants in each playpen and one 'upbringer' to four children. The task of the upbringer is to provide the child with every stimulus needed to develop skills – sensory, motor, linguistic, and cognitive. She is encouraged to express her affection for the children in the way she speaks and acts. Older children of both sexes also take an active part in child rearing, so there can be considerable diffusion of responsibility for child care. Parents share in the education of the child, but there is partial separation of the mother and child from a very early age.

The report of an American group of experts concerned with all aspects of child rearing and child care, following a visit to China, is also interesting, although observations were limited to a small, highly selective sample. It suggests that more than 90 per cent of women under forty-five work full time. After fifty-six days paid maternity leave (at least for women in state factories), mothers return to work, and, especially in cities, the trend is for babies to be cared for in factory or neighbourhood nurseries from the age of two months to three years; they then pass into a kindergarten. During the first year babies are kept in 'feeding stations' close to their mother's place of work and are usually cared for in eight-hour shifts to fit into a mother's work pattern. Physical comfort, hygiene, and nutrition are the prime concerns (Kessen, 1975). With similar reservations to those of the American delegation, personal discussion and observation (in 1979) indicated that the bond between mother and baby is carefully nurtured. It was said to be common practice for babies, swaddled from birth, to sleep with their mothers for the first three months of life. Neither in the countryside, where the grandmother often cares for young children while the mother is at work, nor in the cities, where increasingly there is communal care, does a mother take sole responsibility for child rearing. Fathers also play a prominent part in a system that involves a number of caretakers – yet reports from China unfailingly comment on the healthy, alert, composed, and competent children.

It may be unwise to build overmuch on a few observations of child care in societies that are very different from our own.

There may be other not so readily perceived consequences. Elsewhere, Bettelheim (1971 : 161) reflects on the difficulty he noticed among Kibbutz-reared children in accepting any viewpoint as valid but their own, as a possible result of the style of their upbringing. It may be downright dangerous to extrapolate from societies where there is concensus between caretakers and parents as to how children are to be reared and the society in which they live. The few cases of severe emotional disturbance among Kibbutz children (Bettelheim, 1971 : 173) were observed where there were 'diametrically opposed, pushes and pulls from parents and metapalets' (caretakers).

Thus, recent evidence does little to change Yudkin and Holme's summing up of the situation in 1963 (p. 104):

> though they may be inconclusive, [findings] provide no support for the wilder statements about serious psychological traumata to children or to the prediction of a generation of juvenile delinquents. But neither do they provide us with grounds for complacency.

If present trends continue and more mothers either wish or are obliged by circumstances to work, there is little evidence that they will impair their children by the use of day care, which allows plenty of opportunity for them to play and practice their developing skills and above all, which helps to provide a stable, loving, *total* environment. Such parents may make a positive contribution to their children's well-being both by providing a higher standard of living and by being true to their personal needs, which are met by pursuit of some vocation. Other parents may reasonably take the view that they wish to enjoy the company of their children at home, that the time from birth to five can most profitably be spent in the home with mother. The vast body of accumulating research points to the mother or mother substitute as the key figure in early childhood education, and the mother who wants to enjoy her children as long as she can before she 'loses' them to school at five is arguably providing the soundest foundation for future learning and happiness.

After all, in our society, the mother is in a unique position for influencing her child's development. She is constantly affecting the way her child develops in the way she relates to it. This becomes (David and Appell, 1966) 'a dynamic organizing force in the personality of the child'. In one study, these researchers visited mothers and children in their homes, each visit averaging three hours; there was a further visit to the office by the mother and child which included a period of free play for the child, testing, and a short separation from the mother. The studies clearly showed that:

> all the areas of a child's personality are deeply influenced by the child's interactions with his mother. Although mothers are not aware of it, each one of them makes consistent and significant conscious and unconscious choices as to how she interacts with her child. Her selection depends on whether the behaviour he shows during the interaction arouses her pleasure, indifference or displeasure. (1966 : 182)

Just as effectiveness varies between institutions, so some mothers appear more successful than others in promoting and sustaining a satisfactory mother–child relationship, one resulting in a happy adjustment to life inside and outside the family, the ability to make friends, and to develop all the skills necessary in school and adult life. Some mothers, and children, are predominantly successful in some spheres and not in others.

CLASS AND CULTURAL DIFFERENCES

Leaving aside the question of genetic endowment, explanations for such differences are commonly based on class or cultural differences. A study of 'Three Year Olds in London' (Pollak, 1972) arose from a GP's impression that children of immigrant West Indian parents were noticeably deficient in speech and language attainment and that their general performance was lower than indigenous children. This carefully designed investigation involved exhaustive interviews, examination, and tests of three groups of children; there were seventy-five English children, seventy-five West Indian, and thirteen who could not be placed in either of the first two categories and reflected the cosmopolitan character of the neighbourhood. In a mixed control group Dr Pollak found statistically significant differences in the tests of speech and language and also in tests of adaptive and personal behaviour between groups in the direction she had hypothesized. She considered and rejected the possible genetic and biological explanations and concluded that 'the average West Indian group child was suffering from two kinds of deprivation: i) maternal deprivation, ii) environmental deprivation, in the sense of a lack of environmental stimuli caused by living in inadequate housing conditions'. Dr Pollak explained maternal deprivation in this context by remarking that although the West Indian child was in contact with plenty of adults, he or she lacked the stimulating mother figure with whom he or she could identify: 'No one person would find time to play with him, cuddle him, put him to bed, buy toys for his birthday (or even remember when it was), take him out or just sit and read him a bed-time story. There was no time to explain things to him.' (1972 : 142).

Such research adds to the already substantial body of evidence that suggests the third major theme: that certain sections of the population concentrated among the lower working class and within certain geographical areas, are at an educational disadvantage (Plowden Report, 1967).

There is dramatic evidence that working-class children are less successful in developing certain cognitive skills than are middle-class children. We know from follow-up studies based on data from the National Child Development study of 16,000 children at ages seven and eleven that differences in school attainment between children of different social strata tend not only to be maintained but to increase during this four-year period. Sociological studies do not suggest that working-class children lack a rich culture or the ability to make relationships or are unable to adjust happily within their family and the community. There are no grounds for saying that working-class children are incapable of attaining well.

What is it then that accounts for the observed differences? Explanations usually centre on differences between the life styles and patterns of interaction between middle and working-class families. Different socio-economic groups have been shown to use distinct 'codes' for example. In a series of papers, Bernstein (1962, 1965, 1970) has shown that middle-class children learn, in natural 'conversation' with their mothers, an 'elaborated' code, in which questions and answers are reasoned and explicit. This fashions a more adept tool for use in developing abstract ideas, broadening horizons, and eventual achievement in a society which increasingly depends on literate, numerate, skilled adults. Lower working-class families tend to use a more 'restricted' code which depends, to a greater extent, on gesture and intonation to convey meaning, rather than on complex verbal structures. While this code may be quite adequate for communication within the family and immediate social group, it limits expression of abstract thought, sequential ideas and militates against success in an educational system that is geared to an 'elaborated code'.

A number of ongoing studies point to the tendency for working-class children to be inexplicit and to assume their viewpoint is shared. It is not so much that they are unable to grasp comparable knowledge, but that they do not practice it in the same way or use it for the same purposes. Differing styles of maternal behaviour and 'teaching' methods have been associated with class. One study (Hess and Shipman, 1966) found that a working-class mother was more likely to give orders demanding instant obedience than to explain or to help her child use words for naming objects and expressing ideas. She tended not to explain the consequences of a particular action in terms of what might happen in the future but rather as something that would result in immediate reward or punishment. The researchers found that horizons were therefore likely to be restricted and the child's thinking to remain self-centred.

There is evidence from other sources that parental values vary according to class, and that these values have a fundamental influence on the way children are reared. Cohen (1964) has shown that working-class parents value obedience, neatness, and cleanliness, whereas the middle-class parent is more likely to encourage curiosity, happiness, consideration, and self control. These very values of the working-class parent may militate against the will to achieve while middle-class parents, by emphasizing self discipline rather than external constraints, may be influencing future development in ways that are not immediately obvious.

John and Elizabeth Newson (1976), describing how they began their long-term study of families with young children in Nottingham without any pre-conceived notions of the relevance of social class, found that it emerged as the single most important variable – distinguishing the way mothers responded to their babies from the first weeks onwards. Thus a model based on socio-economic status has become the most usual explanation (apart from natural endowment) for the observed differences in children's achievement.

There are studies, however, which suggest that such a model is not completely satisfactory. 'Class' may be a powerful indicator of cognitive skills, but it is too crude a measure to explain very much by itself. Such skills are usually assessed by middle-class orientated tests; there are sources of happiness other than academic achievement. A more broad-based study (Miller, 1971) aimed to tease out possible reasons for observed social class differences in primary school achievement and investigated a sample of 489 children from two different boroughs in Middlesex. One was a mainly middle-class dormitory area and the other a diversified industrial area. In addition, as well as considering age, sex, family size, number of schools attended, and social class, Dr Miller included an anxiety measure and investigated many facets of family and adult–child relationships. These included the degree of demonstrativeness, child centredness, over-protectiveness, controls, discipline, and parental discord. Results suggested that there may be aspects of child rearing and early relationships between children and parents that will have influenced educational opportunity long before the child gets to school. Positive factors included homes where there was independent thinking and freedom of discussion among all the members and where there was harmony of values between school and home. Adverse factors were strongly dominating parents, inclined to be punitive and autocratic, who tended to make their children feel inferior or worried about the future. While social class remained an important variable, it did not explain the differences; the factors that emerged as associated with high or low achievement in school cut across social class. Varying interpretation of what was meant by parental responsibility and caring clearly resulted in widely differing patterns of behaviour and attention was drawn to the need to know more about the crucial variable of the mother–child relationship.

A series of investigations by B. L. White (1973, 1976) are of potentially outstanding importance on two counts: they draw attention to the crucial nature of the years before three and they move away from the possibly sterile argument that differences are a function of class to the more fruitful area of observational studies of mothers and children that also take emotional states into account. Beginning in 1965, the Harvard Project centred, not on interventionist work, as so many subsequent studies have done, but on 'building the knowledge base'. The aim was ultimately preventive rather than remedial. The researchers first took a sample of some 400 three, four, and five-year-old children from a wide range of background, location, socio-economic status, and ethnicity. These were carefully studied over a two-year period and assessed according to the competence they developed in cognitive and linguistic skills, in social play with other children, and in using their ability and resources. On the basis of observations at this stage, the researchers felt that the qualities that distinguished the most competent six year olds were already clearly present at three.

Subsequent stages of the study, therefore, concentrated on the 0–3 range. The 'most competent children' were matched with the 'least competent' ones and an intensive study made of the mother's interaction with her child(ren) when the next baby was born into the family.

Two factors emerged as of overall importance in early childhood education. One was the development of locomotive skills (learning to walk) and the other was learning to talk. The first enabled the child to extend his or her field of exploration and enlarged the range of stimuli; the second enabled the child to communicate more satisfactorily, to achieve richer personal relationships.

The researchers concentrated on the different ways that mothers handled problems arising from these two developing skills. They did not suggest that certain types of handling caused subsequent differences in competence. They analysed which aspects in child-rearing and in the environment varied between those who developed well and those who did less well. Measures of socio-economic status, family structures, and lifestyles were considered too coarse to account for differences that occurred across families, cultures, and classes. So environment was defined in such a way as to include the child's own experience; the extent of a mother's participation in play experience, how far she directly or indirectly influenced what the child did.

Significant patterns of interaction were found between the groups of mothers whose children developed greater 'competence' and those who developed less well. In terms of quantity alone, the 'competent' children experienced more interaction with their mothers, approximately 41 per cent as against 26 per cent. But the quality and the type of interaction were different too. Most successful relationships depended on a mother who was consistent, who was permissive in that she did not unduly limit the ways in which her child's curiosity could be satisfied.

She provided an environment that was full of objects of interest and she drew her child into collaboration with her in exploration of it. She was the sort of mother who would explain to her child and who would praise achievements. From a very early age (12–15 months), mothers of children who developed well spent longer in activities like 'reading a book together' and doing puzzles (15 per cent of observation hours, while other mothers spent about 5 per cent of their time on such activities). Moreover as the more 'competent' children grew older, there was a sharp decrease in 'low intellectual activities' while mothers of the less competent children continued at about the same level. The mode of interaction was different too; when the 'more competent' children were under two years, mothers were inclined to be restrictive, but after this age, this practice decreased and activity was likely to be encouraged with 'teaching and facilitative techniques', for example, real choices. A reverse pattern emerged with the other mothers, however; they became more restrictive as the child grew older.

The part played by genetic endowment was not clear from the research. It seemed however that direct and indirect action played a formative part in the developing competence; moreover this was not dependent on a high school education, being comfortably off, or even having a father in the home. Of considerably greater importance was the mother's emotional state – no woman who was seriously depressed was able to do a good job; there also seems to be a negative correlation between houseproud and meticulous mothers and happy and competent children. They were also more likely to take risks, that is, they were not over-protective. They talked to their children at a level they could understand and led their child to expect help, but not all the time. Indeed, they did not spend all the day 'rearing their children'; many of them had a part-time job, but they created an environment with plenty of stimulus, with a secure framework and emotional stability.

One particular finding seems to sum up this research with special poignancy; it is that 'more competent' children spent more time in high chairs and the less competent in playpens – that is, mothers of less competent children were primarily concerned with their safety and less with being close to them and providing a stimulating environment. In contrast, mothers of the more competent children were equally conscious of their child's need for stimulus and involvement with their environment. They brought them up to adult height and included them in general activities. Considered from the point of view of the child's experience, it is enlightening to contrast the outlook of the former, restricted in movement by bars, living in a land of giants, where any attempt to look up to their world must impose the physical strain of tipping the head back on the vertebrae, like balancing a big brick on the top of a delicately balanced pile; by contrast, the child in the high chair is more likely to be integrated in the family, to be able to see what is going on, to be talked to, to get attention, and to 'interact' without strain.

CHARACTERISTICS OF FAMILIES WHO DO NOT USE PROVISION

Although far more needs to be known about the nature and origins of disadvantage, the general proposition is clear, that in some strata of our society children from certain families are at an educational disadvantage. In particular, low-income groups who are badly housed and with a large number of children, or one-parent families are at a fundamental disadvantage (Wedge and Prosser, 1973). Yet many of the 'disadvantaged', in spite of alleged greater need, and even where services are available, do not make full use of them. The same study found that one in three disadvantaged children never attended a welfare clinic, whereas of ordinary children only one in five did not attend. Two thirds of ordinary children attended regularly while only one third of the disadvantaged did so. The latter group was also less likely to have received protection against polio, diphtheria, and smallpox. In spite of difficult and limiting home conditions which would make them priority cases, only one in seven, compared with one in five 'non-disadvantaged' children, had any kind of pre-school experience.

THE 'CULTURE OF POVERTY'

It seems that where multiple handicaps prevail, characteristic attitudes towards authority, child care, and education are likely to develop which differ from the values of society that determine educational achievement. This is not to say that such attitudes are wrong, but to observe that in the present system, they limit potential progress. These characteristics bear a marked resemblance to the descriptions given by social anthropologists of poor communities in under-developed countries and collectively defined as the 'culture of poverty'. Oscar Lewis first evoked the term to encapsulate the psychological attitudes that accompany poverty. He studied communities in Mexico City, San Juan, Puerto Rico, and New York City (1961, 1965) and concluded that the hallmarks of such a 'culture' were lack of participation in community undertakings, a minimum of organization outside the extended family, the need to assume adult responsibilities early in life, together with feelings of powerlessness, dependence, and inferiority. Above all Lewis maintained that these characteristics are self perpetuating from generation to generation; it is in this sense that they combine to form a 'culture of poverty', as distinct from poverty itself. Such a 'culture' could clearly have some bearing on use of services.

A distillation of the findings of social scientists regarding the 'psychology of the poor' (Haggstrom, 1964) characterizes them as having interests restricted to themselves and their families; greater importance is attached to skills needed to cope with the present situation than with those needed to progress. Co-operation is often difficult, due to apathy and the lack of appropriate skills or to acceptance of 'things as they are'. Such families do not plan ahead, horizons are foreshortened, and immediate satisfactions and rewards are sought. Unity springs from hostility towards those better off than themselves, by whom they feel exploited. Unable to control their destiny, the 'poor' consider themselves victims of fate, chance, or luck – that is, of external forces, as compared with the better off, who believe that their own decisions affect their lives.

Where such attitudes exist, it is likely they would militate against use of services, including pre-school provision. Education, with its emphasis on deferred rewards, would not be a priority; the experience of many parents in school would confirm belief in its irrelevance to their needs. Given the choice, they would ignore it. Hostility underlying their unity would lead to a feeling of alienation from society, an estrangement from its values and a sense of isolation. This has been described as 'them' and 'us' by Richard Hoggart (1957) when pointing to the small proportion of working-class mothers who took advantage of the services of a baby clinic. Hoggart maintained that any facility provided by authority was mistrusted and shunned. Moreover, a fatalistic view of life that accepted the status quo would discourage parents from seeking out facilities.

This 'psychology of the poor' appears to affect not only the general outlook of parents but also the mother–child relationship. Follow-up studies by Hess and Shipman to those already quoted (1969) showed that a child whose mother feels subject to fate, luck, or chance when he is four years old is more likely to have a low IQ and a poor academic record at age six or seven. Where the consequences of an action are seen in terms of immediate rather than deferred punishment or reward, the child is more likely to relate to authority than to reason, to comply in his behaviour but not to reflect upon it.

This passive tendency is heightened in city and urban poverty as opposed to rural poverty. Graves (1969) compared rural communities in both Spanish America and Uganda. She found, in interviews with mothers, that those in rural areas were more likely to believe their children could be taught skills, and take their share of responsibilities in family life. The city mother had less confidence and this appeared to limit her belief in her children's capacity to cope with new situations and master new skills. Intimidated by her environment, this type of mother withdraw into her family.

What this evidence suggests is that negative attitudes such as those associated with a 'psychology of the poor' could make a fundamental difference to the response of parents to pre-school provision as well as to the crucial mother–child relationship and the child's potential achievement.

Some would no doubt argue that all this has very little relevance to England where, in the welfare state, poverty such as Lewis witnessed in America does not exist. Such a position is only tenable if one defines poverty as an absolute, an arbitrary line below which no income should fall. Such a view does not take sufficiently into account the fact that while the standard of living of the poor may be raised, their situation has not radically changed because the incomes of the rich have been raised in proportion.

An authoritative study of poverty (Townsend, 1979) shows how this has operated in England and points to the current inequalities. The phenomenon is aptly illustrated by the comments made by Ken Coates and Richard Silburn (1970) concerning their interviews with rehoused members of their original sample in St Annes, Nottingham, five years after their study of poverty in the area.

In a nutshell . . . we found that family poverty had increased among them. The numbers of families in poverty had

jumped from a third to a half, while the proportion of the
total child population had increased from 50 per cent to 60
per cent. Increased rents and travelling costs had reduced the
amount of income householders could make available to
meet expenses on food, clothing and other basic necessities.
The whole sample, even when living above the somewhat
arbitrarily determined 'poverty line' . . . had been pushed
down noticeably to it. (1970 : 10)

In the face of such observations, given the present structure of
society and the inflationary spiral, the situation is such that the
separation of the poor from the rest of society will continue both
in terms of material goods and attitudes. It is accepted that the
poor and the better off have their individual life-styles. On one
hand there is the hardening of attitudes towards the poor due to
the importance currently attached to individual effort and
consequent achievement. On the other hand, as Hoggart (1957)
emphasized, when progress and achievement is considered
unattainable, there is a natural reaction against those who have
progressed and a withdrawal from agencies that are thought to
wield power but which cannot be influenced.

Such a situation was described by Coates and Silburn in the St
Annes study. They reported widespread feelings of hopelessness, powerlessness, and despair; they saw that people 'did not
participate to any significant degree in the major institutions of
the larger society, even where basic self interest might be
assumed' (p. 153). Instead there was a fundamental resignation
and acceptance of the situation. Rather than identifying a
'culture of poverty', however, they found that the most poor
were not a homogeneous group; some lived a crisis existence,
others shared certain self-effacing attitudes and modest am-
bitions and such differences could give rise to antagonism
between members of the same community.

EFFECTS OF FEELINGS OF POWERLESSNESS

It seems too that lack of income is not the unique element
associated with the 'psychology of the poor'; since people who
are very badly off are not always despairing and hopeless,
poverty alone is not sufficient explanation.

Perhaps some experiences, to which all people are vulnerable, regardless of 'advantage and disadvantage', which can

generate negative attitudes and feelings of powerlessness similar to those used to describe the 'culture of poverty' are relevant here. These include personal injury, death in the family, chronic ill-health, dismissal from work, and trauma and shock of all kinds. Some studies (Holmes and Rathe, 1967; Brown, Bhrolchain, and Harris, 1975) suggest that wherever events (good or bad) occur and cluster, in which stress is generated or the possibility of effective action is reduced, such a pattern is predictive of future health changes.

The question then arises as to whether such patterns are associated with other responses? One study that suggests they might be, examined the marital background, housing, education, and employment patterns of two groups of women, one of which made use of maternity services and one which failed to do so. When social class, education, and proximity to the clinic were controlled, distinct differences between the groups emerged. Those who made least use of services were markedly younger than women in the other group (between 18—23 years old) and a high proportion of their pregnancies were either illegitimate or conceived before marriage. They were found to live a crisis existence, beset by housing problems, overcrowding, financial difficulties, and frequent sickness — conditions that caused stress and combined to create feelings of powerlessness. Utilizers, on the other hand, had stable housing arrangements, were in regular employment, and were more likely to have planned their marriage and pregnancy (McKinlay and McKinlay, 1972).

Another investigation of mothers' use of preventive health services in Los Angeles (Bullough, 1972) found a relationship between feelings of powerlessness and whether or not the last pregnancy was planned, which applied both below and above the poverty line. All such studies suggest that barriers to utilization of statutory services may exist which result in withdrawal from society. It may be that failure to use pre-school provision may be the result of such an 'alienation' complex.

There are notable examples in this country and America that firmly underline the possibility that feelings associated with poverty can and do exist in our technological society, even though the general level of income of the 'poor' is so much higher than twenty years ago.

In this connection, a recent study which focused in part on the pre-school age children of fifty-six families known to the social services department in a large Midland city is detailed and thought-provoking (Wilson and Herbert, 1978). While the authors also do not subscribe to the 'culture of poverty', they stress the sense of powerlessness, the inexorable pressure of daily living, which drains families of energy and potential. They show how such families adapt to deprivation, to under-privilege and failure by lowered expectations. The account is of particular relevance since each family studied had one child aged three or four who could go to a specially set up playgroup two mornings a week during the summer and autumn terms of the two years fieldwork. Most of the families sent their children to playgroup, but in spite of transport being provided, attendances were so irregular due to ill-health or to children's unwillingness to participate, that adequate observations, records, and tests could be made on only thirty-one out of fifty-six children. They are described as predominantly 'bewildered, lost children, who did not know what to expect, who continued to be worried and who seemed unable to relax − an impression reinforced by their very poor clothing, unkempt appearance and smell' (Wilson and Herbert, 1978 : 65).

Lack of resources is seen as the chief explanation for families' failure to cope with problems, rather than innate fecklessness or irresponsibility. Enlightening comparisons made between these families and those in a study of 700 Nottinghamshire children (Newson and Newson, 1968) show that while child-rearing practices were largely similar to those of non-skilled workers' families, there were aspects of child care that simply could not be compared. Limitations imposed by general poverty − lack of toys, of privacy, of holidays, outings or hobbies − unhappiness increased by stress factors such as extreme want, ill-health, large family size, and handicap, meant that some questions were meaningless for such families.

Such a situation, if it is indeed self-generating, is closely related to the concept of the 'cycle of deprivation' (Sir Keith Joseph, 1972). This catch-phrase reflects the observation that problems are found in the same family generation after generation; it implies that the cause is deprivation transmitted through the family. No doubt genetic considerations play a part, but environmental factors undoubtedly exert a powerful influence. The structure of society itself, supported by law, imposes certain constraints ensuring the persistence of privilege and the unequal distribution of wealth. Some sections of society discriminate against certain social groups, as the very existence of the Race Relations Board testifies; schools are not all equally effective, there is the varied influence of different cultures and even geographical location, as in the attributing of low achievement of Fenland children in the 1930s and '40s to their comparative isolation and in-breeding.

The number and extent of possible factors contributing to such a cycle, assuming it exists, are abundant. The problem remains, however, that if programmes of intervention are, as envisaged in the White Paper and as seven years later is still the case, to be largely based on institutional provision such as nursery classes, schools, and day nurseries, how are these to reach those mothers who are unlikely to take the initiative in making use of facilities, let alone in participating? Do such mothers exist and what are they like?

CHAPTER THREE

Meeting the need

In some areas families who are not being reached and who are unlikely to be reached by provision 'on demand' have been identified and local initiative has been taken to 'meet the need'; almost always the facilities provided lie outside the bounds of statutory provision of nursery classes and schools. People respond spontaneously to a need; they see ways in which their abilities can be used in terms which often bring immediate and obvious satisfaction. They do not always have time and even patience to record and assess their work. Subjective evaluation goes on all the time and changes are made in the light of experience.

The findings of such innovators are often discounted on the grounds that they are anecdotal, but there is a place for 'case histories' which show, first of all, that a need exists which is not being met by the mere extension of nursery school places, and which illustrate some characteristics of those who do not participate. It is possible to touch on only a few such projects, but it is hoped that, although not controlled experiments, they will provide valuable evidence as to how some individuals, authorities, and voluntary bodies have recognized the need for flexibility. In addition, more detailed accounts of approach, organization, and ethos of individuals' groups may suggest possible explanations of the varying degrees of success in achieving mother-involvement observed in the NCB study (Joseph and Parfit, 1972; Ferri and Niblett, 1977).

As has already been pointed out, one problem with Educational Priority Areas is that pockets of disadvantage may go unnoticed; or if not unnoticed, then without special financial help. Ascot is certainly not an area that would be associated in most people's minds with Educational Priority — rather with horse racing and middle-class affluence. Nevertheless, some years ago the Community Liaison Officer for Voluntary Workers there became aware of three categories of family with under-fives who were under stress and needed special help. First there were the single-parent families living in an area where rents were high and often payable by the quarter. Such families often fell behind in payments and found themselves in difficulties. Second, there was a small number of wives of unemployed and those with serious family problems; finally, a group of women isolated in rural areas, often in tied accommodation.

The problem was not a large one, but it was real and persistent. It was realized that much as these mothers might benefit from pre-school provision for their children, they would never take the initiative; nor, with signs of their demoralization apparent, would they have been easily integrated into established nursery groups. In these circumstances, it was decided to try to interest them in a centre for themselves combined with a playgroup for their children. In this project careful records of each family were kept.

Practical problems were considerable, especially with limited resources. Individual mothers were scattered without means of transport; they were characterized by lack of confidence and inability to make personal relationships − often shunned by their immediate neighbours because they were 'going down'. Nevertheless, premises were made available in an old building scheduled for redevelopment. Support was forthcoming from local voluntary bodies and schools. The Rotary Club, for example, organized free transport, mainly by private car; drivers took on a regular commitment and grew to know mothers and children very well. One unlooked-for development was that mothers found it easier to begin to talk on a car journey when there was no necessity for direct eye contact; they were often ashamed of their problems and found it very difficult to talk about them, however much they wanted to do so. The journey was found to give great strength to child, mother, and helper. The same welcoming driver made for continuity between home and playgroup − both a refuge.

Long before this stage was reached, however, the initial contact had been made by social workers or health visitors. They would suggest to mothers that a playgroup was available and that transport could be arranged. This was often followed up by a visit from the Area Liaison Officer, who would chat informally about what went on in the playgroup and how much mothers enjoyed it. Although no money was involved, it was made clear, when the family was introduced to the playgroup, that there were ways in which mothers could contribute to the running of the group and that such help was needed. It was a group run by the mothers, that is, 'All of us'. This experience of belonging to, and being accepted into, a group totally dependent upon oneself for fund raising and continuance, was totally new to these families.

Indeed, this was basic to the whole scheme; a general characteristic of these mothers was that not only were they short of ready money, but they felt they had nothing else to offer. So that they should not be subject to charity – unacceptable to them – it was necessay to find some real contribution they could make. .

This was not difficult. There were many jobs connected with the running of the group which required only time and a little effort. As mothers gained in confidence, they were more willing to accept responsibility. Fund raising events to provide equipment, jumble sales for example, were organized with enthusiasm. Friends were made in the relaxed atmosphere of the mother's room; here they could make a cup of tea, gather round a fire and chat.

The playgroup was in the adjoining room and mothers could come and go as they wished. The rather unprepossessing premises would compare unfavourably with a normal nursery school, but their similarity to the relative chaos at home was an advantage; it made a gradual adjustment possible. The accommodation was not without character, however; being homely and not too immaculate, the children could explore in ways that would not be permitted in a more formal nursery school. There was plenty of space and no need to pack paint and easels, puzzles and prams away between sessions. The main playroom had once been a magistrate's court and was on several levels. The old jury box remained and was full of play possibilities. Best of all, there were several connecting rooms so that mothers and children could carry on a variety of activities without getting in each other's way.

A playgroup such as this is viewed as a 'Halfway House', fulfilling a role similar to a playbus, in that although its physical limitations make it far from the ideal solution, it can act as an initiator and a useful link between an isolated family and eventual integration into an established playgroup or nursery group. It has acted as a catalyst, in that mother and group activity has developed throughout the Rural District Area as a result of this experiment.

In the majority of families, it was not only the child who needed play. The family had needs of its own which could be met through the group. The children were indeed in need of stimulus, freedom of activity, often of a one-to-one relationship with a loving mother figure, together with the comfort and succour of a relaxed atmosphere. Siblings and mothers, too, and in some cases, other adults in the families, needed the group.

In holiday times or when crisis 'struck', young brothers and sisters were always welcome to come and play; proprietorial pride on the part of the initial playgroup attender and the other children was noticed. The sense of 'belonging' was much needed, particularly in single-parent families.

The success of the playgroup was in no small part due to the fact that it could cater for the mother as well as the child and at the same time. Many mothers could not face parting with a much needed baby, because they were 'alone' and lonely. The child, in many cases, represented their only claim to achievement.

Beyond this need of the mothers to be with the child, there is the need to gain practical help which the socially isolated woman does not receive in the normal neighbourly way. The group offered neighbourliness, but at a distance – swopping clothes, giving lifts for shopping, babysitting, and so on. The combination of this sharing of the practicalities of life (the fund-raising jumble sales are integral to this) and the intangible 'belonging' has begun to develop the confidence these women lack.

The need of other adults in the family has also been served by the rippling effect of the group activities. Jumble sales and outings, regular contact, meeting casually in the shops, all contribute to the breakdown of isolation and give the feeling of belonging to a local community.

The playgroup also successfully links people from different backgrounds – the mothers and the drivers, for example, may find that loneliness and feelings of isolation are shared experiences. In an area such as Ascot, it is not easy for women in the late 30s and 40s to find work that is sufficiently rewarding. There is a surplus of able, untrained middle-class women, often held back from further training by resistant husbands and families, whose sole work satisfaction can be gained by voluntary work. These are 'middle-class do-gooders'. Perhaps it could be argued that their needs are as great, but not as obvious, as the mothers of the playgroup children.

Both girls and boys from the local comprehensive school help on a regular basis, not only with the children in the playgroup, but also in the various fund-raising activities. Preparation for their weekly visits as well as their experience with the group considerably widens their horizons. Community work in the sixth form has greatly developed through contact with the playgroup.

The organization of a group such as this depends initially on the driving force of individuals who, aware of a need or problem, inspire others who can make practical contributions towards a solution. They work as a team together in an informal way, without the need for committee procedure. This rather haphazard approach has been found to be a definite asset when trying to interest mothers who are quickly overwhelmed by formal situations and unable to plan very far ahead.

The way in which a mother is first approached, and the way in which she is received is of paramount importance whether the organization is small, as in Ascot, or on a larger scale as in Birmingham. Informality and willingness to listen at all times are therefore key factors too at a comparatively large pioneer family centre in a 'concrete jungle' of houses, maisonettes, and blocks of high-rise flats in Birmingham. Like the Ascot project, this scheme too aims to reach families unlikely to take initiative in seeking out available provisions. Priority is given to children who are at risk by battering or physical neglect, and those severely lacking in stimulation. In addition, priority is also given to children from one-parent families, or whose parents are themselves inadequate, or emotionally disturbed. A number of the children are handicapped, either mentally or physically. In contrast to Ascot, however, co-operation was between the Social Services Department and the National Children's Home who first studied the area and concluded that the prior need was for a day-care centre.

As a result of generous funding, the Family Centre, a National Children's Home and Methodist Church foundation, opened in November 1971; it is a comprehensive unit with three main departments. One section caters for babies of up to fifteen months; then there are two family rooms for twenty-five children from eighteen months to five years. The third section is a nursery classroom for three to five year olds. In addition, there is a medical department, an administrative unit, an office for social workers, and a reception area. The domestic department has a well equipped kitchen and supplies 100 meals a day. There is also a launderette. Such a centre facilitates co-operation between services. The headmistress of the nursery school acts as educational adviser; and in addition to the resident social workers, the services of a doctor, educational psychologist, speech therapist, and teacher of the deaf are involved.

Facilities then are admirable; but the problem is still the same — how to reach the families in most need? As in Ascot, there seem to be two key factors — provision of free transport and the informal friendliness of a team of people working closely together and ready to meet the demand for endless personal contact and the needs of the family as a whole — the over-compensation that seems necessary to begin the momentum of involvement. This is too time-consuming for the statutory agencies.

The Centre's day begins with a collection service at 7.15 am and an hour later, there are already thirty-five children at the Centre. Officially open at 7.30, the Centre can cater for seventy-four pre-school children, of which fifty are placements from the Social Services Department. The children are given baths and medical attention; then comes breakfast — meals play an important part in the programme, as not only are there cases of under-nourishment and feeding problems, but meal-times also provide an opportunity for making friends and good relationships. Children go home at 6.30 pm and there are no residential arrangements; nevertheless, parents are welcome at any time. Sometimes mothers and even whole families spend the day at the Centre — parents then become temporary 'members of staff'. There are also regular group meetings and evening activities — 'Keep Fit', films, dress-making, and weekly hair-dressing; practical discussions on budgeting, basic cookery, etc. are popular and bring the whole family together.

With all these activities and the wide range of facilities, the Centre is able to provide a social, emotional, and educational base for parents and children. Although they live within an Inner City Ring, their situation is not too very different from the families in Ascot; they have the same problems of loneliness, unemployment, and stresses with which they can barely cope. They share too the need for self-respect and the feeling that they have something to contribute. In Ascot, the mother's contribution was personal and practical; in Birmingham, approximately 80 per cent pay something towards the service as it is considered that to give even 50p promotes moral responsibility.

In both these examples, at Ascot and in Birmingham, the specific need was apparent to those who studied the areas. In both cases, provision of facilities resulted in a sufficient number of families making use of them to justify the outlay in terms of time, energy, and money. This was partly due to the degree of co-operation between social workers, health visitors, and playgroup or nursery school staff.

Specific needs amongst childminders have also become apparent to social workers, health visitors, and educationalists. The more progressive local authorities have introduced home visiting schemes, toy libraries, and 'training' courses to support minders and help improve the quality of minding. One particular scheme, funded initially by Trust money involved both the statutory body and a voluntary organization. Some £17,000, left by Miss Bunbury under the trusteeship of Dr John Bowlby and Mrs Nathan Isaacs, enabled the Social Services of several London Boroughs to combine with Inner London Pre-school Playgroups Association in pioneer projects with child-minders.

The first of these was in Lewisham. Here it was recognized that in many respects a minder's situation was similar to that of mothers whose children used and benefited from playgroups and who often found that participation had greatly added to their own enjoyment and understanding of their children's play needs. But it was unlikely that minders would participate in 'traditional' playgroups, if only because income would be eroded by playgroup fees. With the help of Bunbury Trust money, however, it was possible to make places freely available at an informal 'drop-in' centre with playgroup facilities for the minded children. Continuity was assured since the local authority undertook to fund the scheme once it was successfully established.

Three part-time workers, with complementary skills and personalities, worked from 1975 from premises near the main shopping centre in a district where there were known to be many minded children. The team began by visiting registered minders and encouraging them to come to the centre. They also tried to transform a rather large and unprepossessing church hall into a welcoming place with good play facilities for the children. Basic equipment comprised puzzles and constructional toys, sand and water play, dressing up, a home and book corner, painting and dough. Special activities included carpentry, potato cuts, collage, nature table, finger play, music and movement.

The centre opened two mornings a week. On the first day, only one minder and two children came, but within six months numbers had so increased that it was not possible to cater for any more. A common experience, once minders had visited the centre, was that they 'had' to keep coming back because the children had so enjoyed themselves. An effort was made to use generally available play materials; minders were clearly impressed by the children's absorption and began to try out new ideas for play at home. Issues of discipline, diet, and relationships with parents were discussed informally; minders began to value a place where they could meet others with similar interests and problems and where they could get advice. They organized mutual self-help schemes, raised money for new equipment, and began to help each other informally − in short, another dimension was added to their lives. The children seemed to benefit, developing new skills, becoming more outgoing, talkative, and interested in their surroundings.

Constant reassurance and support from the team of workers was necessary for the success of the project. They were also in a position to alert professional workers where there was a need for intervention. Their more usual role, however, where minders lacked confidence, was to give information and to encourage them to seek the help and guidance they needed.

Approximately two thirds of the minders in the catchment area attended the centre. There were still those who came occasionally or not at all. They welcomed the team in their homes, however, and seemed reassured by regular visits from non-authoritarian people. These visits provided opportunities for informal discussion about play and child care and the introduction, when appropriate, of new ideas.

Without this centre most of the children, for whom places in a day nursery were either not available or not desired, would have been without any form of pre-school provision before the statutory school age and some of them could thereby have been at a disadvantage.

Minders are busy people with homes to run. Like many mothers, until they recognize the role of play and the importance of talking to children, they think that seeing to physical needs and affection is all they can contribute. Just as playgroups can help mothers, so such centres may help childminders to appreciate the importance of the job they do.

The minders and the children in their care in Lewisham were registered with the local authority, however; thus they enjoyed the practical and moral support of the visiting officers. But all childminders do not enjoy such support; all authorities do not have visiting officers with special responsibility for minders; social workers usually have very heavy caseloads, and frequently have to concentrate on only the most difficult and intransigent cases. Is the need of those who are not necessarily known to either health visitors or social workers easily identified and met? Can one even assume that what is seen as a need by an observer is necessarily felt as a need by the mothers concerned?

Some insight into the situation with mothers who are not known to social workers is afforded by a study carried out by the Inner London Playgroups Association. A peripatetic supervisor was appointed to set up and monitor the growth of a playgroup in Lambeth when accommodation became available in what appeared to be a needy area (PPA, 1972a). It comprised approximately a square mile of five-storey flats, a few streets of three- and four-storey houses, few amenities, and no open spaces. It was estimated that there were roughly 300 under fives in this district. One nursery school catered for thirty children in the morning and thirty in the afternoon; three playgroups could take up to forty children between them.

The supervisor had had considerable success in starting play-groups in other similar districts. She began in her usual way by knocking on doors to let mothers know there was a hall available for a playgroup and that if they were interested, they were welcome any Tuesday afternoon to talk about it. (Previous experience with other mothers had suggested that this type of in-formal approach was more likely to attract mothers than one meeting at a particular time.) She waited for them fairly confidently, as she had been well received and mothers had ex-pressed enthusiastic interest. On previous occasions, a similar response would have led to a nucleus willing to start a playgroup.

Mothers did not come. Nevertheless, she continued to make contact with them in their homes and 100 informal interviews were completed. Mothers had apparently spoken freely on all aspects of their living conditions, their attitudes to their children, education, and the future — once they knew and trusted her.

Interviewing in depth, though physically and mentally exhausting, was not rewarding. Although welcomed in the homes and taken into the confidence of many mothers, there was no real interest in a playgroup or any other type of pre-school education. As more insight was gained into the families and neighbourhood, the would-be supervisor realized that the situation of some of these mothers was such that they did not recognize their children's needs. Their own preoccupations got in the way. Most of the mothers were young, 18–22. They had left school as early as possible, not always through dislike of it, but because it was the accepted thing and they felt no encouragement was received from home or school to stay on. Marriage was the next 'stage'. Many girls were pregnant when they married and quickly had a second baby. Once married, it was accepted that husbands took responsibility for any social life, attitudes to children, education, and money matters. Flats afforded little privacy; yet many of them felt isolated. They were bored, depressed, and found difficulty in coping, although their situation was not thought to warrant help from social workers. It was simply that the transition from teenage schoolgirl or young wage earner to mother and wife was one for which they were ill-prepared.

The supervisor decided that the problem had been tackled in the wrong way. She started door knocking again, but this time with the mothers in mind and *not* the children. This new approach bore fruit. One Tuesday afternoon in mid-October, nine mothers and twelve children came to the first meeting of the 'Mother's Club'. They decided to take turns in looking after the children and agreed they wanted people to come and talk to them rather than have a 'nattering club'. They were interested in first aid, dressmaking, cuts of meat and fish, other people's jobs, puppet making, and Christmas decorations — that is, nothing directly to do with children. Subsequent attendance fluctuated between six and sixteen, but the nucleus remained, meeting on two afternoons a week.

Problems naturally arose from the arrangements made to

care for the children. After a few weeks, a thought-provoking outing was arranged to Wandsworth, to visit an established playgroup where there was full parental involvement — that is, parents were responsible for administration, finance, and supervision. The visitors had an opportunity of talking to mothers in the playgroup; this led to lively comment and discussion. The provision of interesting play equipment did not go unnoticed; indeed, the stimulus of a visit to a good playgroup did more to set these mothers thinking than any amount of talking had done. At first they were overwhelmed and felt that the gap between what they had to offer and what they had observed was so great that it was unbridgeable.

This was the moment when the idea of a playgroup could begin to grow; their horizons had been extended to include the germ of an idea of something desirable for them and their children. Long-term, caring, sensitive support for both mothers and children was needed. After much discussion, various fund-raising activities were suggested — jumble sales and a dance — and these were enthusiastically supported. A supervisor was appointed; playgroup and mother's meetings functioned in adjoining rooms.

Inevitably there were problems. Some personalities were difficult. The level of equipment and educational expertise, when judged by professional nursery standards, was low. Nevertheless, without the groundwork put in by the supervisor and her ability to put aside pre-conceived ideas, there would have been no recognition of the barriers preventing these mothers from making use of facilities. Their life-style — if judged only by the time they got up in the morning — was not geared to standard hours for pre-schooling, and with provision 'on demand' their children would have remained outside the system altogether because they did not recognize its relevance to their needs.

The importance of 'researching' an area first and assessing local needs is frequently stressed. (The Education White Paper, para. 22: 'the Government hopes that local plans will reflect local needs and resources': Educational Priority, vol. 1 : 106: '. . . The design of a pre-school programme must be preceded by diagnosis of the specific needs of the children for which the programme is designed.') What emerges from the experience in one small area of Inner London suggests that it may be constructive to consider the needs of mothers too. Meeting them where they are and supporting them in activities perhaps far removed from pre-schooling may enable them to reach a stage where they can respond to needs in their children of which they have hitherto been unaware.

Unfortunately, this is a long process and the dynamics of it are not fully understood; those who are aware of the educational advantages of the nursery school for the children, feel that time is too short to concentrate on the mothers, particularly when many teachers have developed skills for dealing with young children and not young adults who often come from very different backgrounds from their own. Experience in Ascot, Birmingham, and Lambeth suggests the need to start long before nursery school age. Preparation for mother 'involvement' may start in the school, the ante- and post-natal period, through one o'clock clubs, mother and baby clubs or, in some areas, possibly home visiting. In the present situation, however, where the provision of nursery schools and classes still does not meet the need of parents who 'demand' the facility, the real issue is blurred. Staff have enough to do coping with full classes and exploring ways of involving parents who have been among the first to come forward and make use of the facilities.

The issue, however, is not with the need for nursery provision, but rather with the extent to which it will be used by the whole community. Given that there will be a small proportion who need very definite supportive help from social workers and play-leaders and a large proportion who will want their children to benefit from pre-school education, how great is the proportion of people between the two who, for a variety of reasons, may hesitate? What kinds of approach will tip the balance in favour of their participation?

It is in this connection that the history of the established group in Wandsworth which was visited by the Lambeth mothers is interesting. It charts the development of what appeared to be an unpromising and inopportune undertaking.

A new tenant on a Council estate had been horrified at women fighting in the courtyard and had been unwilling to let her children play there. She found other mothers who shared her feelings and went to a Tenants' Association meeting to air them. This mother knew nothing about playgroups; she happened to sit next to the deaconness from a local church who suggested a playgroup might help and advised her to contact both 'Save the Children Fund' and the Pre-school Playgroups Association.

The former advised these mothers against starting their own group on the very understandable grounds that they had no professional qualifications and it would be very much less expensive to let SCF run one.

PPA sent down a local mother who gave them the basic information and help they needed to start. They opened in a Church Hall that was soon pulled down; for some time they even met in a garage but finally came to an arrangement with a local church whereby they share a hall with a Montessori school.

This was the genesis of the group that so impressed the mothers from Lambeth; it is a group which, after five years, impresses professionals as well, with its equipment (at least £400 a year is raised through fund raising activities which involve the whole family) and the expertise with which it is used. It required vision, resourcefulness, and determination to achieve the standards set by this group, as well as considerable help from statutory bodies. The qualities of resourcefulness and determination were constant, but the vision changed as horizons widened.

It was perhaps significant that these mothers had been offered the possibility of a playgroup organized by professionals and had rejected it. This seems to imply that these non-middle-class mothers did not wish to hand over their children to outsiders. The supervisor employed by the mothers belonged to the same community. They appreciated her concern for their children and gave her their support and co-operation. Over a period, through helping at 'their' playgroup, many began to see their children's play in a new light. Some who began by simply wanting to get rid of their children subsequently enjoyed their own children and others more than they would have thought possible. New friends were made and added impetus given by attending training courses.

This group is not unique in the area; other similar ones share a strong community feeling and support each other — financially and in other practical ways. For these mothers, the need was met by involvement, but it was a very gradual process which is still evolving. Had they been faced in the beginning with the responsibilities they now assume with confidence, they would have been overwhelmed, as were the mothers from Lambeth. They feel that it was the very fact of 'learning by doing' that helped to bring about their success. (As one mother said, 'People are constantly underestimating us because we live in a deprived area. I know now that I haven't enriched my own children's vocabulary, because I didn't know about talking to them — I and a lot of people like me are willing and able to do it, once we are given the idea.')

The special quality of these playgroups is emphasized by Dr Margaret Pollak's suggestion that 'working class parents in particular have been persuaded to abdicate educational responsibilities in favour of the institution'. She reported that the majority of mothers in a sample in an industrial area of North East Derbyshire professed a complete lack of belief that they themselves possessed any skill or knowledge that might enhance their children's cognitive skill and intellectual development (*The Times Educational Supplement*, February 16, 1973, and quoted by Lady Plowden at the Annual Conference of the Preschool Playgroups Association in Edinburgh, 1973). These conclusions are not confirmed by the experience in Wandsworth.

There is clear evidence, however, that the home is the strongest single factor in relation to educational achievement (Plowden, 1967). Furthermore, programmes that include the mother and are community based are more likely to be successful; the Report on the Red House (1972) claimed that 'with intelligent guidance most parents can acquire sufficient practical knowledge of child development to act as efficient educators . . . there is also evidence that membership of a highly motivated group raises the morale of parents and helps to break the cycle of low aspiration and low educational attainment which has been suggested by various research reports' (p. 13).

It is therefore important to identify any factors that may contribute to participation of such a kind. There is perhaps a clue in the National Children's Bureau Report (Joseph and Parfit, 1972) which showed that there were clear distinctions in the manner in which playgroups were initiated, organized, and staffed. It suggested that attitudes to mothers — whether they are seen as partners or as people for whom a service is provided — determined responses. It seemed that a range of attitudes existed. At one extreme, they were inclined to be paternalistic; initiation was often by a vicar, church worker, or someone who assumed personal responsibility for the administration of the group. Progress was achieved with minimum of delay; the group ran efficiently, probably with trained staff, some with and others without 'parent participation' (p. 17). At the other extreme a group of mothers coming together on an equal footing to organize a playgroup, was more likely to experience difficulty in establishing procedures, making relationships, and in communication, with consequent delays and setbacks (p. 18). It was noted that fewer mothers in high need areas participated and it was therefore suggested that non-participant groups might be more suitable in this situation.

Mothers in the Wandsworth groups doubted this. 'Initiators' accepted that progress in the early stages was often slow, that mistakes were made and time wasted in discussion. They maintained however that the entire group learned from their experience, since they were all involved and took responsibility. This would not, they thought, have been so likely to happen if an individual had assumed personal responsibility. Although, in the early days, children had the disadvantage of poor equipment, indifferent premises, and untrained staff, they benefited from emotional security and a high ratio of adults to children. Many of these shortcomings could have been overcome by the 'right kind of help'. The type of help that was most appreciated was non-authoritarian and non-directive; it was that which gave practical advice, information, and support but which did not try to manipulate or to take away initiative. If the way advice was given led to a sense of purpose, enjoyment, and achievement, it helped to build up confidence that had been eroded by an education that had produced a sense of failure.

In the long term, once insights gained from mothers' group meetings and training courses began to percolate, considerable changes were noted. These were mainly in the way mothers talked to their children, responded to behavioural problems, chose toys and equipment, and in the general degree of sociability, confidence, and interest in education and child development. Above all, it was claimed that these changes affected not only the 'initiators' and those who wanted to be involved, but also those who, at first, would happily have abdicated educational responsibilities. Such changes, moreover, operated not only while the playgroup was in session, but was felt to influence the whole family.

This is a very different conclusion from that of Mrs Monica Else (1969) who studied the extent of supportive relationships generated by playgroups. She interviewed 114 mothers from three urban playgroups located in different types of housing area and found that playgroups tended to reinforce existing patterns of social relations in the community. Those who already felt at ease in formal and social situations were likely to derive most benefit, while those who already had difficulty in finding the informal support they needed, were prevented by these same difficulties from becoming involved with the playgroup.

It is hardly surprising that in a cross section of mothers, the more articulate and confident would be willing to 'take office' – if only because they were more familiar with procedure and felt able to cope with the situation. Nor is it unreasonable to suppose that since they were willing and able to take responsibility, those less confident would not become involved. What was needed, according to the Wandsworth mothers, was a climate in which all mothers are needed and in which they can gain confidence and a sense of belonging.

This is an opinion very similar to those concerned with the Ascot experiment. Although it was accepted that there were some mothers who could not participate, it was thought that there were many others who initially did not wish to do so because they felt inadequate and lacked confidence; the mere idea of committees and committee procedures was enough to deter such mothers. Fatigue, ill-health, stress of all kinds was felt to militate against involvement. Yet, in retrospect, the experience of mothers in the Wandsworth group would testify to the view that, expected to take an interest, helped to understand and cope with their children better, together with the kind of support received from other mothers and supervisors, this type of involvement has had a profoundly beneficial effect on their lives.

The consensus of opinion of staff and mothers in these case studies was that it is not so much a question of structure of organization, but of the basic attitudes within that organization. Initiators can be mothers, church workers, PPA, or statutory bodies; success in involving those who would not normally participate depends on the attitudes within the groups. An amalgam of statutory/voluntary provision may in some projects offer the best type of help; the voluntary workers tempering bureaucracy by their warmth and spontaneous caring. Parent expectation, the way in which horizons are gradually extended, and the degree to which parents are supported, their initiative encouraged and their confidence increased, are the crucial factors. The role of the supervisor is seen as reaching out through the children to the parents and the community.

Such an approach is often unacceptable to the trained nursery teacher, whose special skills lie in creating a stimulating and educative environment for the young child; they do not usually extend this activity to mothers. Many schools welcome parents and try to improve home – school relations, but the onus is on parents to respond. Although some parents do help in the classroom, they are likely to be those who already have some training or natural interest and ability. According to the Report of the National Union of Teachers (1974), teachers welcome parental support and are prepared to put their training and experience at the disposal of parents. Teachers see their role as primarily concerned with the social education of the young and preparation for school; while they seek to develop a good relationship between school and home, they expect to establish this link through friendly relationships and a welcoming school atmosphere. Yet it is made clear in the *Study of Nursery Education*, Schools Council Working Paper 41 (1972), that attitudes are basically authoritarian and child-centred.

But if, as these case studies suggest, parental participation of at least a proportion of the 'disadvantaged' is not just the corollary of generally friendly attitudes, but entails a fundamental difference in approach, then 'parental participation' will mean either a change in attitude, or involvement only for those parents who already have the confidence and status to cope with a 'school' atmosphere; those who feel they have nothing to contribute will withdraw from the situation. Excuses for non-participation may be given which simply mask the real reasons. These may be related to lack of confidence, feelings of hopelessness and alienation rather than lack of ability.

Of course, such anecdotal evidence provides no more than interesting examples of individual experiences; one cannot generalize from it. The investigations that follow, although essentially still case studies since they concentrate on small groups, go one stage further. They introduce an element of objective measurement and by studying *all* the mothers or minders with children eligible to use pre-school provision designed to meet their needs, they offer a more clearly signposted perspective.

PART TWO

A STUDY OF PARENTAL RESPONSE TO PRE-SCHOOLING

CHAPTER FOUR

'Hillcroft'

BACKGROUND TO THE STUDY

Previous studies which have touched on problems of demand and utilization of pre-school provision have concentrated on geographical areas where findings could be overlaid or distorted by extreme conditions such as bad housing, overcrowding, and lack of social amenity — all reasons that are frequently advanced to explain lack of enthusiasm. Although such problems may well be important, it was thought preferable to study a community without marked advantages or disadvantages, but distinguished by the fact that pre-school provision designed to meet local needs would become newly available in it.

Fortuitously, in 1972, the Council of the London Borough of Hillingdon decided to allocate £21,000 (later rising to £65,000) to provide custom-built premises intended primarily for use as playgroups on seven council estates designated as being 'in special need'. This referred to estates where there was a high concentration of children, an active tenants' association, and no pre-school provision; it did not reflect poor standards of housing or social deprivation.

Such a development met the basic requirements for study. Facilities designed to meet local need were to be introduced where there was no existing provision. The decision to do so was taken after pressure both from tenants for this particular type of pre-schooling and following an 'expert' assessment of needs by a working party set up by the Council. The catchment areas of each unit were clearly defined and socially homogeneous; the estates, in a relatively favoured outer London borough, did not include high-rise flats. Premises were to be centrally sited and heavily subsidized by the Local Authority, though not run by the Council. It would be possible to interview mothers, all of whom could be assured of a place for their children, before the playgroup opened. Hence, responses could not be subjective reactions to a particular teacher or playgroup leader.

An initial investigation in the first project area to be completed clarified the design of the main study and ironed out technical problems.

AIMS AND SCOPE OF THE STUDY

It was then decided to focus on mothers with three- and four-year-old children on the second estate in which a unit was installed. There would therefore be no control over numbers; all the mothers with a child eligible to use the playgroup would comprise the sample.

The intention was to describe the total picture. Then, once the playgroup opened, to divide mothers into three groups on the basis of their response to it and to isolate outstanding characteristics of each group:

Group 1 – those who were hesitant about enrolling on the waiting list and who ultimately did not take up a place for their child.

Group II – those who had kept their pre-school children at home, but said they welcomed the new facility, had placed their child's name on the waiting list, and took up a place at the playgroup.

Group III – those who already sent their children to pre-school facilities outside the immediate neighbourhood and continued to do so.

Overall, the study was to be exploratory, not definitive, qualitative rather than quantitative.

The study area

'Hillcroft' was defined by the catchment area of both the proposed playgroup and the local primary school. It fell in the social service area with a much higher proportion of children-in-care cases than would be expected on the basis of relative population size. It is only fair to say, however, that the administrative social work area included estates outside 'Hillcroft' itself and that these seemed to generate most concern. It was dominated by an estate completed in 1969: built of pre-cast concrete, blocks of three-storey flats were arranged in a series of 'closes'. Each block had a central staircase which served three flats on each floor; the middle flat in every case was one-bedroomed and intended for the elderly. They had small private balconies. Flats on either side were two-bedroomed family flats and their balconies were not enclosed but formed part of a 'landing' at the top of each stairway.

All family flats were light and airy, centrally heated, and built to the same design. An L-shaped hall gave access to one double and one single bedroom, a bathroom, and separate lavatory. There was a large, well-proportioned living room and a con-necting door to a kitchen/diner. Amenities included universal provision of an electric clothes drier, waste chutes for refuse disposal, and 'pram' sheds at ground level for tenants on the upper floors. There were ample parking and garage facilities.

In the centre of each close was an ornamental area, partially enclosed by low brick walls, irregularly placed, and planted inside with trees and shrubs. There were also a few saplings on the open green spaces between the blocks of flats. Centrally placed was a small concrete play area, with a rusty old engine and a few swings. Close by, on some open ground, the Council had recently opened an adventure playground, but this was not intended for younger children.

In addition to the new estate, another area of older council housing was included in the study area. This property was built about 1952 and comprised semi-detached terraced houses in red brick; each had an enclosed garden. The 'estate' had a modern look and gave the impression of being well-tended. There were also eight blocks of older flats built on three floors and separated from each other by green open spaces. Each of these flats had a tiny enclosed garden where washing could be hung and children could play. The only private housing was a very small development of detached houses in a cul-de-sac near the school.

A well-stocked supermarket was sited in the centre of the new estate, close to the children's play area and the rent office. Prices compared favourably with those in the nearest shopping centre, about ten minutes walk away. Here there were several supermarkets, a good selection of small shops, library and post office, clinic and Citizen's Advice Bureau, together with bus and train routes. Behind the main shopping centre lay a small recreation field and park. There was no cinema in the locality and no community hall; there were, however, two licensed social clubs and a number of pubs within walking distance.

Apart from the British Legion, there was no social centre where parents could go with their young children.

Physical needs, then, were well catered for in that there was opportunity for employment, good accommodation, excellent clinic and hospital provision, and accessible social amenities. Some institutions which might have helped draw people into community life were too far away to play any significant part. A number of Catholic families, for example, expressed regret that their church was over half an hour's walk away; they just could not join in activities when their children were young. Thus, although not inaccessible, 'Hillcroft' gave the impression of being cut off from the larger community and yet not to have developed a community life of its own.

Such was the backcloth against which the study of the new playgroup developed.

The Council's proposals

The Tenants' Association publicized a series of meetings when the Council's proposals were explained by the Borough Pre-school Playgroups Adviser. The Tenants' Association was very active and concerned with the welfare of residents in all age groups. It dealt with grievances among tenants, organized social events, and circularized a newsletter. It had been particularly forceful in its demands for a playgroup, had expressed willingness to take responsibility for developing it, and consequently played a key role in communicating local authority intentions.

No rent would be charged by the Council for the premises; free heating and general maintenance would be provided, the Tenants' Association being solely responsible for replacement of small items and for cleaning. Tenants were encouraged to raise funds for specific purposes, but there was an initial grant of £100 for equipment. The Council expected that the playgroup would cater for estate and non-estate children where these fell within the catchment area or were within reasonable walking distance. The anticipated ratio of estate to non-estate children was 3:1. If tenants wished to use the premises for purposes other than the playgroup, then it was unlikely that youth activities would be encouraged, but smaller committee meetings, those for senior citizens, mother and toddler groups, or opportunity groups would be encouraged.

Tenants' reactions

General reactions ranged from enthusiasm for a 'fantastic' and 'extraordinary' offer − 'just what we need', to a more grudging response that 'if that is what the Council is determined to do, we might as well go along with it' − but with reservations.

Lack of sympathy for the idea came mainly from tenants who had no young children and who were worried about noise in respect of the elderly or shift workers. Some were concerned about the degree of responsibility involved and the economic viability of the playgroup; others opposed a move that might encourage children from outside to come and play on their territory. 'We have enough of our own.'

It was evident that there was some reluctance on the part of mothers to 'take office'. However, the Advisor had created a pleasantly informal atmosphere and went on to explain more fully what was involved. Eventually eight mothers volunteered to serve on the committee and a chairman, secretary, and treasurer were elected. This committee threw itself into fund raising and gathering of equipment with great enthusiasm. Fathers too were involved in making and repairing toys. A trained supervisor was appointed and a monthly newsletter circulated to all mothers on the estate.

The role of the Borough Advisor was crucial; she was able to offer guidance in choices of equipment and in the type of toy the playgroup would need. She established excellent relations, both with the Tenants' Association and with individual mothers, combining a businesslike, forward-looking procedure with an informal and supportive approach which she adjusted to meet differing needs. Her role assumed even greater importance due to building delays and consequent disappointments which dogged the project. It was inevitable that even where there was great enthusiasm, initial interest and involvement was eroded by frustration and misunderstanding in the absence of any visible signs of progress. In an increasingly depressing situation, when one hold-up followed another, she organized meetings for mothers in their own homes. On these occasions, there was an opportunity to discuss aspects of playgroup practice and a chance to handle and talk about material and equipment before the playgroup opened.

This was the period when mothers were interviewed in their own homes.

Finding the sample and gathering information

Spot checks had suggested that lists of families with under fives supplied by the Tenants' Association, by health visitors, and the Education Authority omitted a worrying number of families. Accordingly a preliminary door-to-door survey pinpointed all the mothers with under fives. There were two interviewers, both women. One was young, in the same age range as most of the mothers, the other was middle-aged (S.S.). Thus mothers had a choice of two people they could talk to − where one interviewer failed, the other succeeded. Ten families refused information, out of a total of 729, but it was known from neighbours which of these families had young children, and they were included in the list of mothers to be interviewed. It was decided to talk in depth with the seventy-seven mothers who had children aged three and four who were therefore eligible to use the new playgroup. All but one mother agreed to the interviews, most of which were tape recorded and lasted at least one hour, many of them longer.

The interview schedule

A semi-structured interview schedule was developed. It covered size and composition of family, ages of parents and children, schooling and attitudes to education, occupation, health, income, and housing. It explored family relationships, friendship patterns, and social habits as well as a mother's perception of the young child's needs and her relationship with her children. One section was concerned with the use of pre-school provision and the extent to which mothers thought that existing or proposed provision met their needs. Incorporated, though administered separately, was a Grid designed to assess mothers' attitudes to playgroup practice (Saxby, 1973) and the Rotter I-E Scale (Rotter, 1966). This American measure had, in many other studies, proved useful in pinpointing attitudes associated with the 'Culture of Poverty'.

The interviews

After a period of initial suspicion, mothers were helpful and responsive. Even those who had slammed the door or refused to talk in the preliminary survey were welcoming once they began to know and trust the interviewers. All those who had at first refused to co-operate were reached.

It appeared that the main reason for reluctance to answer the door to casual callers was the heavy pressure of door-to-door salesmen to which the new estate in particular had been subject since its earliest days. It was also found that 'students' were ostensibly 'doing a survey on children for a university course'. They were really selling encyclopaedias. One mother was quite unable to give her mind to the interview on a first visit; she was totally overwhelmed by the realization that she and her husband had signed for close on £200 worth of books which they could not possibly afford. 'But they looked so nice . . . whatever will we do?' Concurrently another firm was also 'doing a survey of children'; their real purpose was to prepare the ground for a home photographer.

Such a background to the interviews meant that the first few minutes were crucial in establishing rapport with whoever answered the door. In practice, it was found necessary to respond to whatever situation presented itself and to the mother as a person. It might be that she needed reassurance that we were not selling anything or, in some cases, she needed practical help. This ranged from keeping an eye on, or playing with her children while she coped with some domestic chore, to taking her and her offspring to the casualty department of the local hospital.

FAMILIES IN 'HILLCROFT'

i. Housing

Council housing policy went some way to controlling family composition. It stipulated that families occupying two-bedroomed flats on the new estate would be eligible for a house if they had two children of different sex, once the younger had reached the age of one year. Although not all the families eligible for larger accommodation had been moved, such a policy not only biased the sample against large families but also included families whose size was to some extent influenced by it. In order to obtain a house, for example, some families admitted to having more children than they otherwise might have done; when two or three children of the same sex were born in the same family, this could be considered a misfortune and a blow to hopes of a house and garden. The total number of boys and girls was nicely balanced with forty-one boys and forty-two girls.

Families with young children were concentrated in the new

flats (also Council housing policy) — 78 per cent; approximately one quarter (22 per cent) of under fives lived off the new estate. Only 13 per cent lived in houses with an enclosed garden or outdoor playspace. It seemed that the majority of people living in houses had moved in during the early 1950s, when their own children were young, and they had already brought up their families.

There was clearly a division in the minds of some who lived off the new estate as to the 'status' of the two types of dwelling. A typical response was 'You won't find no young 'uns here abouts — you'd best go over there' (indicating the new estate). There was a noticeable number of gratuitous comments implying that people in the new flats came from London, or at least 'not from round here', that they had a lot of children and were 'rough'.

The new estate had been built just over five years and most families (81 per cent) had lived at their present address between two and five years. The majority of parents seemed to have had settled childhoods; that is, with no moves. Contrary to the impression gained by comments on the adjoining estate (mainly houses), and even from social workers and health visitors, most of the families with children eligible to use the new playgroup were local. Only 15 per cent had come from outside the area, mostly rehoused from Inner London.

Where the new estate was concerned, a distinction was often made between the accommodation inside and the external appearance and amenity. 'I love my flat, but if only it was somewhere else, anywhere else', and another typical remark, 'once you get in and shut the door, its alright — the flats inside are very nice really, but . . .'.

Reservations sprang from two sources. One was the loneliness of mothers who had been rehoused from London. They missed the variety of city life and their own families. 'There's not enough for my age group' (the twenties), 'it's terrible, you get so depressed; they're a funny lot here — even for a game of bingo you've got to go two connections, and the journey takes more than the games you play'; 'Most days, I go back to me mam' (in Wandsworth, London).

The other source of reservation was the desire for a garden or at least some enclosed space, where children could play. A clear cut difference emerged between those who lived in flats and those who had a house. Perhaps it was best summed up by a mother who had been moved from a flat to a house. She had a

boy and a girl, both under five, and had been in her new home
for two months: 'It's made a wonderful difference to all of us;
my husband says I'm a different person. And I'm off pills, aren't
I? The children can play in the garden; look they're digging
now, and I never dare let them out of the flat.'

ii. Patterns of employment and economic status

The questions of working mothers and employment for mothers
was approached in a number of ways. Mothers were asked
whether they worked and about the nature of such work as well
as whether they would like to work outside the home and what
the 'ideal' pre-school provision would be.

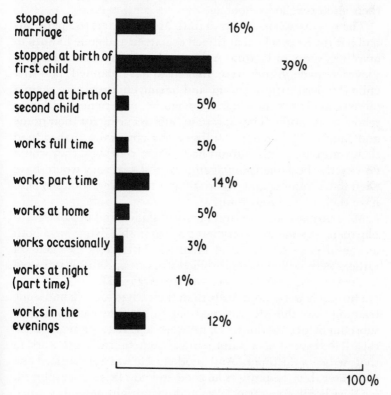

Figure 1   *Employment of mothers ('Hillcroft')*

Patterns of employment will obviously vary from district to
district. It is possible that if 'Hillcroft' were close to factories

where highly paid, congenial jobs were available or if the financial situation were tighter, the proportion of working mothers might be different. As it was, the employment pattern (see *Figure 1*) was in line with national figures of 5–6 per cent of mothers with under fives working full time, but it revealed a larger proportion working part time – 35 per cent as compared with a national average of 26 per cent (Bone, 1977).

For most mothers, there was not the pressure to work; nor were there the incentives of high wages and convenient hours. The prevalent desire (74 per cent) was for a 'little job' during school hours once their children had started school, but 72 per cent were adamant that even if there were local provision to look after their under fives, they would not think of going out before their child reached school age.

The reason was not hard to find. Most mothers (63 per cent) had left the local school at fifteen or sixteen and gone to work in an office, shop, or factory. A similar proportion married before they were twenty; they were unlikely to have planned their first child (70 per cent). Marriage and having children gave them a sense of achievement which they had not experienced either at school or at 'work'. They saw their 'job' as caring for their home and family. Most seemed fulfilled thereby. Even if they 'had their time over again', almost half (49 per cent) said they would do exactly the same thing again; the rest said they would have liked some training and would still want to marry, though not to have their children so young.

Most husbands could find plenty of skilled and unskilled employment at what was considered a reasonable living wage both at the airport and at local factories. Fifty-eight per cent of fathers were skilled or semi-skilled workers and this is reflected in the training they had received (see *Figure 2*).

Husbands were more likely than their wives to have had some training, but this often turned out to be different from their subsequent occupations. There were a variety of reasons for this. 'He trained as a paint sprayer, but he can't get work in that, so he's a dustman.' And another: 'He was apprenticed as a carpenter, but the pay was no good and now he's self-employed. He does home decorating. We're doing alright now.' It seemed that breaking off apprenticeship often coincided with marriage and starting a family.

The majority of mothers (64 per cent) considered that they had 'enough to live on'. There was, however, some reluctance to admit to specific sums over £35. It was the 'self-employed' or those who were supplementing their income 'on the side' to whom this applied. Such incomes were subject to considerable fluctuation and, taken overall, were unlikely to amount to more than an average of £40 a week.

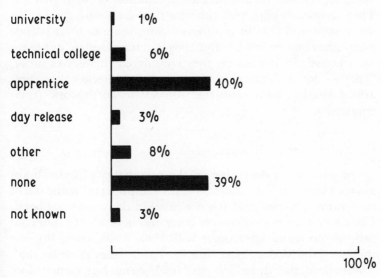

university 1%

technical college 6%

apprentice 40%

day release 3%

other 8%

none 39%

not known 3%

100%

Figure 2   Father's training ('Hillcroft')

As perceived in the home, the economic level was high: 74 per cent had washing machines, fridge, dryer, and electric mixer. All but three families had television, usually colour; those who did not, said the decision was deliberate. As these were also amongst the few families who stood apart because they had hobbies or outside interests (e.g. cultivating an allotment for vegetable freezing; designing and fitting out their own motorized caravan), the statement seemed in keeping with their life style. Freezers were not generally considered a luxury. Most families (60 per cent) ran a car and 40 per cent had a telephone. It was clear that practically all the mothers took pride and pleasure in their homes and possessions. A few, even in the higher income bracket, that is over £35 a week, were uncomfortable because they had run into hire purchase debt. It was, of course, sometimes difficult to judge financial positions accurately from furnishing and appliances. The general impression, however, was of young couples who were reasonably well off and whose money was mainly spent on their homes and children.

This impression was sustained by comments made about the flats and houses. There was little doubt that for most parents, the flats were their first real home; previously, they had been living in rented, furnished accommodation or with parents. They frequently expressed the view that 'flats were good value for money' and that in comparison with some of their friends whom they had envied because they had managed to 'put down on a house', in retrospect, they considered themselves lucky. 'They've got a right millstone round their necks; they can't afford another baby, and the wife *has* to go to work' (their emphasis).

iii. Attitudes to neighbours

Obviously, much depended on the personality of individuals; almost exactly half the mothers in the sample were 'in and out of each other's houses' and felt 'we're all in the same boat here'. They could be matched with other mothers who encouraged little or no social intercourse with their neighbours, because they considered that 'once you let 'em in, they're never out'. There were also those few who held themselves rather aloof because they did not like the estate and preferred to make their friends outside it, and those they tended to ostracize − the 'roughs'.

If a mother wanted to be friendly, there was someone to be friendly with; if, however, she wanted to 'keep herself to herself', she could. There was little doubt that mothers in some blocks were more outgoing than others, and there were some who felt isolated in blocks where perhaps there were no others with young children.

There was some evidence of a difference in attitude between those families who were 'locals' and those who were not. This was evident even within the new estate: 'there's none from London in this block, you know, and it makes a difference!' (this mother was explaining her friendly attitude to her neighbours). But other mothers from London, even though they had reservations about local amenities and missed their own families, had made friends with their neighbours. 'I wouldn't change mine for the world; she's smashing, blimey, she's nearly raised my Debbie.'

iv. Mothers' daily routine

Once a mother had finished her housework, she had very little else, apart from shopping, which she felt she had to do. Most mothers (78 per cent) said they spent an hour or more playing with their children each day; the form this play took varied from involvement in games to active encouragement while the children played. 'Even if I don't actually play with them, I'll give them a broom or dustpan and brush and let them play with it.'

Mothers' most usual practice was to keep children in the flats in the mornings, while they 'did their work', and in the afternoons to join in games and play together with the children on the grass. On sunny afternoons, this worked well; sometimes mothers would take turns to look after children. Where a mother had made friends, this sort of arrangement would continue indoors in the winter months.

The visual impression gained from several weeks of summer visiting on the new estate, of mothers in deck chairs and children happily engaged in water play, could be misleading, however. It left out of account those mothers who did not feel able to join in and those few, who, even in hot, sticky weather, remained indoors with the windows shut and curtains drawn. It is not possible to say exactly how many mothers this applied to: approximately 52 per cent 'kept themselves to themselves' and 'did not mix'; but naturally, some of these had friends off the estate whom they visited, or they might choose 'to go to the park', swimming or other activities. Non-social activities off the estate were mainly confined to the park (57 per cent said they went regularly, at least two or three times a week); swimming (20 per cent used the baths weekly, apparently on father's initiative) and shopping.

But it was quite evident that flat-bound mothers did exist. Interviewers found them at home and were told 'I was here three months before I dare open the door', and another 'He [her four year old] stands with his nose on the window all the time — he looks at the other children, you see, but I just couldn't go down there'.

Rather than 'sit about', mothers who had been brought up in the district would visit or be visited by their family and friends. Most meetings were in each others homes. The majority of mothers saw their own mothers once a week or more (60 per cent and the proportion rose to 80 per cent, when relatives were included in social visits).

Sport, bingo, and the pub played very little part in social life. Entertaining was far more likely to be done at home: indeed, many sitting rooms had well-stocked fitted bars hung with trophies and souvenirs from foreign holidays, a priority for dusting each day. (A regular annual holiday was enjoyed by 46 per cent and a package tour abroad was normal.) Evenings otherwise would be spent watching television, playing cards, or 'catching up with the ironing'. Most parents seemed keen on Do It Yourself. Fathers were practical and flats were papered and painted regularly. Even where parents could go out together in the evening, that is, where relatives or friends would baby-sit (72 per cent), mothers often said they preferred to stay at home. There was little temptation, it seemed, to join any of the evening classes offered in the vicinity on a wide range of subjects — only five mothers had attended a class in the previous two years. Mothers did not normally go out in the evening except on special occasions or to 'pop next door' to a tupperware party or see a friend.

Very few mothers said they read for pleasure. A minority took womens magazines: 'I like the stories', 'They take you out of yourself'. As *Table 1* below shows, there was wide variation in newspaper reading habits. Mothers were almost equally divided between those who read the local paper and those who did not. Nearly all those who read a daily newspaper took the *Sun* or the *Daily Mirror*, while the *News of the World* was the most popular Sunday paper.

TABLE 1   *Readership of newspapers ('Hillcroft')*

daily papers			Sunday papers		
paper	no. of readers	%	paper	no. of readers	%
none	20	26	none	26	34
Times/Guardian	2	3	Sunday Times/	4	5
Telegraph	1	1	Observer		
Mail/Express	4	5	Sunday Telegraph	0	0
Sun/Mirror	50	65	News of the World	28	36
			Sunday Mirror/	19	25
			People/Express		
totals	77	100		77	100

v. Fathers' role

Some husbands (41 per cent) went out on their own, mainly to the pub, one or two nights a week; but most fathers took an active part in the home as well as playing their primary role of wage earner. They shared the household chores, cooking, and looking after children (see *Figure 3*) and this applied particularly to those who were shift workers. This was considered an advantage, since the family could often go out together on weekdays. Fathers were most likely to be involved in care of the children. They both played with them and looked after them more than helping with housework, cooking, and shopping. This may have reflected the degree of caring which both parents felt for their children.

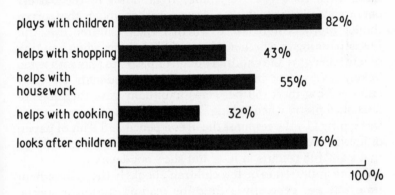

Figure 3   *Father's role in relation to child care and household chores ('Hillcroft')*

vi. Childrens' activities

a. *indoors*

Most mothers (62 per cent) let their children play wherever they wished in the house or flat. 'What I say is, it's a home, and we go where we like in it, so why shouldn't they?' A smaller group of mothers (22 per cent) organized a bedroom as a play area; some had been furnished with great care and were full of toys. Where there were several children in a family or 'friends' who came in to play, this arrangement seemed to work satisfactorily. But where there was only one child, the bedroom became rather a storage area and toys were brought into the living room or kitchen to be 'with mum' (13 per cent). Very few, only 2 per cent (all found amongst the house dwellers), had any separate play area – these were 'garden rooms'.

Mothers seemed to think that one of the advantages of flat living was that there were other children around for their youngsters to play with. But in spite of predominantly friendly attitudes to neighbours, 38 per cent had not made friends sufficiently well to say that their children had any one outside the family to play with.

The range of toys for indoor play was wide and it was evident that a great deal of money was spent in small everyday toys, as well as expensive items like dolls prams. This mother's list was typical of toys considered desirable: 'She's got dolls, a lovely cot, guns, cars; she's got everything, right down to the battery operated washing machine, crockery washer-upper, that sort of thing.' Mothers were asked whether their children ever did finger painting or whether they used big brushes when painting or if mother gave the children dough or pastry to play with when baking. Very few mothers actually made dough for their children, but most (69 per cent) habitually gave them bits of uncooked pastry when baking. The general reaction to painting was typified by the response 'he likes a pencil and a bit of paper' or illustrated by this comment: 'I've got a big paint-box in there, that's got 108 colours in it – but she's not keen'.

There appeared to be few children's books in the homes. Bedtime was not generally a time for reading stories or special ritual. 'I read if he wants me to, but he usually just falls asleep.' It seemed more likely to be 'Look at your book' (and keep quiet).

Few mothers (7 per cent) had ever been to the local library either for themselves or their children – although there was a children's section and regular 'Story time'. A number of mothers voiced concern at their children's destructiveness: 'the only thing about getting a book from the library is if a kid rips it'. Destructiveness may account for the observed paucity of books in the homes, given that 80 per cent of mothers said they had bought a book during the previous three weeks – mainly *Rupert Bear* or the 'Ladybird' series on sale in the local supermarket.

Colour television was to be found in most homes; a subjective impression was that it was usually on, though not necessarily watched. Undoubtedly children watched it (64 per cent at least one hour a day) but mothers said they seldom sat and watched with them. It was considered an advantage for the children to have television, but it was something they could watch for a while when the fancy took them — rather a background accompaniment. Several mothers said it was 'company' and lessened the likelihood of hearing what was going on in the adjoining flat. Television could act as a two-way 'scrambler'.

Noise was a source of difficulty. Children are naturally energetic; most had a tricycle or scooter, but often were not allowed to ride it outside because of 'rough' children, danger on the road, or the weather. They would therefore tear round on their bikes from one room to another with the consequent thump every time they rode over the rise in each doorway. On the ground floor, this was not too resounding, but on the middle and top floors, it could lead to tension for mothers and neighbours. This was not always so. 'Dick and Jan are as noisy as we are, so there's no complaints'; but where there were elderly or childless neighbours, mothers were often very much on edge. Even where there were children on both floors, tension could arise from lack of soundproofing. 'Her children are early risers and when my husband tries to get a bit of sleep [shift-worker], they're rushing round and shouting and water running, but what can you do — she's got two children and she's a heavy person.' All neighbours were not as accommodating as this one; another mother who made her children's clothes said that she had only to get her machine out, even in the afternoon or early evening, for her neighbour to be banging on the ceiling, or coming down 'swearing through the letterbox'.

b. *outdoors*

Outdoor play apparatus was poor, if judged by the availability of sand, water, swings, slides or climbing frames, and bikes. Most children had bikes or scooters, but on the new estate or in the flats many were only allowed to ride them round the flat or under supervision. Only houses with gardens afforded opportunity for sand, slides, or climbing frames. Yet children, who were allowed to play outside by themselves on the estate displayed ingenuity in finding a variety of natural activities for themselves; these, with lower standards of hygiene and safety, were natural parallels of much 'play apparatus'. They would balance along the top of low walls, swing on bars dividing the green areas from pavements, slide down the garage ramps, dig around the trees and shrubs, and play with water trickling from open pipes. They created their own 'adventure playground'.

Outside play created most tension for mothers, but much depended on where exactly a flat was situated and, perhaps more important, the mother's way of dealing with a problem. Stairs were one example. Two mothers, each with one child, in what appeared to be very similar circumstances three flights up, reacted completely differently. 'The very first thing I did when I came here,' said one, 'was to teach her how to climb the stairs and go down' (the child was eighteen months old). The other mother, who had been living in the flats since her child was one year old, felt unable to let her child negotiate the stairs alone at four years old. She was afraid, not only of the danger of falling but of the hazards of play in the open plan area.

Mothers were virtually united in their condemnation of the so-called 'children's play area' (all but two said they would not let their children go there). They objected to broken bottles, to the bigger, rougher children, to the fact that it was not enclosed, and some, that undesirable strangers lurked in the vicinity. Nor were balconies satisfactory play spaces (92 per cent). They had several disadvantages. They were not enclosed, but were rather 'landings' which served the entrances to three flats. There was no guarantee that children would not overcome any home made barriers and wander away or fall down stairs. Finally, since balconies were directly outside windows of flats for the elderly, there was the problem of noise. The only outside play space left for children in flats were the roads, car-parks, and shared green space. It was nowhere enclosed and for many mothers (approximately half), it was impossible to hear, see, or get to a child quickly in an emergency. The great majority of mothers (86 per cent) said that outside play space was unsafe and a further 11 per cent that it was 'fairly safe', leaving 2 per cent who considered it 'safe'. But these figures do not quite tie up with the proportion who nevertheless let their children play outside on the road and car-parks (39 per cent), as well as on the open green space (86 per cent). This may reflect the policy of some to encourage a child to cope with its environment, whatever it is, from the earliest opportunity, or indifference. In others, it may obscure tensions generated by letting a child play in circumstances that do not permit peace of mind.

vii. Discipline

When asked about the ways they disciplined their children,

most mothers (61 per cent) said they would never threaten a child with any other person, although some used father as a deterrent (23 per cent). The prevalent view (90 per cent) was that parents not only often were wrong but admitted they were wrong to their children. Mothers also thought it better to tell children the truth when they asked 'embarrassing' questions (86 per cent). When a child was naughty, the most usual punishment was a smack; mothers accepted this as reasonable and salutary (53 per cent). Some mothers, particularly where they felt they had hot tempers, preferred 'temporary banishment' (25 per cent). When a child came to his mother and complained of quarrels with other children, the normal expedient was to 'hit back' (52 per cent). One mother explained that she 'used to encourage him to let other children have turns and to give way, not to hit others. He was very good about it', but now she 'realized that this was the wrong thing. In order to survive outside, whatever I would like him to do, I've got to get him to hit back and stick up for himself.'

viii. Health

Overall, health in 'Hillcroft' seemed good, certainly as far as the children were concerned. The majority (71 per cent) were 'never ill'; there was a handful (6 per cent) of children with reported eye trouble, hearing difficulty, and speech defect and only two children who were physically or mentally handicapped. Although there were seven children who were cited as having a speech defect, there were others who, had they been observed by a playgroup supervisor, would almost certainly have been recommended for specialist advice.

About half the mothers (52 per cent) still paid a yearly visit to the clinic. Even those who did not do so still seemed to have a very warm feeling towards the health visitor whom they felt they knew and to whom many would go for help. Of the 50 per cent who would go to an official body for help, half would choose the 'welfare' and the other half said they would go to the Citizen's Advice Bureau. Obviously, those mothers who had young babies still had stronger links with the clinic. Less than half the mothers (46 per cent) had taken their children to the dentist during the previous twelve months, but a few mothers said too, that they would take the children but not go themselves, 'because of the expense'. The idea of dental checks was not universal or even commonly accepted — as one mother said: 'Why frighten him? Why take him to the dentist when he hasn't got anything wrong?'

SUMMARY

The residents of 'Hillcroft' formed a fairly homogeneous, working-class community as far as socio-economic status, family life, child rearing practice, and material prosperity were concerned.

They tended to have roots in the community, to have limited educational backgrounds, to have a restricted social life that focused strongly on the home, and to place their priorities in material possessions rather than less measureable long-term gains. For most of them, their council flats or houses were their first homes and valued as such. Just as they enjoyed being at home, so too they enjoyed the company of their children.

The next important question concerned the general attitude towards pre-schooling. Hitherto, parents had had virtually no choice in the matter, but local pressure groups favoured playgroup provision. What picture would emerge when the views of all the parents whose children might benefit were taken into consideration?

CHAPTER FIVE

'Hillcroft' and pre-school provision

THE EXISTING SITUATION

When it came to pre-schooling, the chief problem for mothers hitherto was the distance they had been obliged to travel. There still was no easily accessible day care or nursery school provision in 'Hillcroft'. The nearest nursery school was attached to the primary school in an adjacent catchment area. In cases of very special need, children from the study area might be allowed to attend, but pressure for places was extremely high. Day nursery facilities were available in similar circumstances, and attendance might mean up to a thirty-minute walk for the mother. The nearest playgroups had long waiting lists and also entailed considerable effort on a mother's part to get her child there and back.

It is hardly surprising, therefore, that 82 per cent of children made no use of any form of pre-school provision. The generally expressed view was that mothers did not want their children to start school full-time sooner than was necessary. Mothers saw pre-schooling as an introduction to the 'big school' and a weaning away from them – a necessary evil. This reflected their enjoyment and acceptance of under fives at home.

DESIRED PROVISION

As to 'desired provision', *Table 2* over shows that the majority of mothers did not envisage sending their three-year-old children to any form of provision for more than two or three half days a week. At age three, about one fifth would have preferred five half days and only one mother 'ideally' wanted full-time provision. Mothers felt their children would benefit from more sessions once they reached the age of four, but still proportions were low; just under one third required five half days (31 per cent) and fewer still full-time attendance (11 per cent).

The majority of mothers stressed the importance of choice for everybody. Total disagreement with pre-schooling or desire for radically different facilities were expressed by eight mothers (10 per cent). Reaction to the possibility of home visiting was unfavourable — 'people would be coming round poking their noses' — but this was probably a reflection of the general antipathy towards callers. Most mothers simply stressed the importance of choice for everybody.

TABLE 2   *Desired form of pre-school provision for children aged three and four ('Hillcroft')*

type of provision	3 year olds	%	4 year olds	%
nursery school	8	10	12	16
nursery class	21	27	30	39
hall playgroup	27	35	21	27
home playgroup	4	6	2	3
childminder	0	0	0	0
other (relig.)	6	8	5	6
day care	1	1	2	3
none	10	13	5	6
total	77	100	77	100

Here, as elsewhere, where numbers are small, percentage statements can be misleading, but they are given to draw attention to the general characteristics of the data. There were apparent discrepancies between the type of provision desired and the number of half days for which it was required. Nevertheless, there was reason to think that mothers perceived the needs of their older children as different from that of three year olds. Some mothers, for example, were quite clear that they would prefer state provision at either nursery class or 'school', but maintained that they did not want their children to attend for more than three or four half days, or alternatively, they wanted it full-time.

It appeared that a class attached to an infant school appealed to mothers because they saw the function of pre-schooling as preparatory to the 'big school' and thought it would accustom the children to it if the buildings were close together. There was also the point that where older children in the same family attended the same premises, collection was easier. For three year olds a playgroup, as opposed to nursery school or class, was attractive as preparation for school.

'EXPRESSED' DEMAND

Marked differences can be expected when comparing a small local sample with a national estimate as there will be wide regional variations. Nevertheless, using the Plowden estimate as a yardstick serves to highlight one local variation. In view of the increased pressure of public opinion for pre-school provision and the national trend towards more women working at least part-time, it would not have been surprising had 'expressed demand' (waiting list) been greater than the Plowden estimate of take-up (90 per cent of four year olds and 50 per cent of three year olds who would require five half days a week) and had more than 15 per cent of mothers (Plowden estimate) expressed a desire for full-time day care either because they were working or wished to work.

The waiting list did not reflect general increased public demand for pre-school provision, however, but the demand for full-time provision for four year olds (10 per cent) was less than the Plowden estimate.

The most striking feature of the response at this early stage in the study was the proportion of mothers, almost one third of the sample (30 per cent) who said they did not wish to use any pre-school facilities − a proportion reminiscent of the Lambeth study referred to in Chapter 1 (page 13). One further reflection is that 'Hillcroft' was a very different area from Lambeth in that it was not recognized as one of high deprivation. To draw attention to the existence of a group of mothers who did not make use of provision, however, is in no sense a criticism of them, nor is there any implication that they should use provision.

MOTHERS' VIEW OF PRE-SCHOOL PROVISION

In addition to gauging the nature and extent of demand, an attempt was made to assess the relative importance mothers attached to various aspects of pre-school provision. It appeared that facilities were valued for their potential benefit to children and not to mothers. Enabling mothers to obtain advice from other mothers and the supervisor, to make friends, or to have any time away from their children did not rate highly. Enabling a child to play with other children and to learn through play were of paramount importance; 'a lasting educational advantage' rated slightly lower. Advantages for mothers and an opportunity for messy play rated lowest of all and may reflect mothers' lack of experience of the scope of and reason for such activities for under fives.*

REASONS GIVEN FOR NOT USING PROVISION HITHERTO

Given that the vocal reaction to the proposed new facility was mainly favourable, and that pre-school provision was generally seen as 'desirable', why, hitherto, had so few mothers made the effort to go further afield for something that they considered would benefit their children? What were the chief reasons for not making the effort?

Expense appeared to be a minor consideration (8/77); mothers nevertheless welcomed the subsidized provision. While only a small proportion (4 per cent) said they would not send their child unless the playgroup was free, the rest said they were content either to pay a small sum − 15p (44 per cent) − or even pay 35p or more. The most striking aspect of this was the small proportion of mothers who thought it should be free; most mothers seemed to want to pay something.

Was it something about the provision itself that influenced mothers? Few (8/77) expressed outright disapproval of pre-schooling. In an attempt to assess how far existing provision would meet their needs, mothers were asked about a number of ancilliary services. The possibility of meals appealed to approximately one third of mothers but did not draw an immediate enthusiastic response. Most seemed to enjoy cooking;

---

* Children learn through play. In modern towns and cities, opportunities to play with things like earth, sand, pebbles, and water no longer occur naturally in the environment.

Sand, water, dough, and glue in playgroups and nursery schools are substitutes for this missing experience. Such activities not only provide a creative and emotional outlet, but they can also help children begin to understand and to control the world about them.

In the same way, painting, including finger-painting, is a satisfying activity if carefully organized. It encourages children to appreciate the neglected sense of touch, to become aware of and to enjoy colours, to experiment with them and to make patterns, and to express their feelings and imagination, reliving things that are important to them but which they may find difficult to express in any other way.

feeding their families was seen as an integral part of their job: 'What I say is, its my job and I like to see them sit down and eat' and again 'We don't eat out of a tin here . . . they've got to start with school and school dinners soon enough.' 'I hated school dinners.'

A pick-up service would have been more appreciated (46/77). 'It would make all the difference having someone I could rely on to take Keith there and back − come the afternoon, I'm flaked out', and another 'if I could go too, I might stay and help; other mothers stay and they've asked me to, but by the time I've pegged up there [town centre] I just want to sit down'.

An even larger proportion of mothers wanted some form of supervised play during the holidays (56/77) − 'That'd be marvellous'. . . 'Holiday times drive us all mad' . . . 'The older kids get rough and start with the little ones' . . . 'I can't let Maria [3 year old] out at all in the holidays − they'd scalp her'.

As to their own involvement in a group preventing them sending their child, three out of seventy-seven mothers said that mother involvement would stop them using the facility; these were all one-parent families. A wide range of hopes and fears applied to the remainder. Their children were the pivot of their interest and mothers wanted to be involved, though not necessarily on a rota. Well over half (57 per cent) expressed a desire to help in this way; however, since the playgroup was seen as a means of accustoming children to be away from them for short periods, some felt that to stay there would defeat the purpose. Mothers were, however, willing and interested to help behind the scenes (making toys, mending, washing clothes, or preparing the mid-morning break); it was noticeable that the jobs they saw themselves doing were menial and self-effacing. Even those who confided that they wished they had 'stayed on at school' and that they would have 'liked to work with children' were too lacking in confidence in themselves to think they could take part in the administration of the playgroup or even 'take a course'. Those who were more socially inclined, however, were interested in fund-raising projects.

By far the most frequent reason given for failure to use provision hitherto was distance (44/77). Indeed, those mothers who did take their children to existing groups often had to leave home at 8.15 am, walk for thirty minutes and walk back. By this time, they had to begin to think about collection. It is quite understandable that such a procedure would be unattractive unless a mother were convinced of the benefit. Many mothers would find it totally impractical.

Perhaps the most potentially significant response was that 37 per cent of mothers said that pre-school provision was not important enough to bother about anyway. 'I wouldn't go out of my way to send her to a playgroup' said one mother, 'she has plenty of people to play with her — we all know how to stick bits of paper down for kids to paint and that'. What remained to be seen was how these mothers would react when provision was available within a few minutes walk; would there still be a wide margin of mothers who saw the provision as an irrelevance?

THE NEW PLAYGROUP

The playgroup opened in February 1974; fees were 15p a session (half day), payable monthly or per term. It offered the possibility of attendance two or three half days a week for all three- and four-year-old children whose parents wished it. The organizing committee hoped that mothers would wish to become involved in the work, but there was no obligation on them to do so.

In the week prior to opening, all interested families were welcomed to two open evenings by invitation of the Mothers' Committee and the Tenants' Association. Both these occasions were well attended: each time, approximately thirty parents took the opportunity of meeting the supervisor, asking questions, and inspecting the premises.

The units had been specially designed for use as a playgroup with large, low windows on one side which gave access to a covered play space and a small fenced area of grass and trees. Doors on one side of the room led to a storage room, a staff or 'quiet' room, and staff cloakrooms. On the opposite side was a kitchen equipped to provide refreshments, but not hot meals. There was also a lobby with access to the side of the building and children's cloakrooms and toilets. The playroom was equipped with a large, low level sink and water supply; the room was designed to be partitioned off into play corners, and special gaily coloured board for hanging pictures, paintings, and collages at child height lined the walls. Safety was a feature of these units; heating was principally by an electric under-floor system and windows were of 'unbreakable' material.

Allocation of mothers to a group according to their response to the playgroup

Once the playgroup opened, it was possible to allocate mothers to one of three groups according to what they actually did when they had an alternative and not according to their stated intention. The three groups within the study were therefore:

Group I − those families who made no use of the new provision (except those who already went elsewhere)   22/77
Group II − those who made use of the new facilities   37/77
Group III − those who continued to make use of pre-school facilities outside the area.   18/77

In view of the earlier demand for a playgroup, the size of Group I in relation to the sample (29 per cent) was larger than might have been expected; but clearly much depended not just on the size of the group, but on the characteristics, attitudes, and felt needs of its individual members.

Major findings and material from the tapescripts alone are described here with the aim of presenting results in a readable, non-technical form. The research worker who is interested in the details of analyses used throughout the studies will find them outlined in Appendix 1a and fully reported elsewhere (Shinman, 1978).

Statistical terms and tables are kept to a minimum. The word 'significant' in the text should be noted, however; it refers to the arbitrary probability levels, set by convention. The 5 per cent level of significance indicates differences which could only happen by chance five times out of one hundred. The 1 per cent level offers a higher degree of confidence that there is less probability of error − variation would occur only once in 100. Where differences between groups are described, it can be assumed that these have been tested. Where measures of association have been used, any correlation of .3 or higher denoted a positive association and is 'significant'. No causal relationship can be inferred.

Major differences between the groups

Following analysis, certain major differences emerged within the framework of the three groups mentioned above. Although the ultimate focus of attention was on families who did not participate (Group I), characteristics of mothers in the other groups were also of interest. Those mothers who already used some form of provision outside the immediate neighbourhood (Group III), for example, differed from the other two groups in some important respects.

i. *working mothers*

One of the general characteristics of mothers in 'Hillcroft', already referred to in the last chapter, was the disproportionately small number who went out to work. Those who did so were concentrated in Group III (existing users); even so, and given that they used day-care facilities, only three out of eighteen mothers in this group worked full time. One of the working mothers put it this way:

> I found I was wandering round the flat thinking, 'I want this and that', and inwardly I was blaming her [her daughter], and that's why I decided I had to do something. From my point of view it works out better I think, although I do feel I've lost something in the last year. I was fortunate enough to have her until she was three and a half, but it was such a trial. I don't like going to work — I hate it. But when Jenny goes to school I don't want her to be the only one with no shoes on her feet. It's not going to make her happy. All this business about rags and happiness just isn't true.

And another:

> As regards work, I haven't got a choice there. Either I do that and we eat, or else we go back to the breadline. I did it for a year, but if you're at home all day living on Social Security, you're not giving your child love, because you're looking round the flat all the time thinking, 'I haven't got a three-piece suite, what am I going to do?', and this reacts on the child.

In the Lambeth Study, in which the inception of a new playgroup was monitored (Shinman, 1978: App. XI) it was found that a substantial proportion of mothers who, when first interviewed said that they were not working, were in fact doing so. With this experience in mind, extreme caution was needed in interpreting the responses in 'Hillcroft'. It seemed, however, that where there was no economic necessity to work, mothers were happy not to do so. Where mothers on their own were helped by their parents or supported by boy friends or former husbands, it seems they chose not to work.

Group III included all those mothers who for reasons of poor health, family difficulties, or need to work, used day-care facilities, and those who for similar reasons made use of playgroups as well as those who made a particular effort to seek out playgroup provision because they thought it beneficial for their children.

A substantial proportion of mothers in this group could be considered 'special cases'. One mother, for example, spent the day caring for an aged, invalid relative who lived some distance away; she therefore found it easier to take her little girl to a nearby playgroup. Another mother herself worked as a nursery nurse and took her child with her. Others again were so depressed or unable to cope that their children had been recommended for day care by social workers or health visitors.

ii. *family size*

Size of family has been associated in numerous studies with poor health, low attainment, and educational disadvantage. When family size within the three groups in 'Hillcroft' was considered, further differences emerged.

Mothers already using pre-school provision (Group III) tended to have smaller families than those in Groups I and II. Furthermore, there was a clear tendency for larger families to be disproportionately represented among families who did not participate (Group I). This is even more remarkable because it was Council policy to rehouse families with children of different sex, once the younger had reached the age of one year. Although not all families in this category had been rehoused, the sample was clearly biased against large families.

There was also a disproportionately large number of families with only one child among existing users (Group III). It could be said that, in general, in Group III one- and two-children families predominated while in Group I there were more two- and three-children families. It might be argued that this was to be expected in the knowledge that Group III included a number of one-parent families. Yet one-parent families are not necessarily smaller than nuclear or two-parent families. In an important study of one-parent families (Ferri, 1976) there was no significant difference in family size between fatherless and two-parent families, although there was a tendency for families in which the father had died or where the child was illegitimate to be smaller. There was no such tendency in families which were fatherless due to marital breakdown. A significant difference in family size was, however, found between families who were motherless and two-parent families; but by definition, such families did not feature in the groups in this study.

iii.   *age of mothers*

It would not be unreasonable to expect that where families were on average larger (Group I), mothers would on average tend to be older. Yet although a significant difference did emerge in relation to mothers' ages, it was in the direction opposite from that which might have been anticipated. Group I mothers tended also to be younger than those in the other two groups.

Mothers were also asked whether they had planned their first baby; a question asked with some diffidence and one which it was thought might cause resentment or evasion. But the general response appeared to be more frank and forthcoming than had been expected; indeed, the information was usually volunteered, and responses made it clear that it was understood to mean 'were you pregnant when you married?'. It seemed that a greater proportion of mothers in Group I not only tended to be younger than average when they married but not to have planned their first baby; 82 per cent as compared with 63 per cent in Group II and 39 per cent in Group III (see *Table 3*).

TABLE 3   *Age at which mother had her first baby ('Hillcroft')*

	age			
group	16−17	18−20	21−24	total
I (non-users)	10 (91%)	9 (25%)	3 (10%)	22 (29%)
II (new users)	0 (0%)	19 (53%)	18 (60%)	37 (48%)
III (existing users)	1 (9%)	8 (22%)	9 (30%)	18 (23%)
total	11 (100%)	36 (100%)	30 (100%)	77 (100%)
total as % of sample	14%	47%	39%	100%

Yet, despite the fact that four-fifths of them said they were pregnant when they married, Group I mothers seemed to have shared the same type of social background with the rest of the sample. Their childhoods were, like those of mothers in the other groups, predominantly settled, and like the other mothers, they went to their local secondary school, and stayed in formal education until the age of fifteen or sixteen. None of them stayed until the age of seventeen or eighteen (compared with 3 per cent of Group II mothers and 17 per cent of Group III mothers) or subsequently went on to university (as contrasted with 6 per cent of those in Group III). In spite of this apparent homogeneity, however, their lives after they left school tended to diverge from the pattern of Group II and III mothers. A larger proportion of Group I did not work between leaving school and having their first, probably unplanned, baby (73 per cent had no job before becoming pregnant, compared with 54 per cent in Group II and 56 per cent in Group III); they started their families younger.

iv. *mothers' health*

As has already been described, the general health of mothers was reported as 'good'; but it did vary between the three Groups, though not 'significantly'. There were more mothers with 'poor' health in Group I and III and fewer with 'good' health in these two groups. This was perhaps not surprising in view of the possible strain of bringing up several under fives. Although also not 'significantly' different, there was a greater number of 'pill takers' in Group III, possibly a reflection of stress in one-parent families. Although numbers were negligible, there were more speech defects among children in Groups I and III (of the total of seven cases, three were in Group I and three in Group III). The only mentally and physically handicapped children occurred in Group I; the nature of the handicap in these cases was not such that they could not have attended a pre-school playgroup or nursery. Indeed, playgroup had been recommended by the Health Visitor, but it was advice that the mothers had not felt able to take.

v. *fathers' occupation*

Fathers' occupation is often considered an indicator, not only of income and the consequent standard of living, but also of the level of education or training and skills within the family, attitudes to education, child rearing, even the probability that children of manual workers are likely to weigh less and be shorter than those of middle-class fathers.

The parents of families in 'Hillcroft' were predominantly working-class. Consequently, it was to be expected that no significant class differences emerged between the groups. A larger proportion, however, of those who made use of pre-school provision were in occupations requiring special training. Group III (existing users) included 17 per cent in non-manual occupations and proportionately fewer in the lower manual grades.

On reflection, a better indicator of social class than 'fathers' occupation' might have been 'occupation of main bread-winner', since the former question effectively excluded mothers-on-their-own (28 per cent of Group III), that is 10 per cent of the total sample.

Nevertheless, whilst no significant differences emerged between the groups, the existence of sub-groups of lower occupational status in Groups I and II suggested that these families might be expected to be in the lowest income groups and also be less sympathetic towards education and long-term goals.

It is in these sub-groups that we would expect to find the least well off, where it would be likely that mothers would be 'driven' to supplement the family income. After all, the provision, although subsidized by the Council, was not free; expense could still be a very real stumbling block, particularly in view of the larger than average families among non-users.

vi. *income levels*

It appears that in spite of the apparent lack of fathers' training and education, families' incomes in Group I compared quite favourably with those in the other groups. It was in Groups II and III where mothers in the lowest income groups were to be found and where it was 'necessary for mothers to work', that is, the one-parent families (see *Figure 4*).

Expense, then, does not seem to have been an operative factor in preventing mothers coming forward for places. The majority (82 per cent) of those who did not participate (Group I) and 88 per cent of those who did (Group II) stated that money was not a problem. Taken as an economic indicator rather than a social or cultural one, ownership of a car or telephone showed no significant differences between the groups. (Approximately 60 per cent in all groups had a car, but 56 per cent of Group III had a telephone, compared with about 36 per cent in the other two groups.)

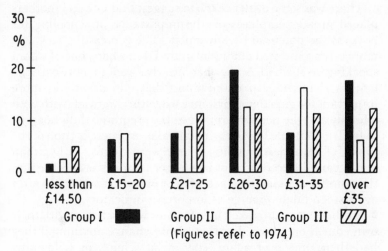

Figure 4 *Weekly income levels of Groups I, II, and III ('Hillcroft')*

vii. *attitudes to education*

There is, however, the further possibility that as more Group I mothers fell into the lower sociological grouping, it might be surmised that their attitudes to education might be different from those, found mainly amongst Group III, who had themselves stayed on at school after sixteen. A measure of this assumption might be responses to questions about the raising of the school leaving age, about the relative importance of education for boys and girls, and their views on their own education.

Fewer mothers in Group I were positive as to the benefits of staying on at school and more of them immediately responded that it was 'a bad thing'. Not only were there more mothers in Group I who were opposed to the raising of school leaving age, but there were more who fell into the 'don't knows' — which may have indicated that they had not thought about it, were not prepared to think about it, or did not really care much one way or the other. They seemed to feel that if a child were clever, it should be given the chance to 'get on'; but there was a general scepticism about the value of book learning, or rather an ambivalence towards it. Mothers wanted 'the best' for their children, but this was seen in terms of a comfortable standard of living which did not depend on being 'good at school' (reference: the income levels of Group I families).

There was some evidence too to suggest that Group I mothers placed greater emphasis on the importance of schooling for boys, as the potential breadwinners. The contrasting view was more often expressed amongst Group III mothers, one of whom speaking, as she said, 'somewhat bitterly', went to more extreme lengths than most in maintaining that education was more important for girls than boys since when they were left with both a family and the need to support it, they required skills not only to fulfil a dual role but to earn high salaries — a reflection of the plight of fatherless families. These were trends, rather than 'significant differences', but in a larger sample it is possible that the number of years spent at school or in further education after age sixteen might emerge as important indicators.

Mothers were also asked how far they were satisfied with their own education — whether they would change anything if they had their time over again, stay on at school, or follow any special training. Although again no significant differences emerged, it seemed that there was a trend for mothers who did not come forward (Group I) to be satisfied with life as it was or to express an almost stoical unwillingness to think about change. 'What I say is, you make your mistakes when you're young and you're stuck with them. It's no good grousing.' Those who had already made the effort to go outside the area for provision (Group III mothers), on the other hand, were either more ambitious or in a position where acquisition of skills would materially alter their standard of living. Earlier attitudes to schooling and education had therefore changed and they regretted what were now seen as missed opportunities.

A strikingly consistent variation in such attitudes between the groups suggests that Group I families regarded the value of education rather less than others. Taken in conjunction with the fact that Group I mothers did not pursue their own education, this may make us suspect that their values lie more in 'short term horizons' than in 'deferred rewards'.

viii. *a culture of poverty?*

Aside from the question of material poverty, which did not apply to Group I, the analysis so far had extracted a number of characteristics or trends suggestive of a 'culture of poverty' in that group; particularly the truncated education and lack of specific training, early marriage, early and often pre-marital pregnancy, larger families, and less concern with education and

long-term goals. In addition to these features, there was a disproportionate number of mothers in Group I compared with
the other groups, who were opposed to pre-school provision
by the Council; they preferred the idea of provision run by
the community, the tenants' associations, or committee-run
groups. Since a characteristic of the 'culture of poverty' is a
feeling of 'us' and 'them' together with mistrust of, and antagonism towards, authority, there would seem to be some such
ethos among at least some of those who do not use pre-school
provision.

A similar interpretation could be put on the finding that
when faced with an emergency or when they needed help,
Group I mothers would be more likely to go to their doctors or
clinic, as opposed to the Health Visitor or Citizens' Advice
Bureau. Group III mothers were more likely to use the CAB or
the clinic. Here again, it could be argued that some mothers in
Group I were displaying anti-authority characteristics – in
their response to the CAB for example.

Yet, while the sample as a whole showed a tendency to feelings
of hopelessness and excessive belief in fate, luck, and chance –
as measured on an American test which in many other studies
had proved useful in highlighting attitudes associated with a
'culture of poverty' (Rotter, 1966) – this test yielded no indication of any significant differences between the three groups of
mothers regarding the extent to which they felt they exercised
control over their own destinies. There was scant evidence for a
'culture of poverty' associated with unresponsive families. The
flavour of comments that punctuated general conversation
about use of 'outside' help suggested far more positive and independent attitudes.

There were those that expressed a mother's conviction that to
ask for outside help from an agency like the Citizen's Advice
Bureau was somehow a confession of failure: 'I'd never go there
[CAB], that's for people who can't stand on their own feet. If
we've got problems – and who hasn't? – we'll sort it out for
ourselves and not go running to them.' There was a dislike of
anything that drew attention to possible problems; it seemed
that to be seen going to an advice centre or for an official visitor
to be observed at their door was undesirable. To go to the clinic,
however, where anyone with children could go without exciting
undue comment, was easier; while the doctor offered complete
confidentiality and a one-to-one relationship. The personality

of individual welfare workers and doctors was also relevant in interpreting this finding; the names of particular doctors and health visitors recurred with comments like: 'You can tell him anything and he'll listen' and 'You don't feel a fool when you try to tell him something', 'I can talk to her — she's got no side — when you meet her out shopping, she always stops and chats, not like the other one who . . . I wouldn't have anything to do with her.'

ix. *attitudes to neighbours*

There were other characteristics of Group I mothers which were not necessarily a feature of the 'culture of poverty'. Another element was the attitude of mothers towards their neighbours. Group II mothers (those who took up places at the new play-groups) seem to have been much more friendly than either Group I or Group III mothers; they chatted with their neighbours, visited each other, shopped together, and had mutual baby sitting arrangements. But a disproportionate number of mothers in Group I were comparatively isolated within the community. Some 'kept themselves to themselves'; they would say 'hello' and be willing to help in an emergency, but they did not invite neighbours in or habitually 'pop round'. Others 'didn't mix at all' — they seldom, if ever, passed the time of day; they did not know who their neighbours were, and they did not wish to become involved with them. Moreover, Group I mothers, in addition to a marked tendency to cut themselves off from neighbours, were also unlikely to have much contact with their own mothers or with relatives. They saw them 'seldom' (once or twice a year) or 'never'; they 'lived too far away' and mothers said they did not correspond or keep in touch by phone. The same type of comments applied to other relatives. In contrast, those mothers who used provision, particularly those who used the new playgroup, were likely to see their own mothers 'several times a week'; if they lived too far away for this, they exchanged visits, phoned, or wrote to each other. They also saw other relatives, notably sisters and aunts, 'at least once or twice a fortnight'.

x. *location of provision*

One possible explanation for feelings of isolation, or indeed for not using provision, might hinge on the type of dwelling and its exact whereabouts. In 'Hillcroft' there was little evidence to suggest that these were major problems. No family in either Group I (those who did not participate) or Group II (participants) lived more than five minutes walk away from the playgroup. Ease of access was something that all mothers had in common. Thus, greater interest focused on the type of accommodation and, in the case of flats, on the height a family lived from the ground. Yet no particular pattern could be found; mothers living on the top floors of the blocks of flats (three storeys up) were just as likely to use the playgroup as those living on the ground floors.

SUMMARY

Preliminary analyses of the three groups of mothers based on their response to the playgroup disclosed findings that shifted the focus for explanations of lack of enthusiasm for pre-school provision away from low status and income, from inconvenient location of premises, negative attitudes to education, and a 'culture of poverty'. Aspects of family structure, social networks, and attitudes to the way provision was administered emerged as of greater relevance.

TABLE 4 *Major characteristics of mothers in relation to use of pre-school provision ('Hillcroft')*

group	major characteristics
I (N = 22) non-utilizers	above average family size (2 or 3 + children) dislike of neighbours mother's youth at marriage mother pregnant before marriage mother below average age when first child born mother's present age below average father below average age at marriage parents opposed to council run provision
II (N = 37) new utilizers	mother friendly with neighbours mother older at marriage father above average age at marriage preference for council run or owner – supervisor administration of provision
III (N = 18) existing utilizers	smaller family size (1 child family) mother in employment (mainly part time) preference for council run/owner – supervisor supervision one-parent family

As *Table 4* shows, mothers who did not use the new playgroup (Group I) were characterized by larger families — that is three or more children, dislike of neighbours, and mothers' comparative youth both at marriage and when her first child was born. Fathers also tended to be younger than average when they married. Parents were predominantly opposed to council run provision, preferring a community-oriented administration or owner-supervision.

Parents of children who used the new playgroup (Group II) tended to have been above the average age when they married. These families were distinguished by their friendliness and sociability and their preference for council run or owner — supervisor administration of provision.

Families in Group III (those who already used provision) were smaller. They were also characterized by preference for council run or owner — supervisor administration. Mothers were more likely to be employed outside the home in a part-time capacity.

The initial objective of teasing out some of the characteristics of mothers who chose not to use provision had been achieved, but, as so often happens, findings also raised new questions. Subsequent exploration of differences within the groups themselves suggested that many issues could be considered in quite another and more illuminating way. It is that stage of identifying the nature and needs of some of the smaller groups that is the subject of the next chapter.

CHAPTER SIX

A change of view

Exploratory studies are rather like peeling an onion; once the outer skin is removed, new layers are revealed. Likewise, once the sample was broken down into the three groups, as described in the last chapter, new contours were revealed.

AN INDEX OF MATERNAL ALIENATION?

It now appeared that the sample was not as homogeneous as had at first appeared. For example, mothers who did not use provision (Group I) were characterized by larger than average families — yet there were also a number of one-child families in that group. The possible existence of smaller groups, masked by the gross differences that had already emerged, was also noted among mothers who already used pre-school provision outside the immediate neighbourhood (Group III). They were predominately in the low income bracket, but some of them were among the more well-to-do in the sample.

Such clues were followed up by intensive examination of each of the three major groups. This showed that there might be at least two important sub-groups of mothers in each of the three main groups, that is six sub-groups; and that some of their salient characteristics were of considerable relevance to demand and utilization of services. The stages by which these conclusions are reached are outlined here, but are fully reported elsewhere (Shinman, 1978).

Analysis began with the eighteen families who already went outside the area for pre-school provision (Group III). It showed that there were five mothers whose extreme responses to some potentially important questions were not only consistent amongst themselves, but collectively different from other families in the group.

Seven key characteristics initially pin-pointed these mothers. They were:

1. dislike of messy play
2. the youth of the mother when she married
3. dislike of neighbours
4. comparative isolation from family and friends
5. lack of child-centredness.
6. little time available for relaxed play with her children
7. a 'less mature' mother – child relationship

It seemed reasonable to assume that if these characteristics existed in an extreme form, then mothers in general might vary in the extent to which they portrayed them.

There was indeed considerable variation among the mothers in Group III, and so it was decided to give all eighteen a cumulative score on the seven characteristics. A mother's response could fall into one of three categories for each characteristic and could score 1, 2, or 3 respectively. The definition of each category is given in Appendix I. The lowest cumulative score was 7 and the highest 19, with the five mothers who had been the focus of attention being the highest scorers.

The seven characteristics were tentatively called the Index of Maternal Alienation (IMA) and, experimentally, the group of eighteen mothers was sub-divided into those who tended to have low alienation scores (LA) and those who tended towards high alienation scores (HA). This exploratory step generated some thought-provoking observations.

All but one of the one-parent families, for example, were found among the High Alienation (HA) sub-group. They were subject to considerable pressures and had problems to contend with which did not figure in the experience of the Low Alienation (LA) mothers. One mother explained how she had to get her child ready for the day nursery before she went to work herself. 'She needs clean clothes every day and there's the washing and that . . . There's the housework to do when I get home at night – I don't even bother cooking a meal . . . I just don't feel like it.' Another mother, even though at home and living on social security also could not summon up enough effort to cook a meal: 'I haven't cooked a meal in months – sometimes we go round me mums, but we don't get on.' Yet another said they were 'up to our eyes in debt'; her husband, it turned out, was a gambler and the reasons for her edginess and increasing apathy were not hard to understand.

Another telling difference between LA and HA mothers

concerned the ways in which they had first come to make use of pre-schooling for their children. The overwhelming majority of those in the LA sub-group had taken their own steps to seek out provision. In contrast, significantly, five out of the seven mothers who had taken up pre-school places following intervention by some outside agency were in the HA sub-group. Health visitors, social workers, or doctors had been instrumental in getting their child to playgroup, nursery school, or day care.

Thus differences in two fundamental respects — whether a one- or two-parent family and whether provision had been sought on a mother's own initiative or at the instigation of a helping agency — suggested the existence of at least two subgroups amongst those who already sent their children to some form of pre-schooling outside the immediate neighbourhood.

Next, Group II was considered on the basis of the IMA. The cumulative scores of mothers who came forward and made use of the new playgroup showed a slightly wider range than those in Group III, from 7 to 20 points; yet the proportion of HA mothers was smaller.

The most illuminating development, however, was that checks were made twice during the course of the first term as to who was attending the playgroup and any reasons for not attending. Significantly, the only changes that occurred concerned children with HA mothers, who consequently shared IMA characteristics of HA mothers in Group III. The latter, however, were known to social workers and receiving support from the statutory authority.

Altogether, there were eight families whose children could be classed as non-starters or spasmodic users. Seven of these had HA mothers. One family had moved out of the district; another had said they were moving out but had not done so and had made no attempt to return to the playgroup. Two further children, it was understood, were starting school — but they had not done so. Three children left after a few weeks because of alleged difficulties with other children in the group. One child, although still on the register, was an irregular attender.

Just as the cumulative score on the IMA seemed to differentiate between mothers in Group III who used pre-school facilities on their own initiative and those who used them only at the instigation of some external agency, so too among Group II mothers, it seemed to differentiate between those who continued to use provision purposefully and those who, although they made some initial use of it, eventually dropped away.

On the face of it, the IMA, concerned with characteristics that could be described as aspects of 'stress' and 'alienation', might be related to uptake and continued use of pre-school provision.

When it came to examining Group I, however, there was a problem. By definition, none of the mothers had responded positively to any pre-school facility. There were eleven LA and eleven HA mothers. Scores ranged between 8 and 21 points. Yet it was impossible to link these with any particular behaviours towards provision. But it was quite obvious that amongst those mothers who chose not to use pre-schooling, at least half shared some stress characteristics with HA mothers in the other two major groups.

Detailed examination of all the data on the basis of the IMA followed. It helped to substantiate the existence and clarify the characteristics of two sub-groups of mothers within each of the three main groups. Different patterns in at least two areas of major importance emerged when one looked at the LA and HA mothers. These were family structure and occupational and financial status.

FAMILY STRUCTURE

High Alienation (HA) mothers in Group I were mainly very young, but all of them had more than one child. In spite of their youth at marriage (all had married and had their first child by the time they were eighteen), mothers had gone on to have another child soon after the first. They still had many child-bearing years ahead of them. Low Alienation (LA) mothers were older (twenty-two or more) when they married and had their first child; there was usually a two-year gap between children and most mothers said they had now completed their families.

Grounds for believing that different attitudes towards marriage and child bearing characterized these two sub-groups were strengthened by consideration of whether or not a mother had anticipated marriage. Nearly two thirds of all the mothers in 'Hillcroft' said they were pregnant before they married; from the willingness with which the information was given, for the majority, it seemed that no particular stigma was attached to this. However, it is noteworthy, especially in view of their youth, that 100 per cent of HA mothers who made no use of pre-school provision fell in this category. These points helped to consolidate the view that although mothers in Group I all rejected pre-school provision, their characteristics in terms of family size, planning, and attitudes were very different.

OCCUPATIONAL AND ECONOMIC STATUS

The knowledge that large families and lone parents are groups in the population at large who suffer from financial hardship, raised the question of the economic pattern between LA and HA mothers. Unfortunately, discussion of income levels is complicated by the rate of inflation in the last few years. Constant re-adjustment of what might be considered a living wage is required. Mothers were interviewed when prices were just beginning to rise, but before the oil crisis of 1973/4 and major increases in the cost of living had made any real impact. Only those receiving less than £20 a week said they found it 'very difficult' to manage, apart from the few cases where there was some particular difficulty in that family.

Bearing this in mind, the earlier finding that mothers in Group I (those with the largest families) were among the most well off, was substantiated. But fathers in this group with LA wives were more likely to earn an 'average living wage', the most usual being £26–£30 a week. In contrast, those with HA wives tended towards the higher income group with incomes of £36 plus. So HA mothers in this Group were characterized by larger than average families but not by financial hardship.

Group III, on the other hand, was found to include the lowest incomes of the three major Groups, as well as the highest. Here again, division of the Group into LA and HA mothers was instructive. It showed those in the first category to have the greater proportion of high incomes (£36 or more weekly); these were the professional or managerial people in the sample. The lower paid predominated among HA mothers.

Division of Group II in this way was also thought-provoking. It suggested that the very poorest families in the sample were concentrated among those who started, but did not continue, to use the playgroup. If there is one sub-set that would be inhibited from using pre-school facilities for financial reasons, it would include some of these parents.

Portraits of each of the six sub-groups formed by the division of the three main groups by the IMA were gradually built up from analysis, from the tapescripts, and from personal notes made at the time of interviews. These permit the more rounded pictures that follow.

Group I(a)   'Low Alienation' mothers who used no form of provision – (child-centred decision)

Enjoyment of children's company permeated the conversation of mothers in this sub-group. 'I'm one of those women, I enjoy having children around me'; and another, 'If anyone's going to play with my children, it's going to be me'. They had some social life themselves, and the children were integrated in it. 'We go round to a friend who's got a garden about three times a week, and then on Tuesday and Thursday, I'm shopping in the town. We take them out a lot in the evenings though, to the woods or somewhere.'

Such remarks were clearly compatible with the finding that mothers were unique in making daily use of the park in summer and enjoying regular outings to the swimming baths. Further light was thrown on their life style in that the smallest proportion of mothers of any sub-group said they watched television regularly and the largest proportion of them fell in the 'hardly ever watch television' category. Their social integration was also underlined by the fact that 90 per cent of mothers called upon relatives or friends for babysitting, compared with about 53 per cent in other sub-sets.

At first glance the two characteristic attitudes that distinguished mothers' views of pre-schooling seemed rather odd in view of their not using provision – namely willingness to take a course and assume responsibility and the importance attributed to the playgroup as enabling a child to practise balance and co-ordination. Both characteristics could stem from mothers' awareness of the possibility of playgroup or other pre-school provision and their conscious decision against it. Should the need arise, they were quite confident in their own capabilities and competence to assume responsibility. Indeed, this was exactly what they were already doing. They found other aspects of playgroup practice either of 'no overwhelming importance' or of 'great importance', but such as could be equally or better handled in the home. One mother put it this way:

The little girl upstairs goes to one [playgroup], and her mother told me to go along with her to see what I thought of it. But I didn't think it was all that good. The kids didn't seem to want to do anything, although they'd got plenty of amenities there. I find when I've had children in they just like to dress up and sing songs and that kind of thing, but there, they just let them get on with their own thing. The boys played with cars, the girls with necklaces, some with prams and painting — that kind of thing. If all they are going to do is play with cars and things, they might just as well be at home.

This same mother was very emphatic that she would never permit water play and referring to pastry, dough, and plasticine, said, 'Oh, I never let them get hold of *that*'. A very few mothers in this sub-set did seem to be excessively houseproud, but most were warm, caring people who had weighed up the case for pre-school provision and, for them, found it wanting. They wanted their children at home and felt they could give them everything necessary.

Mothers were not isolated — most had family in the vicinity, but several voiced their dislike of their school days and this may have influenced them in their desire to keep their children out of any activity associated with it for as long as possible. 'What I say is, they start school quite soon enough at five.' Most had quite enjoyed school, however, and wanted their children to enjoy it too and were confident they would do so.

The main difference between these mothers and others who made positive use of pre-school provision appeared to be that those in this sub-set had decided that they were 'happy as they were' and for a variety of reasons, chose not to make use of the provision. As one said:

It's hard to explain. I suppose I'm being a bit selfish on her behalf, really, but when she goes out to play there are quite a few rough children and they fight, and I didn't know whether she would be any better off at playschool or better where I could keep an eye on her. Also, carrying the baby, it would be difficult to get there and once he comes it will be just one mad rush until we get a system going. Then, I thought, well, she's four now and all being well she'll be at school next year.

Another put it this way: 'I'm quite happy. If you're on your own, and you've got to go out to work then it's different; you've got to put them in a nursery or something like that, but if you're at home, then I don't see any need for it until they are older.' It was only when children reached the statutory school age at five that mothers in this sub-set would consider the possibility of going out to work and then only if the hours would enable them to be at home when their children came home from school and during school holidays.

Group I(b)   'High Alienation' mothers who used no form of provision – (mother-centred decision)

The two recurring themes in conversations with this sub-set of mothers were, first, their withdrawal from the community and, second, their distrust of anything 'educational'. Reluctance to get involved with others meant that these mothers were among the most difficult to reach initially; when, eventually, they agreed to talk, their comments were punctuated with remarks like: 'We keep ourselves to ourselves', 'we've learnt by experience, it doesn't do to be friendly', 'there's no one'd talk to you here'.

Apathy and fear seemed to underlie much of what was said – 'All I want 'em to do is to sit down and watch telly. I just can't cope with them. I know it isn't right, but there you are.' This mother, like a strikingly large proportion of mothers in the sub-set, had three children under five; she, however, was certainly not enjoying their company. She said the doctor had tried to get her to take pills, but she has resisted the suggestion. 'You've got to soldier on and put up with it . . . I think now I've made a terrible mistake [marriage], but I'm stuck with it.' One might have though that a playgroup was just what this mother might have appreciated. In theory, she did: she was not one of those who did not 'approve of pre-school provision' – on the contrary; but she was not able to make the initial effort to get there or to face the additional strain of meeting new people.

Mothers in this sub-group were likely to have left school as soon as they could; marriage was seen by them, at that time, as highly desirable, but many of them appeared to have been precipitated into it without any real idea of what it involved. They were still clear, however, that school had nothing to commend it. Although not significant at this level, mothers seemed more likely to consider education more important for boys, 'as they would be the breadwinners', but their underlying attitude towards education seemed to be one of distrust and dislike. Speaking of her schooldays, this mother was fairly typical in her reaction: 'I know I didn't like it at all . . . I hated exams − if you're like me, and at the end of an hour there was nothing written down, well . . . you know, it was all there, it just went. It was terrifying. It frightens you. Especially the quiet, when you're not allowed to talk and you're not allowed to look round the room.' Analysis had suggested that unhappiness at school generated a lack of confidence in 'education' and left such mothers ill-equipped to cope with problems and tensions which are part of married life and raising a family. The consequent stress seemed overwhelming and appeared to erode hope of happiness and fulfilment.

Not unnaturally, mothers looked back to their childhood experiences and both pleasant and unpleasant associations influenced their thinking of what was or was not desirable for their children. Learning and places or objects associated with it, like playgroups or libraries, were seen as irrelevant and to be avoided. Illustrating the point, this same mother, who had so hated and feared school to the extent that her attitude to pre-schooling was antagonized by it, had a completely different childhood experience of dentists. 'I remember, when I was little, I had to have an awful lot done, and I had a really good dentist. I had an accident with my teeth when I was about three. He was really good; I had to have gas and he wouldn't put the thing over my face because he thought it would frighten me, so he used to take the thing off and wave the tube around in front of me.' This mother was almost unique in the sample in saying 'I think they ought to have a check up, say, every six months. So that they wouldn't be frightened when they did have to go.'

But it was not always associations with the past that influenced mothers. They could be caught in a depressive spiral of events which resulted in their withdrawal with their children into their home, and cutting themselves off from outside activity. Shortage of ready cash and the strain of coping with several under fives most probably explained the sub-group's 'poor health' and the likelihood that they would take their annual holiday by odd days out. But such an observation does not adequately convey the way in which mothers were often trapped between circumstances and their own legitimate desires. One mother, for example, said she had needed to go out to work for financial reasons. But she, didn't find it a good thing . . . I don't like the idea. I had no one to look after him, so he had to go to the day nursery. Although they were very good and it was very well done – for Johnnie, I don't know whether it's the same for all children – well, I wasn't his mother in the end, if you know what I mean. I was just a weekend drudge or whatever you like to call it, and anything I said, he just wouldn't do. The girl down there who used to see him all week was more his mother than I was. He got so tired and so did I. I took him away and he was back to normal within a week.

But having taken the step because she felt it was right for her child, this mother was under considerable personal strain; apart from being 'bored with the children and house and things', she found it difficult to make ends meet. 'I cut out on things, I can't manage at all; I cut out on meat and fruit – I get it once a week when I have money and by the end of the week, I'm broke and just can't afford it. I cut out on food because you've got to pay rent and bills.' Her husband was 'one for the cards' and they were behind with hire purchase debts: 'I sometimes wonder why I bother at all.' This mother, too, who might have benefited by the new provision did not make use of it. In spite of her admitted financial limitations, she did not want a free service and felt that mothers who wanted the provision should be willing to pay something towards it. For herself, it was no longer 'worth the bother'.

Group II(a)   'Low Alienation' mothers – regular users of the new playgroup

Mothers in this sub-group showed a marked contrast with those in the last group by their open, friendly attitude both to each other and their initial response to the interviewers. They were among the first to know all about the proposals for a playgroup on the 'neighbours grapevine', as well as through the Tenants' Association magazine. Boredom often dogged these mothers; 'Come in', would be the usual greeting to the interviewer, with the door opened wide from the first moment. 'Time is something we've got plenty of', or 'It's you – I met you round my friend's – remember?', or 'No need to come back later; come in now, kettle's on!'. They were well organized and after housework was done, enjoyed a cup of coffee in each other's flats or playing with their children. Some mothers in this group felt isolated within their 'block', but had particular friends or family nearby. Their feelings were perhaps voiced by the mother who said, 'I'd like something for the mothers, because we get so lonely and we don't make friends that easily. If only we had somewhere we could go and sit and know there was someone else to keep an eye on the children.'

As well as welcoming the idea of a playgroup, most of these mothers would also welcome an informal 'club' for mothers with younger children, perhaps with occasional talks, but mainly 'come as you go'. Circumstances permitting, mothers were eager to take an active part in the proposed playgroup. However, they were often diffident about their own capabilities and would need encouragement to participate. They did not appear keen to go out to work: 'I wouldn't go out to work unless I was really desperate', or, 'Perhaps a little job between ten and two when he starts school, but I wouldn't leave him before them', or again, 'It would be nice to have enough for some new clothes and not baby talk all the time, but they're only yours until they start school, aren't they, and I don't want to miss a minute'.

Yet attitudes could change over quite a short period. Another mother, for example, talking about whether, if there were provision for her children to be looked after all the time she would make use of it, said, 'I wouldn't now, but I have been back to work since I had my little girl, when she was eighteen months old. I wouldn't leave them now, but at that time I needed to go back. She was looked after by a child minder because I was so low and cheesed off being at home.' (She had married at eighteen when she was already pregnant.)

For these mothers, then, involvement in the playgroup made very good sense. They were willing to make an effort for something they considered beneficial for their children. They did not wish 'just to be rid of them'. 'If he went all day, I'd be even more bored. Come to think of it, one or two mornings a week is all he needs.' Indeed, they were likely to have organized the flat for the children's play as well as for their own convenience.

The thing is, their bedroom is a perpetual junk heap. They've got two big toy boxes but you'll find there are more toys out of it than in it. But I let them do what they like in there. I decorate their room, but it wasn't worth it, because she gets a bit pencil happy on the walls. There's usually a bit of a fight about who's going to clear it up and who's going to do this and who's going to do that, but I end up doing it anyway. There's always children in, especially during school holidays. Other children know I let them do what they like in their bedroom and they like it. But I think, they're happy and it keeps them out of my way if I'm trying to do something, and then I get less agitated. We're all happy that way.

Perhaps the feelings of mothers like those who welcomed and made use of playgroup provision on their doorstep, were best summed up by a playgroup committee member-to-be, who said: 'I want the playgroup for her, not for me − it wouldn't hurt for two hours a day − it gets them ready for school. I'm willing to pay. Fifteen pence is quite cheap. I can afford six shillings a day − neither of us smoke − or I'd give something up.'

Group II(b) 'High Alienation' mothers − non-starters or spasmodic users of the new playgroup

The most striking thing about mothers in this sub-group was that, although they gave high priority to playgroups, they also said they were prepared to go the shortest distance of any group of mothers for such provision. Yet, when a playgroup was available nearby, they made initial use of it, but they did not, as a group, persist. A detailed examination showed that 43 per cent received £21 − £25 a week and 38 per cent £20 or less, so low income emerged as the most important dimension for understanding this group of mothers.

The only other characteristic which singled them out was the regularity with which parents went out together in the evening. This should, perhaps, be linked to the fact that nearly half the sub-group were low-paid workers. Some of the remarks made by mothers suggest that they felt stifled and frustrated by the struggle to make ends meet and that their temperamental response to their situation was to 'get away from it all' (meaning the flat and children) at least once a week or 'to break out and have a mad binge'. One mother said: 'We sit and look at the four walls and we can't stand it a minute longer. We know we shouldn't, but we've just got to get out and go somewhere, anywhere . . .' It is a matter for conjecture as to where this unsettled attitude has its roots. One possibility might be a link between the reported greater mobility in childhood of both parents than those in any other sub-group. This did not reach a statistically significant level, but it was a striking fact that less than one third of fathers and mothers in this sub-group, as compared with approximately two thirds in all other groups, had a settled childhood. One further point is that these parents said they usually got a friend or neighbour to baby-sit for them. Although there were no systematic data collected and it may have been coincidence, visits where it was either known or suspected that children had been left alone without baby-sitters, were to families in this sub-group. The apparent in-difference of some mothers in this group was typified by one who said: 'I wouldn't lift a finger to send her [her three and a half year old]; but if the other kids go over there, I expect she'll tag along too — I'm not having her here [the flat] all day, that's for sure.'

Group III(a) 'Low Alienation' mothers – the initiative takers

A key feature was that these mothers tended to be the oldest of all in the sample. Both parents were likely to have stayed at school longer, to have been older when they married, and older when their first child was born. They were characterized by fairly comfortable living standards and included all the 'owner–occupiers' in the sample.

It is arguable that their own extended education (in com-parison with the rest of the sample) influenced their attitude to pre-schooling. They appeared ambitious for their children and to think that a few mornings a week at a playgroup would help prepare them for separation from home when 'big school' started. Benefits were primarily seen as social: 'I'm not sending her to a playgroup so that she can walk out a genius, just so that she can develop the most natural way.' With one exception, mothers wanted to be involved in the playgroup and aware of the special skills to be expected in playleaders.

> When she first went there, it was really worth it: she used to stand back and watch, but after the first few weeks, she was really a leader there. The woman that was running it then really knew what she was doing — everybody fitted in. Nobody was forced to do anything, but she managed to get us all doing what she wanted . . . I think it taught me quite a lot. One thing was to write these small letters again. When I first went there, I was putting the names at the top of the

papers and she [playleader] came up to me and said, 'Not capitals!'. Then I really had to think how to do the small letters again. I got ideas how to let Fiona do things . . . things like singing number songs — I think that's marvellous. We all used to talk about what things they would do when they went to school, so I feel I'm half way to getting Fiona ready for school.

A few mothers were more aware of reading and numbers: 'Some people think that learning is just how to put one brick on top of another, but when my child puts one brick on top of another, I want her to say, "There's two".'

Although mothers did not themselves see the value of attendance at playgroups as of primary importance for them, yet remarks such as these reveal that they had learned something about enjoyable and beneficial pre-school activities which had enabled them to extend the play experience of their children at home. These were the mothers who were significantly more likely to use finger paints and large brushes, and tolerate and understand 'messy play'. These mothers were able and prepared to pay to get what they wanted for their children. They were also prepared and able to make a considerable effort to go out of the immediate area for such provision. This meant a lengthy walk or even a cycle ride. No one had the use of a car. The bus service was unsatisfactory.

Some mothers felt that provision outside the district was an advantage. They disliked the estate and did not wish to mix with their neighbours. Some went so far as to say that they would never send their children to a playgroup on the estate because of 'roughness' or because they thought there was an advantage in a 'change of scene'. Indeed, although ten mothers made use of playgroups outside the area, only two of these eventually changed to local provision. This, of course, could also have been because they did not wish to move a child who was happily settled and who would probably be starting school shortly.

But although they were inclined 'to keep themselves to themselves', mothers were not socially isolated. They had friends whom they visited and they 'got out and about as a family' at weekends. With the exception of one mother who said frankly that she was 'not keen on young children' and just had to go out to work 'to keep sane' (although she behaved very warmly with her child during interview), mothers were home-orientated.

Those who did work found part-time employment until their child reached school age. It was noticeable, however, that they had broader interests than mothers in the rest of the sample — reading (use of library), gardening, and practical handicrafts figured uniquely in their account of how they spent their evenings, rather than 'just television'.

Group III(b) 'High Alienation' mothers — pre-school users, following intervention by a helping agency

This sub-set included a large proportion of one-parent families, which made it a 'special case'; their difficulties have already been described. Many lived on Social Security, but the feelings of all mothers in this position were perhaps summed up by one who, towards the end of the interview said:

> Let's face it, with the playgroup down there, I'll want to keep my business to myself. I think I'm always wary of who I'm talking to. It's the authorities and I know I've got to depend on them for money to keep the children. I'm always worried about when the social security people are going to call . . . they make you feel so guilty and then you've got to prove yourself innocent. They ask you if you've got any savings and if you have, they'll stop your money, so you can't try and get anything behind you. If anyone gives you a present, you're frightened in case they see it.

But it is not only 'mothers alone' who may be under considerable strain. Mothers who have the 'support' of their husbands may, through lack of education, temperament, youth, or ill-health, feel themselves inadequate to cope, even though their families are, as in this sub-group, smaller than average. Marital support may, of course, be only nominal — fathers may themselves be invalids, they may be gamblers, drinkers, wastrels, or even wife beaters. Women do not wish to admit to such backgrounds; the result sometimes appears to be a withdrawal from society and friends, an alienation from those in authority.

SUMMARY AND CONCLUSION

The pictures that emerged from both statistical analysis and from more anecdotal material were highly compatible. They suggested that the simple dichotomy of use/non-use of pre-school provision was not necessarily the most illuminating way of thinking about problems of poor response to services.

Mothers' responses on the Index of Maternal Alienation (IMA) revealed two sub-sets within each of the three major groups. In some important respects — concerning attitudes to child care and the degree of isolation in the community — all the Low Alienation (LA) mothers had more in common with each other than with other mothers in their respective major group. Similarly, all the High Alienation (HA) mothers could be considered as a group, with very different pre-occupations and attitudes from mothers who responded in the same way to the possibility of pre-school provision for their children. Thus, the sample might, with advantage, be considered as two major groups (see *Table 5*).

TABLE 5   *Groupings within the sample defined by the Index of Maternal Alienation (IMA) ('Hillcroft')*

(a)		(b)	
major groups	low alienation (LA) group (tendency to positive attitudes)	high alienation (HA) group (tendency to negative attitudes)	total in major group
I (non-users)	11 (25%)	11 (33%)	22 (29%)
II (new users)	24 (55%)	13 (40%)	37 (48%)
III (existing users)	9 (20%)	9 (27%)	18 (23%)
total	44 (100%)	33 (100%)	77 (100%)
total as % of sample	57%	43%	100%

The first group, all the LA mothers together, formed 57 per cent of the sample. Of these, 25 per cent opted out of provision, feeling they could provide a satisfactory pre-school environment in the home without the need to attend external facilities; 55 per cent took advantage of the new playgroup; whilst 20 per cent were already using some form of pre-schooling. While the actual response to provision varied, these mothers tended to be positive in their attitudes.

The second group, all the HA mothers together, formed 43 per cent of the sample. Of these, 33 per cent opted out; 40 per cent started to use the new playgroup but soon dropped away, whilst 27 per cent were already using pre-school facilities — but as the result of intervention by some helping agency. Stress and alienation were associated with a tendency towards more negative attitudes.

Main distinguishing features of the new classification

Four main facets of family life emerged as of major importance in describing these two groups, all the LA mothers together being called the Positive Group and all the HA mothers the Negative Group. These facets were family structure, socio-economic background, the degree of isolation and alienation felt by the mothers and, finally, differences in attitudes towards the child and its perceived needs.

The positive grouping

Mothers in the more positive group tended to have married and started their families in their early twenties. They were two-parent families and comparatively well off. If mothers worked, it was 'to meet others' or 'for an outside interest'. They had a choice in the matter. Fathers' training, occupation, and the use made of further education classes all showed a trend to the advantage of this group.

There was a sense of 'partnership' in marriage, in that fathers shared in the cooking and shopping, as well as in looking after the children. They also made it possible for their wives to go out on their own regularly and to have a break from the household routine. Parents tended to be stay-at-home, however, enjoying home based activities such as do-it-yourself, reading, and hobbies. Health was generally good but, in an emergency, mothers relied on their own mothers. They had a circle of family and friends.

A number of characteristics centred on mothers' attitudes to their children. Understanding and tolerance of messy play, use of finger painting, dough or playing with pastry while mother was baking, were more frequently found among 'positive' mothers. The latter were also more likely to take their children swimming regularly in summer and to show reluctance to allow their under fives to play unsupervised in roads and car parks.

There was almost the same proportion among both 'positive'

and 'negative' mothers for whom the child 'came first'. The majority of children were 'integrated' in both groups, but there were no children who 'came last' among the more positive mothers.

The negative grouping

A strikingly different picture of the other group emerged. One-parent families were concentrated in significant numbers among the more 'negative' mothers as well as those who had married and had their first child in their teens. Family incomes were lower and more mothers would go out to work 'for money'.

When 'mothers alone' were excluded from the analysis, incomes were still below average. Health of both fathers and mothers was frequently reported as below par. Few mothers saw a dentist regularly. This could be due to disregard of the importance of dental checks, but it could also be due to expense. More than one mother volunteered that she saw to it that her child went to the dentist, but although she knew she ought to go herself, she 'kept putting it off because of the expense'. There were, of course, other practical difficulties involved − waiting for buses, cost of transport, the need to find someone to look after her child, or the business of taking it with her. Lower income may also have contributed to the comparatively small proportion of parents who took an annual holiday and to their being less likely to use their central heating or have a car. Although all flats were supplied with central heating, not all tenants availed themselves of it.

When only two-parents families were considered, a characteristic life-style was apparent in which roles were clearly defined between breadwinner and housewife. Both parents, however, were likely to go out together once or twice a week − 'nowhere in particular, just out' or 'we go down the town and look in the shop windows' or 'down the pub, if we're not skint'.

Mothers in this group tended to feel isolated. It was apparent from replies to the question: 'To whom do you turn for help in the long term?' They seemed to depend most on their husbands, but no one said they would turn to friends or neighbours for help. All those mothers who had lost their own mothers by bereavement were in this group, but this gap did not appear to have been filled by contact with other relatives or friends. More than half the mothers, when asked whether, if they had their time over again, they would change their lives in any way, wished they 'had done otherwise'. They said they were un-happy. Yet there was no indication of a 'culture of poverty'. It may be unwise, however, to assume the irrelevance of belief in 'luck, fate, or chance' and a sense of powerlessness. The American test which was used (Rotter, 1966) may have been inappropriate for use in Britain.

Nevertheless, some characteristics seemed to reflect aliena-tion from family and friends. These included dislike of the area, accommodation, and neighbours. Mothers did not welcome callers at the door; they were unlikely to be members of the Tenants' Association. They also expressed little desire to become involved in playgroup activities. This applied not only to the mother on her own, who was obliged to work and was therefore not free to participate, but also to the mother who was unhappy or overburdened. The prospect of involvement, for her, seemed just another chore.

The education of both parents seemed to have been trun-cated in comparison with those in the more 'positive' group. Mothers had little or no work experience before marriage and starting their families. Yet family size, which was so important a feature in identifying some of the sub-sets, showed no sig-nificant differences between the two groups. Nevertheless, 'negative' mothers tended to have little or no time for relaxed play with their children during the day time; they were likely to allow them to play in the roads unchaparoned. A variety of pressures militated against their enjoyment of their children's company. In some cases, they seemed so pre-occupied with their own problems as to be oblivious of those of their children.

These are the mothers who should be the focus of attention in a caring society. Yet, in this comparatively privileged com-munity, only 27 per cent of them said they had any form of external support. The others cut themselves off from family and friends; they were not known to social workers and over one third of them had had no contact with health visitors during the previous eighteen months – even those who had very young babies.

Whilst mothers had every right to reject help, it was clear that many did not know what was available or that they reacted against the particular form of support open to them. In so doing, some of the principles of the rights of children, as laid down in the International Declaration (1979), were being violated.

Crucial questions remained unanswered. To what extent was this a localized situation? Would the Index of Maternal Alienation which was seemingly a key to understanding mothers in this community, be as meaningful in other contexts?

PART THREE

NEW PROVISION IN A DIFFERENT CONTEXT

CHAPTER SEVEN

Childminding in 'Kingswell' and 'Higham'

The study of mothers' response to the playgroup in 'Hillcroft' had suggested the need to follow it up by looking at response in other settings. Consequently, it was decided to test the predictive value of the Index of Maternal Alienation as it appeared in the context of childminding. In setting the stage for this development, this chapter falls into three sections: a rationale of the next steps in the investigation, an outline of how they were carried out, and a descriptive analysis of two new samples.

Before this, however, it is important to take account of the strong evidence that exists of an overall increase in the proportion of women working or wishing to work full time outside the home. Recent projections (*Department of Employment Gazette*, June 28, 1977, p. 587 quoted by the Equal Opportunities Commission, 1978) suggested that the biggest increase in the total labour force is expected to be among married women. This could create increased demand for day-care facilities which is unlikely to be met. As long ago as 1974, the office of Population Censuses and Surveys found that only one third of mothers who expressed a wish for day care for their children had actually been able to find it. Currently, full-time provision in local authority day nurseries is available for only 2 per cent of mothers with children aged three and four (Hansard, 1978). The goal of approximately 8 per cent of day nursery places per 1000 children under five seems unlikely to be reached in the current financial climate.

Such considerations emphasize the fact that government policy has, since the war, been at variance with a marked social trend. Day nursery provision has been reduced rather than expanded; it is mainly available for priority cases.

Given insufficient places to meet demand, there is ample evidence (Jackson, 1979) that many mothers fall back on childminders. These are defined, under the 1968 *Health Services and Public Health Act*, as any one who 'for reward, takes any child to whom they are not related into their homes and cares for him for two hours or more during the day'. Childminders are normally, though not necessarily, women. They are required to register with the local authority social services department. It is the responsibility of the local authority to inspect homes and to ensure they meet statutory health and safety regulations.

Much of the available evidence (Jackson, 1979; N.E.R.D.T., 1974, 1976; Community Relations Commission, 1975; London Council of Social Services, 1977) however, suggests that in spite of statutory oversight, there is considerable variation in the quality of care offered by childminders. There are also marked differences between local authorities as to the amount of supervision and support they provide. Most importantly, a significant number of children is involved; one estimate varies between 100,000 children and twice that number if unregistered and therefore illegal childminders are included (Jackson, 1979 : 176). A more conservative estimate (Local Authority Associations Study, 1977) based on Department of Health and Social Security projections refers to 64,500 children with registered minders.

Such a situation makes many people uneasy about childminding as a service for working mothers. There is scant research evidence to counter the conclusion of the Seebohm Committee (1968 : 59) that 'Many children under five are being minded daily in conditions which not only endanger their health and safety, but also impair their emotional and intellectual development'. Indeed, of the few available studies, one (Mayall and Petrie, 1977), is particularly worrying. It concerned an 'unusually favoured sample of 39 daily minders from four London Boroughs' and painted a picture of, 'sad, passive children, of anxious harassed mothers and hard-pressed minders insensitive to children's needs and distrustful of mothers — who in turn are resentful of the minders' (p. 11).

In view of the disturbing implications of the Mayall and Petrie study, and the small number of minders on which they based their assertions, it is especially important to know how childminders might react to services designed to help children in their care.

Consequently, the two follow-up studies to 'Hillcroft' are particularly relevant to this question. They were carried out with two different groups of mothers who were also child-minders in priority areas of Inner London, 'Kingswell', and 'Higham'.

In both these areas, projects were to be set up by a voluntary agency with the active co-operation of Social Services departments. The intention was to start informal centres which combined play facilities for the minded children with a welcoming 'club' for childminders and the possibility of informal training. The overall aims were to foster a sense of group identity among childminders and, where necessary, to improve the quality of minding.

At first sight, this might seem an unlikely context in which to pursue the investigation of response to provision. Marked contrasts could be expected between 'Hillcroft' and the two child-minder samples. The situation of a mother at home with her own child or children differed in some important respects from that of a childminder looking after other people's children as well as her own. Disparity between the comparatively comfortable mothers in 'Hillcroft' and minders living in underprivileged areas could make comparison between the groups inappropriate. Similarly, variables which could not be controlled in the two childminder projects, such as the personality of individual workers or local conditions, also meant that comparison might be unprofitable.

Yet answers to the key question 'Who would come forward to use provision?' could usefully be explored since the following criteria were met: all three schemes were forms of innovatory pre-schooling designed to meet a specific local need where there had previously been no provision at all. Premises were conveniently sited for the people they were to serve. The samples comprised *all* those within the defined catchment areas with children eligible to avail themselves of the opportunities offered. All mothers and childminders were notified about the projects in writing and by personal contact. Socio-economic backgrounds were 'working class', and due to housing and registration policies in the respective boroughs, there were normally not more than three children involved with each mother. Facilities were either free (childminder centres) or heavily subsidized (Hillcroft); the local authority co-operated with, but did not initiate or run the schemes.

These considerations outweighed the drawbacks, and the main objective could be pursued. Would minders who did not make use of the centres exhibit characteristics similar to the more 'alienated' mothers in 'Hillcroft'? In addition, the necessary task of gathering data on all the registered childminders in two clearly defined areas, as a preliminary to an analysis of response to provision, promised valuable incidental information.

The studies, by focusing on attempts to provide or extend services to help childminders and to improve the quality of care, would draw attention to how far such services appealed to those it was most hoped to attract. In so doing, possible inhibiting factors might be pinpointed and understanding of the issues broadened.

These, then, were the main arguments for pursuing this particular line of enquiry. As in any investigation, however, there were problems and limitations. The next section, in outlining how the studies were conducted, will be particularly concerned with techniques and interpretation of terms.

RESEARCH METHOD

i. The sample

The first task, finding the samples, was comparatively simple. Local Authority lists of registered minders and those in the process of registration were checked. This process revealed that approximately half the minders, in both areas, had either given up, moved, or died. It reflected both the instability of the child-minding service and the difficulties experienced hitherto by Social Services in maintaining regular visits. The revised lists comprised the samples.

ii. The schedule

A schedule was developed to provide a framework for the collection of information (Shinman, 1978: Appendix VI : 516). It incorporated the Index of Maternal Alienation (IMA), but gave the individual items no special emphasis. 'Age mother married' was excluded, but a minder's age was known from social service records.

The variable 'Type of administration preferred' distinguished, in the 'Hillcroft' study, between desire for council sponsored provision and that run by a community or independent group. It was included as an indication of attitudes to 'authority'. In 'Hillcroft', the question had been asked by an independent interviewer before the playgroup opened. In 'Kingswell' and 'Higham', however, there was a problem. Interviewing took place when the childminder centres were already open; it could have been divisive to draw attention to different types of administration. The project workers were employed by a voluntary body and such a question could have been construed as encouraging criticism of the local authority.

Instead, another variable was chosen to serve as a possible indicator of preference for a particular type of administration. It centred on a topic of current concern among childminders, 'whether minders should be paid by social services'. The current practice was for direct payments by parents. It was supposed that those minders most resistent to oversight by the local authority, and to erosion of their own autonomy, would resist the idea.

Other topics, as in the 'Hillcroft' schedule, covered family structure, environment, health, and socio-economic status. In addition, items of particular relevance to childminding concerned a minder's perception of her role, her attitudes and behaviour to her own and the minded children, to parents, and to social services.

In order to organize the information, each attitude or situation was defined on a five-point scale. A score of three indicated the mid-position, 1 and 5 indicated the respective extremes and 2 and 4 tendencies towards those extremes. Regarding quality of care, for example, a score of 5 indicated a minder who appeared to the project workers to show considerable confidence and competence in coping with the children in her care, whether at home or at the centres. She was warm and responsive; she also provided and used stimulating play materials with the children. Such a minder showed sympathy and understanding for parents of the minded children, for the minded children themselves, and an awareness of how her own child might feel. The other extreme (score 1) referred to an apparently stressful, difficult, or unbalanced relationship between minder and child, perhaps excessively permissive or lacking in consistency. Little attempt would be made by the minder to communicate constructively with parents. Standards of hygiene or diet might be poor; children might spend much of the day with little to interest them. Such situations were considered detrimental to the minder—child relationship. Between these two extremes, was the 'average' minder and those who tended to one or other extreme.

The unreliability of such scales, particularly when used for a number of differing aspects of child care, has to be acknowledged. At the same time, however, emphasis has to be placed on the exploratory nature of the whole exercise.

iii. Interpreting the terms

A basic problem was interpreting the role of childminder — a point of fundamental importance in assessment. What, initially, seemed quite straightforward, emerged as a complex problem. One difficulty is that there is no general agreement as to what the role is. Much public discussion of childminding has political overtones. In the present economic and social climate, various factions argue the case for and against it as an acceptable form of day care. It is seen by some (Department of Health and Social Security, 1976) as low-cost day care. Others (Hannon, 1978; Mayall and Petrie, 1977) consider that without training, salaries, and resources commensurate with their responsibilities, childminders cannot be expected to offer satisfactory provision. Some people value the childminder for what is seen as her non-institutional, motherly qualities, others see her as a means of intervening in disadvantage — a key figure in compensatory education. There is, however, a common tendency to cast her *either* in the role of 'mother' *or* 'teacher', or simultaneously in both. There is insufficient recognition that she is neither.

Mayall and Petrie (1977), for example, argue that a childminder is a substitute mother rather than a nursery nurse or teacher. These researchers rated minders according to the number of interactions initiated by the child with its mother and with the minder. They found significantly less interaction between children and minders than between children and mothers; they concluded that a minder's strengths were not those of a mother substitute.

At the same time, some of the other measures used, notably the provision of a range of toys designed to develop different skills, seemed more related to the theoretical knowledge one might expect from teachers and from the resources of a nursery or playgroup. In this direction, too, they found childminders wanting.

The point of view taken in the present studies was that the childminder's role is unique. It lies somewhere between the two extremes of mother and teacher, tending to one or other role in particular spheres.

Dimensions in which there are clear and generally accepted distinctions between mothering and teaching may help to clarify this point. Katz (1980) has drawn attention to several such dimensions; she has argued, for example, that the mothering role is diffuse whereas the teacher's function is specific and implies the setting of goals and objectives. The relationship between a mother and child is likely to be permanent and intimate, whereas a teacher's interest in individual children will probably be of a transitory nature. A mother is concerned primarily with her own child or children and her responses are likely to be spontaneous, emotionally charged, and impulsive. The teacher, in contrast, has to cultivate professional objectivity or at least 'detached concern' for the children in her care; she is likely to invite professional criticism if she manifests overt emotional involvement with children or assumes responsibility for socialization which belongs to the family. Her responsibility for the group demands a degree of impartiality which is not associated with motherhood.

Such an analysis brings into focus several areas in childminding which give rise to much tension and misunderstanding. In this perspective, the position taken was that a minder's relationship with a minded child should *not* tend too strongly towards the maternal role. There are dangers in usurping a mother's place made vulnerable by the long hours she spends away from her child. Consequently, it was the generally supportive, concerned, befriending role of the childminders towards the child *and the child's family* which was taken as the ideal.

It also seemed unrealistic to make the range of toys a minder had at her disposal a major basis for assessment. It was thought preferable to observe how a minder used what equipment she had. Did she use available resources, like toy libraries? To what extent would she go out of her way for the benefit of the children in her care? The amount of time a minder spent playing with children, her attitudes to 'messy' play and how she talked with her charges were taken into account.

This does not imply the view that childminders should be full-time child care experts, nor that they should necessarily provide a wide range of equipment in their homes. The model adopted more closely resembled that described in the Harvard Pre-school studies and described in Chapter 2, p. 32–5, as typifying mothers of 'more competent' children. It was not considered that there was 'one type of "good" minder'; rather that within the broad framework of health and safety standards, there were differing styles more or less suited for particular families.

iv. Gathering the information

Basic background data were supplied from Social Service records, providing that confidentiality was assured.

Much additional information was gathered by the project workers, who were particularly opposed to asking specific, probing, or delicate questions. They preferred to get to know the minders well and to concentrate on building a secure relationship with each individual, essentially non-threatening in character. This was relevant to their primary task of developing the centres.

The decision not to rely exclusively on standard procedure or single interviews was borne out by subsequently experienced difficulty of getting at the facts. The following extracts from notes made at the time illustrate the problem.

> *Extract 1.*   'This minder has told a different tale to everyone and we can never be sure we will hear the same story from one time to another. Today she told X that she had decided to come clean.'
>
> *Extract 2.*   'Mrs K has been registered with social services and visited by them for some years. I found today she was not the person registered by them at all.'
>
> *Extract 3.*   'Mrs B is registered for three children. This is a charade played for the benefit of social services. She tells us "now that we are friends", that she minds many more regularly and up to sixteen on occasions.'

It became evident that no classification could justifiably be made after one interview. Information was therefore gathered in a series of extended informal interviews. It was dependent on what was volunteered rather than extracted, but this, as it turned out, was very comprehensive. Furthermore, it was only passed on for monitoring purposes if minders were willing. Assured of confidentiality, they all agreed in the hope it would help towards a wider appreciation of their problems and a greater awareness of the issues.

Most of the information hinged on what the minder herself said or did, but there were some important areas which depended on the project worker's observation and judgement. There were therefore not only problems of imperfect reliability, but the dangers of subjectivity and of the risks inherent in any face-to-face situation. Interviewers can alienate people as well as distort or misinterpret facts. Interviewees may respond in ways they think are acceptable or give misleading information.

Clearly such sources of bias can never be eliminated, but steps were taken to minimize them. Project workers were aware of ways they might inadvertently influence responses, questions were approached in a variety of ways and checks were built into the studies. Among the most useful checks was the practice of tape recording discussions concerning interpretations of terms. These could be analysed for possible misunderstandings, and used for reference between workers in the two separate schemes.

Building the knowledge base extended over eighteen months of contact at the centres and unscheduled home visiting every two or three weeks. All the minders who could have used the centres were taken into account, not just those who chose to do so. Thus, assessment was the result of knowledge over time and of concensus opinion.

v. The centres

Free, informal centres were open two sessions each week. Every registered minder was told about them individually and consulted about days and times convenient for her.

The centres offered a minder an opportunity to get out of the house and to meet others with similar interests and concerns. She could relax over a cup of tea for as long or short a time as she wished, able to keep an eye on the children at play in the care of a trained playleader; from watching their activities, as well as from discussion with other minders and the project workers, a minder could pick up new ideas for use at home.

The project workers divided their time, as seemed best to them, between informal discussion with minders and playing with the children. Great care was taken to provide attractive and absorbing play facilities, a stimulating environment for babies and toddlers through to rising fives. Many activities were completely new to them and beyond the scope of most minders to provide in their own homes. In addition to larger equipment like climbing frame and slide, each centre provided opportunities to paint with large brushes and to explore different textures and properties of wet and dry sand, of dough and clay. As well as water play, there was a popular 'home' corner, which included a carpenter's bench. Books, table toys, and activities such as singing and imaginative play were also novel ideas for some minders.

Children were not the only focus of attention, however. Project workers were as much concerned with creating a favourable climate for minders to develop. Although the ethos of the centres was clearly beyond the scope of these studies to evaluate, their atmosphere and the ideas they embodied would almost certainly influence minders' response. If only to give some inkling of the type of provision on offer, it is therefore worth outlining the main assumptions and expectations that were shared by the project workers. These viewpoints were based on learning theory, 'Rogerian' therapy, and experience with playgroups and self-help groups; they were as follows:

a. that initially energies would be focused on getting to know minders and understand their problems;
b. that home visits were of fundamental importance for the insights they offered and for creating friendly relationships with minders;
c. that the skills of the project workers lay in recognizing individual needs, providing appropriate guidance, and keeping long-term goals in mind;
d. that the ultimate objectives were to make minders more aware of the importance of their work and to encourage and inspire them to want to learn more about it;
e. that those minders most in need of change would also tend to be those who had disliked school. The method most likely to break through barriers created by this was not necessarily a formal one, although that might be what was expected;
f. that a climate of mutual respect in which all felt comfortable and confident was essential before any real learning could take place;
g. that there was no point in imparting knowledge regardless of whether or not minders were ready to use it;
h. that there was room for different styles of learning. For

example, some minders were extremely capable and provided excellent models; others would learn through observation or through discussion or by direct acquisition of
information. Others, again, would learn by doing, and by
making mistakes;

i. that if minders were happy and satisfied at each stage of
development, then they would continually adjust their behaviour and actions in a positive way;

j. that if minders expressed a desire for a more formal
approach, they would either be encouraged to enrol for
courses run by the Pre-school Playgroups Association or the
style of the centres would change accordingly;

k. that change would take a long time and that progress would
not be steady;

l. that if too much were expected too quickly, then there would
be defensive withdrawal from the centres, or superficial
interest expressed in new ideas, with no carry over into the
home.

The foregoing points throw some light on important aspects of
the centres which could effect take-up. What remained to be
seen, of course, was how minders would react when the centres
opened.

vi. Criteria of success

After eighteen months, attendance at the centres was taken as
one criteria of success. Attendance was categorized as follows:

1. never attends;
2. attends only rarely — that is, two or three times a term and
on special occasions (parties or jumble sales);
3. attends every two or three weeks;
4. usually comes (normally once a week, but easily put off by
weather, colds, etc.);
5. regular attender, once or twice weekly — not easily discouraged.

Analysis focused on the characteristics associated with utilization of the centres and on the predictive value of the IMA in
identifying non-users who might be a cause for concern. A
number of different statistical methods were used to tease out
such characteristics and the implications they might have for
the success of future schemes (Appendix I).

Other criteria related to changes in attitude and practice; they were therefore incidental to the main concern of this book.

The spirit in which the two investigations were carried out was exploratory, both as regards the relevance of the Index of Maternal Alienation (IMA) and in understanding issues in this complex field. In breaking new ground, there has usually to be some compromise. Given the limits set by resources, the procedures adopted had certain advantages. Chief among these was that a more qualitative and accurate overall picture might emerge than was likely with standard sample survey methods. It is to that picture we shall now turn.

CHILDMINDING AS OBSERVED IN 'KINGSWELL' AND 'HIGHAM'

A preliminary task was to consider the initial impressions made by the two groups of childminders on the project workers during the first three months of the projects.

Were there any major features in common? Where did the groups differ? How did they stand in relation to current issues and how far did the general impression of the groups tally with that given in the Mayall and Petrie study? Would any aspect be likely to militate against use of provision? These questions are the concern of the next section and discussion will concentrate in particular on variables that were particularly important in 'Hillcroft'.

Similarities between the samples

Superficially, both 'Kingswell' and 'Higham' had much in common. They were in priority areas of Inner London and each covered approximately one square mile. Conditions were thought to be such as to generate large numbers of child-minders: the only day nurseries were oversubscribed, there were known to be many single parent families, and an above average proportion of under fives in relation to the total population in each borough.

It is not surprising, therefore, that when local authority lists of registered minders were checked and brought up to date, there was about the same number of mothers caring for other people's children, as well as their own, in each area. They could not properly be called groups, however, since minders were often unaware of each other's existence, even when living in close proximity. Approximately 14 per cent, in both areas, had previously been unregistered. This was mainly due to ignorance of the legal obligation on them to register with the local authority.

Council policy, in both boroughs, was to register a minder for a maximum of three children, including her own. Registration for more children was exceptional; it was occasionally permitted to prevent family break-up or in some special circumstance. Within that framework, in 'Kingswell', thirty-eight minders were registered for 105 minded children (a ratio of 1 : 2.76), while thirty 'Higham' minders were together responsible for eighty-five children (a ratio of 1 : 2.65).

After several visits to each minder, when the children in her care were also present, the general impression of the minded children in both areas was of healthy, normal under fives. Emotional and physical needs were usually met. There were a few obviously difficult and disturbed youngsters, as well as some who seemed unduly withdrawn or ailing (about 14 per cent in each area); it was too soon, however, to know whether such manifestations were due to something in the child's home background or the daytime environment. 'Sad, passive children' were in a small minority. Although worrying, they did not dominate the emerging picture, as might have been expected from the introduction to the Mayall and Petrie study.

A more general cause for concern was the lack of stimulating play afforded the children as well as some minders' apparent unfamiliarity with the importance of talking with young children. Yet this concern was recognized as an educationally oriented judgement. It was relevant if childminding was to be considered a professional service, but it was hardly a basis for criticism of a cross section of mothers, most of whom had had no formal preparation for the job. All had the experience of bringing up their own children, however. While some minders in Kingswell (15 per cent) had taken part in informal discussions organized by the local authority, most said they saw little point in formal training. They felt their experience as mothers was sufficient qualification for the job. Moreover, evenings were valued for relaxation with the family. Days were already fully occupied.

Indeed, only a small minority were active outside the home, involved in the local community, in vocational or leisure pursuits. Four or five helped, in a voluntary capacity with spastics, in youth clubs, or hospitals. One minder made soft toys, another jewellery; a few had cars or caravans and managed to get out of London at weekends or for holidays.

If, as this suggests, life was circumscribed by a job that severely limited the time minders had for themselves, why did they do it? In view of suggestions in the press that minders were 'in it for the money', implying that they cared less about the children, this was an important question. The extent to which a minder was child-oriented could clearly affect her view of the centres.

Reasons for minding

The overwhelming majority of minders in both Kingswell and Higham initially said they started and continued to mind for the money.

This was difficult to understand, in view of the availability of other jobs and the generally agreed evidence of poor financial rewards in childminding. According to the LCSS Report (1977), the average a minder might expect to get was 5 pence an hour. In Kingswell and Higham, weekly pay for one child varied between £4.50 and £5.00. Assuming she was registered for three children, out of a total of not more than £15, a minder had to find all her expenses – feed the children, pay for overheads like gas and electricity, wear and tear of the furniture, bus fares, and refreshments on outings. Even in 1975, such an income could hardly produce handsome profits.

Moreover, most minders seemed agreed that income was irregular, 'You never know when they'll turn up, so you can't rely on it'. A usual response was 'We'd survive without it [the money], but it provides the extras'.

It was particularly interesting, therefore, when, towards the end of the first three months of regular visiting, minders, who perhaps began to feel more confident in themselves and in the project workers, began to give different reasons. In order of frequency, these were:

1. because they liked chidren;
2. to help a friend;
3. mother wanted to stay at home;
4. money, and
5. in response to personal crisis like the death of a husband or relative.

This seemed to reflect the need to fill an emotional void, rather than to meet a cash crisis. More often than one might suppose from the initial responses, the underlying need and desire emerged to have young children about them — a genuine interest in home making and a motherly instinct.

The situation in Higham was of even greater relevance to the finding (Mayall and Petrie, 1977 : 29) that nearly one-third of minders in their sample had definite plans for going back to work once their own child started pre-school or primary school. The implication was that many minders simply did the job as long as it suited their family requirements and without a sense of commitment. It is worth noting, therefore, that in Higham, where 75 per cent of minders were without under fives of their own and could have gone out to work, they had not done so. The average length of time minders had been caring for other people's children was seven years and, as *Table 6* suggests, money became less important with the passage of time and liking for children was more often the motivating force.

TABLE 6   *Reasons given for childminding ('Kingswell' and 'Higham')*

reason	for starting %	for continuing %
money	50	27
help a friend	12	34
suited family needs		
(mother wanted to stay at home)	25	28
health visitor suggested it	25	1
company for own child under 5	19	6
likes children	19	66
no other job open (applied to		
non-English speakers)	9	4
personal crisis (to fill an emotional		
gap following bereavement)	9	1

*Note: Several minders gave more than one reason — this is reflected in the percentages

A related question concerned minders' perceptions of child-minding as a job. This was a common topic of conversation and a remarkably similar and stable spread of attitudes became apparent between the two samples.

Approximately 45 per cent of minders in both Kingswell and Higham accepted childminding as a good neighbourly act, which provided pin money and which they carried out responsibly, as far as they could with very little support, guidance, or recognition. Some of the more articulate minders (about 35 per cent) considered they were doing a very worthwhile and rewarding job, but that they were widely underrated and misunderstood. A minority (not more than 20 per cent) thought their work 'of little importance'.

Patterns of the working day

Whatever their attitude to childminding, the pattern of the working day could clearly affect use of provision.

Common to all was an early start to the day. Children arrived between seven and nine in the morning. They were washed and given breakfast, sometimes with the minders' own family and sometimes after the family had gone to school or work. How a minder's day developed depended largely on the ages of her own and the minded children. For minders with young school-age children, everything tended to revolve round taking them to and from school; minders with under fives only had greater latitude.

Most minders said they did their housework in the morning and then went out shopping. If they cared for babies, they were in the habit of letting them sleep in the afternoon. Cooking, shopping, and cleaning took up a major part of a minder's time, just as it did with mothers in 'Hillcroft'.

At about 3.30 or 4 pm the number of children in some homes showed a dramatic increase. Not only did the minder's own school age children return, but part-time minded children arrived. They were usually children who had known the minder since babyhood and whose parents were still at work.

This practice was discouraged by social services, but it was apparent that at least 40 per cent of minders in both Kingswell and Higham accepted part-time minded children. They were not always included on the official list of registered children, however. One minder, registered for two children, coped confidently with up to ten children after school. This was exceptional, but up to five or six children was quite normal.

Here again, if childminders are seen as a professional service for under fives, an influx of older children is likely to detract from the quality of personal attention they can give; but in the context of a family and assuming competent oversight, such groupings could provide a natural and beneficial experience for all the children. In 'Higham' and 'Kingswell', rather than an indictment of the minders concerned, acceptance of part-time minded children seems as much a reflection of the lack of adequate provision for 'latchkey' children. In its absence, many minders were providing a social service.

Minded children were usually collected about 6 pm. Some husbands, about 16 per cent in both samples, did not wish to see any trace of children when they arrived home from work. Husbands of just over half the minders took no active part in looking after children, but were said to be understanding and supportive of their wives. They could also be relied on to help with shopping and general chores. The remaining husbands (about one third) played a more positive role; they helped care for the children, played with them, and took them on outings. This applied particularly to husbands who were shift-workers.

Even at this early stage, the importance of husbands' attitudes was quite evident. Consider, for example, the influence they exert over a minder's relationship with parents. When a child arrives in the morning, the mother is likely to be in a hurry to get to work. In the evening, she may be tired, but not under so much pressure; this is the best time for her to talk to the minder. The minder, however, has family pre-occupations looming. If, in addition, she has a husband who is unsympathetic and intolerant towards her job, it can create tensions which make her reluctant to take time with the departing mother and child. A crucial opportunity for deepening relationships is lost. As it was, there was a high correlation (.7) between minders who said they enjoyed positive, happy relationships with parents, and positive attitudes on the part of husbands towards childminding.

Features common to both samples which might influence response to provision

From all this several important elements could be identified which might affect response to provision. Convenient opening times and location of premises were obvious, but as in 'Hillcroft', they were to some extent controlled in these studies. Of greater importance was the stage of development of the minder's own family, as well as the number and ages of the minded children.

As minders were home oriented, husbands' views had to be considered. Some parents, too (about 10 per cent) were said by minders to be unhappy if they took the children out of the house. Project workers, after they had met and talked with each minder on several occasions, were strongly of the opinion that shyness and lack of confidence could also be obstacles to the use of the centres.

Areas of contrast between the samples

There were other features, more apparent in one sample or the other, which could also influence response to provision.

housing

Living conditions, for example, varied considerably between the two areas, but both were very different from 'Hillcroft'.

Kingswell was comparatively favoured. Houses were, in the main, substantial and well cared for, even though many were occupied by several families. There was one pre-war council estate, past its prime. Parks, excellent shopping facilities, and social amenities were all within easy access.

The majority of minders were well-housed, and as *Table 7* shows, at least had access to a garden. Even so, an equivalent number of children to more than one nursery class were cared for in physical conditions which the project workers would not have accepted for their own children. Four minders (nine children) were living in sub-standard housing with leaking roofs and defective plumbing, and ten minders (twenty-six children) coped with cramped conditions in which there was very little play space for the children.

'Higham' presented a striking contrast. General conditions were poor, 1971 Census figures giving 10 per cent of families as housed in statutorily overcrowded conditions, and 44 per cent without basic amenities of running hot water, bath, and indoor lavatory. Now (1975) much of the area was being redeveloped, but there was a somewhat run-down, pre-war estate which housed 4–5,000 families. Streets of decaying Victorian houses, punctuated by building sites, contributed to the air of desolation associated with inner city redevelopment. There were no open green spaces or modern shopping areas nearby.

A particular problem stemmed from the influx of single parent families and rehoused families with young children and a consequent need for day care. Many young and single parent families were placed in short-life property. Social Services had a high referral rate of an average of forty new applicants each week.

TABLE 7   *Housing in 'Kingswell' and 'Higham'*

classification	'Kingswell' no.	%	'Higham' no.	%
housing tenure				
owner occupied	24	(62)	15	(47)
private rented	7	(19)	6	(19)
council rented	7	(19)	11	(34)
total	38	(100)	32	(100)
type of accommodation				
self-contained	33	(87)	28	(88)
multi-occupied	2	(5)	0	(0)
shared living quarters	3	(8)	4	(12)
total	38	(100)	32	(100)
outside play-space				
house with garden (enclosed)	15	(40)	6	(19)
house or flat with access to play-space	9	(24)	7	(22)
no access to outside play-space	14	(36)	19	(59)
total	38	(100)	32	(100)

The type of accommodation registered for childminding reflected the picture outlined above. *Table 7* sets out the proportion of minders living in different categories of housing, but the figures do not adequately convey the restricted conditions in which some minders were struggling to cope with young children.

As one might expect from the general description, problems were more acute in 'Higham'. Approximately half the minders seemed well-housed by local standards. The other half were battling on in conditions which, while commonplace in the area, left much to be desired. As might be expected in a densely populated area, few minders had a house with a garden, or a flat with outside playspace. As *Table 7* shows, almost 60 per cent of minders had nowhere outside where the children could play and a further 13 per cent (those living in flats above ground level) were considerably restricted.

All this suggested that the centres could meet a real need for somewhere for the children to play, and it was thought that the children cared for by such minders were amongst those who stood to benefit most.

family patterns

Other circumstances which could affect demand and utilization of services, related to family patterns. Some of these are set out in *Table 8* below. They are selected for discussion either because, like mothers' age, they were variables of some relevance in Hillcroft, or because, like race and language, they were new and possibly important elements in the issue of non take-up.

TABLE 8   *Family patterns in 'Higham' and 'Kingswell'*

classification	'Kingswell' no.	%	'Higham' no.	%
(a) minder's nationality				
English	26	(68)	18	(56)
West Indian	8	(21)	3	(9)
Irish	1	(3)	6	(19)
European	3	(8)	3	(10)
others	0	(0)	2	(6)
total	38	(100)	32	(100)
(b) minder's status				
1st marriage	33	(87)	27	(84)
2nd marriage	3	(8)	0	(0)
divorced/separated	2	(5)	4	(13)
widowed	0	(0)	1	(3)
total	38	(100)	32	(100)
(c) minder's age groupings				
22−25	5	(13)	2	(6)
26−35	15	(40)	6	(19)
36−45	12	(32)	13	(41)
46−55	4	(10)	7	(22)
56 +	2	(5)	4	(12)
total	38	(100)	32	(100)
(d) husband's employment				
full time	34	(89)	22	(69)
part time, retired	3	(8)	2	(6)
invalid	0	(0)	5	(15)
dead or separated	1	(3)	3	(10)
total	38	(100)	32	(100)

i. *cultural background*

While the majority of minders in both areas were English, the mix of nationalities in 'Higham' contributed to the more cosmopolitan character of the sample (*Table 8(a)*). There was an even greater proportion of non-English speaking children in their care, so it was an open question whether language difficulties would be a particular feature among 'Higham' minders and inhibit use of the centres. Language barriers were less likely in 'Kingswell' with its comparatively large West Indian group, mainly of second generation immigrants. Cultural differences were not as diverse as in 'Higham', but the possibility of colour prejudice entering the dynamics of the developing centres could not be ruled out.

ii. *age and family composition*

Another striking contrast between the two samples was the average age of minders. If findings in 'Hillcroft' were anything to go by, characteristics relating to age and family composition might turn out to have an important bearing on use of provision.

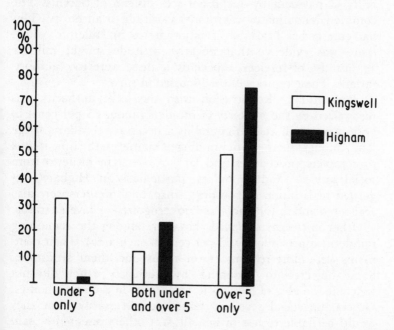

Figure 5 *Percentages of families in relation to children's ages*

In 'Kingswell', most minders were aged between 26—45. The typical family comprised father, out at work all day, and mother with two young school age children to care for. Half the mothers also had under fives at home.

By contrast, minders in 'Higham' were, on average, older — between 36—60, with few in the youngest age groupings. A probable reflection of this was the comparatively large proportion of husbands who were retired or invalids. The typical minder had a larger family than her counterpart in 'Kingswell' (three or four children). These children were likely to be at secondary school or already working, and as *Figure 5* indicates, only 25 per cent of minders had their own under fives at home.

iii.   *attitudes to 'authority'*

Turning now to issues that pre-occupied minders in the first three months of the projects, three inter-related topics in which negative attitudes were strongly associated together suggested themselves as potentially important in relation to response to provision. These were registration, overminding, and the possibility of payment by Social Services instead of parents. The common denominator was minder's attitude to 'authority'. This had emerged as a variable of major interest in 'Hillcroft', where there was evidence that negative attitudes might militate against use of services, especially if these were too 'authoritarian'. These topics will be discussed in turn.

a. *Registration*. Registration with the local authority was recognized by the majority of minders (about 65 per cent) in both 'Kingswell' and 'Higham' as a necessary corollary of the job. Amongst them, criticism hinged mainly on the time it took to complete procedures and lack of oversight hitherto from social services. Some minders, particularly in 'Higham', regarded registration as pointless, since 'bad' minders were also registered and thus it conferred no recognized or coveted status.

Other criticisms surfaced, however, among the remaining minders (approximately 35 per cent in each area). Their comments were more reminiscent of an 'us' and 'them' syndrome. Some objected to 'snooping' by 'authority'; they did not welcome the idea of being told what to do in their own homes. Others, on social security, feared (unnecessarily) that they would be liable to loss of benefit. Yet others resented or said they could not afford modifications to their premises necessary to comply with safety regulations. These same minders also tended to be upset or dismayed by compulsory X-rays and health checks.

b. *Overminding*. Indications of an anti-'authority' element were borne out by an analysis of attitudes to overminding, that is the practice of taking in more than the permitted number of children. A commonly held view, as for example Mayall and Petrie (1977 : 30) is that overminding is often the minder's response to low pay.

In 'Higham' and 'Kingswell' almost all the minders, at one time or another, expressed considerable dissatisfaction with rates of pay and the lack of standardized practice. Evidence was far from conclusive, however, that those who overminded turned to it deliberately and exclusively for financial reasons. At least three different attitudes were identified underlying the same practice.

Most minders (about 55 per cent in both areas) respected the guidelines laid down for their benefit and that of the children in their care. They did not overmind.

A small group (about 15 per cent) persisted in overminding, in spite of being warned by local authority childminder workers against it. These minders were almost certainly doing it to help make ends meet, since they were significantly likely to be among the few (some 16 per cent) who also said they had early morning and evening jobs. Such work, also discouraged by social services, was mainly cleaning offices, shift work in factories, or as night staff in hospitals.

The issue was more complex for a third group (about 30 per cent). Such minders were not anti-authority *per se*, but manifestly followed an independent line if it seemed right to them. They were known, at least occasionally, to take on more children than they were registered for, but for reasons other than money. They were often older women who had raised their own large families, competent and confident that they could cope. Their persistence in overminding reflected, in their view, a responsible and rational response to a child's needs, often in circumstances that gave no time to contact social services. Such minders sometimes felt strongly that they could be penalized for something which, while not ideal, was better than the alternative. Speaking of one minder who was known to overmind, another commented 'If you shut her down, those children will be shut in the house and mum will go to work. It may be diabolical in her home, but surely its better to be diabolical together than shut up in a house alone.'

c. *Payment by Social Services*. Finally, there was the question of whether minders wished to be paid by social services or by parents. The reported success of a salaried scheme by child-minders (The Groveway Project: Willmott and Challis, 1977), coupled with difficulties experienced over the existing system, led to much discussion of the pros and cons of introducing a similar scheme. A possible reflection of the hassle 'Higham' minders felt over parents and problems arising from cultural diversity, was that 81 per cent favoured payment by social services. The rest said they got on well with parents and saw no reason to change.

In 'Kingswell' however, three distinct groups were identified. Some minders (44 per cent) wanted the security of being employed by the local authority. A small group (18 per cent) felt that the suggested measure would deprive them of direct dealings with parents, essential both for the well-being of the child and the minder's own satisfaction in the job. Others again (38 per cent) valued their autonomy and simply said they did not wish to be employed by anyone.

iv. *quality of care*

The overall picture, after three months intensive visiting and discussion, suggested to the project workers that those minders who were worrying in one respect, tended also to be worrying in most others. These were mothers who were often under con-siderable strain, who did not recognize the importance of the job and consequently set themselves low standards. They were the ones who spoke of difficulties with parents, of longstanding health problems, including 'depression'. They seemed fre-quently under the weather, if not actually ill; and were also likely to speak of little support, either active or moral, from their husbands. They accounted for between 15 and 20 per cent. Their existence emphasized deficiencies in the system of registration and the laws relating to childminders − the lack of oversight by parents and social services. It drew attention to social and economic pressures which obliged people to put up with unsatisfactory conditions.

In marked contrast, other minders (about 25 to 30 per cent) created a positive and happy environment. They organized their day so that they could both keep house and manage to spend time with individual children. 'If a child walks up with a book, if it's your own and you're busy, you say "in a minute". With minded children, you have certain times each day when you sit down with them.' And again: 'If a minded child comes up when you're busy, even so, who else has he got to ask? So you pick him up and cuddle him.'

This left about half the minders who tended to one or other extreme and who afforded a less rich environment, providing little in the way of stimulating play. They characteristically showed a strong sense of responsibility towards the minded children, however, and often seemed to go out of their way to feed and clothe any children they felt were neglected by their parents, as well as offering help to the parents themselves.

The new centres, in the judgement of Social Services, had a great deal to offer minders and the children in their care. What remained to be seen was how far they would appeal to those they most hoped to attract.

SUMMARY

A preliminary study of all the registered minders in two small areas of Inner London suggested uncohesive groups of mothers at home, doing a similar job, but largely unaware of each others' existence.

The differing mix of nationalities and stages of family development found in each area, emphasized the dangers of generalizing from one group to another. Minders in 'Kingswell' tended to be younger, to have smaller families comprising school-age children or under fives at home. In contrast, 'Higham' minders were more likely to have older school age children or wage-earning adolescents at home. Families, on average, were larger.

As to quality of care, children's emotional and physical needs were, with a few exceptions, satisfactorily met. The range of stimulating play on offer, with some notable exceptions, was extremely limited. This observation, however, has to be seen in the context of limited resources, meagre external support, and no formal preparation for the job.

There was clear evidence of many problems relating to looking after other people's children; sources of stress existed over and above those of living in poor housing or associated with mothers at home with young children.

A complex picture emerged. There was some evidence to suggest that several variables which in 'Hillcroft' had proved important in relation to take up of provision, might also be relevant here. What was needed was some way of ordering the information and providing a more secure basis for discussion. Results of such an approach will be the subject of the next chapter.

CHAPTER EIGHT

A fresh perspective on childminders

The foregoing descriptive analysis, based on three months' home visiting and work at the centres, drew attention to possible explanations for disregard of provision. Following on from the 'Hillcroft' study, those it was expected might be most important turned on aspects of stress, alienation, and of family composition. In samples as different as 'Kingswell' and 'Higham', however, other reasons could not be discounted.

Both centres appeared successful in so far as they attracted as many, sometimes more, minders than the project workers could cope with satisfactorily. It was nevertheless clear that about one third of minders, among whom were many who had said they would use the centres, did not come forward to do so. At a purely subjective level, workers said they thought practical difficulties and lack of confidence were the most likely explanations. Yet it was impossible at face value to be sure what was of crucial importance in inhibiting or encouraging use.

This is where a formal, statistically-oriented approach was needed to obtain a more objective and parsimonious account of the evidence. The fruits of such a strategy form the basis of this chapter. An outline of the contribution of the Index of Maternal Alienation (IMA) will open the way to a summary of the main characteristics associated with minders who did not come to the centres. Finally, some issues arising from the studies will be discussed and the main points summarized.

Before this, however, it is interesting to note that some of the characteristics that turned out to be most important in 'Hillcroft' (the Index of Maternal Alienation) were also relevant in 'Kingswell' and 'Higham'. When childminders were subdivided into categories of low and high alienation, the picture that emerged, even at the anecdotal level, to some extent validated the IMA.

Table 9 shows the sub-groups formed by the distribution of scores on the IMA for the combined samples. Identical headings are used to those in 'Hillcroft' for ease of reference (cf. p. 114). The table indicates that, according to scores recorded towards the end of the first six months, one third of minders tended to have more negative attitudes towards child care and to be more alienated.

Within Group I (non-users) and Group II (new users), scores on the IMA distinguish those minders who tended towards more positive attitudes and those with more negative tendencies. Sub-group IIIa, although poorly represented in the childminder samples, is included because a parallel exists between mothers in 'Hillcroft' who went out of their way to find pre-school provision and minders who used playgroups. Later experience suggests that in other areas, a considerable proportion of minders may belong in this sub-group. Sub-group IIIb comprises minders, who like the mothers in IIIb in 'Hillcroft' could be considered clients of Social Services.

TABLE 9   *'Kingswell' and 'Higham' samples combined, showing the distribution of scores on the Index of Maternal Alienation*

	low alienation scores		high alienation scores		total	
	no.	%	no.	%	no.	%
Group I non-users	5	(7)	11	(16)	16	(23)
Group II users	37	(53)	9	(13)	46	(66)
Group III existing playgroup users	5	(7)	3	(4)	8	(11)
total	47	(67)	23	(33)	70	(100)

Clearly, since each category actually includes quite a spread of scores for each characteristic, some traits are more or less pronounced in some minders than in others within any one sub-group. Of course, once people are categorized, the danger of 'discovering' things that fit, and disregarding those that do not, has to be recognized. Nevertheless, in presenting the typologies that follow, the salient and recurring characteristics associated with each sub-group were remarkably consistent in matters beyond those relating directly to the IMA. Moreover, descriptions were based on anecdotal material recorded by people who had no notion at the time of the existence of such sub-groups or of the implications of the IMA.

TYPOLOGIES OF THE SIX SUB-GROUPS

Sub-group Ia: 'Low alienation' minders who used no form of provision – child centred decision

Minders in this group seemed glad to have visitors who shared their interest and concern in children. Although they tended to keep 'themselves to themselves', they were not without friends. Occasionally one or two childminders living close together arranged joint outings or made other reciprocal arrangements. They were welcoming and fairly business like with parents; there were few complaints about 'troubles' with the minded children or their parents. Some minders took their children on the recommendation of social services, others advertised or found them independently. They tended to be 'non-joiners', whether a playgroup or a 'professional' association.

These were among the childminders who were likely to have organized their homes round the children, to have extended the house to provide a playroom or better kitchen facilities. Husbands clearly played a major role in such decisions. They also came into the conversation with comments like, 'He always does the shopping for me' . . . 'I never have to worry if I feel a bit off colour, he'll always help out' . . . 'He loves having the kids as much as I do'.

Minders in this group frequently expressed their very positive enjoyment in the children. It was reflected in the pleasure they showed in some new achievement, the way they greeted a mother with the 'news' when she arrived in the evening. These minders tended to include the minded child and his mother: 'We've been baking this afternoon – you'll stay and have a cuppa', or 'Mark's got something special in a bag for mummy to take home.' They seemed to like cooking and spoke of the satisfaction they derived from feeding the family and the minded children.

One seldom found painting or messy play encouraged. 'I don't think they need any of that – my kids got on all right without it' or 'well, we do a bit of painting sometimes, but you've got to watch the walls. I'm not keen.' A few minders went out of their way to make sure the children had the benefit of a 'home playgroup' and, with limited resources, made an effort to provide a wide range of play activities. Their warmth and sense of responsibility were undeniable.

Such minders saw the centres as superfluous to their needs and to those of the children. To take the children to centres was to negate their contract with parents to care for the children in their own homes.

Sub-group Ib: 'High alienation' minders who used no form of provision – minder centred decision

As in 'Hillcroft', this was a sub-group that gave rise to disquiet. The minders concerned were likely to be living in poorer accommodation and to be among the more difficult to reach. Some of them had been registered since before the re-organization that followed the Seebohm Report; and they were retained on the list to 'keep a foot in the door'. An unexpectedly high proportion of them were not welcoming to visitors. Strangers knocking on the door were clearly suspect and a slight movement behind net curtains might be the only sign of life.

Inside, heating was often inadequate. Rooms tended to be barren and dingy with a lack of stimulating play for the children. They might expect to spend most of the day in such a room, perhaps with a settee and a television set, possibly a few plastic toys. 'I give them lots of cuddles and they've got the tele', or again 'I mainly have babies. They sleep a lot. They don't need much else do they?'

It seemed that this sub-group was defined as much by the parents who sought the services of its members, as by the minders themselves. There seemed to be some linkage between the two. Whereas minders in the 'a' sub-groups often took their minded children through social services, those in this sub-group more often found their children independently.

Somehow parents knew about these minders who usually seemed to be well supplied with children. To mothers in distress, even such provision could be a godsend. 'I opened the door' said one minder, 'there was a woman standing there with a baby in her arms and tears down her face. She thrust the baby at me, "a friend said you'd look after it. I've got to go or I'll get the sack" and she rushed away. I ask you, what could I do? What would you have done?'

It seemed that descriptions of parents did much to explain these minders. One example was a lone mother, separated from her husband and not in contact with social services. She was one of a group of squatters living in one room at the top of an insalubrious house. When she cooked, it was on a gas stove on the landing. The lavatory was two floors below and shared. She would have liked a day nursery for her little girl, but she worked unusual hours and had to travel to work. A childminder was the only alternative she could think of and she had heard of this one 'on the grapevine'. 'She's got her points, though I do worry . . . I don't think she feeds her properly and I do worry.'

Another example, of parents this time, who were not eligible for day nursery provision. They also lived in poor housing which they tried hard to make attractive. Both felt they needed to work. They were even pleased with the attention their child was getting. 'She [the minder] makes a real fuss of him, she gives him the food I make and she doesn't mind if I'm a bit late and do my bit of shopping on the way home. She's my mate and we have a good natter − it works out quite well really *and* she doesn't cost as much as my friends pay.'

Parents like these arguably had little choice and the gap between their lifestyle and that of the minder was often negligible.

Sub-group IIa: 'Low alienation' minders − regular users of the centres

These minders, the largest single sub-group, tended to be the most outgoing and friendly in the samples. Some, like minders in Ia had organized their homes for looking after small groups of young children. Yet they preferred to come to the centres because they found the children enjoyed it and benefited from the experience. There was a wider range of activities than they could, or perhaps wished, to provide themselves. They often commented how much they liked to see their friends and meet new people.

Others lived in comparatively cramped conditions. It was a welcome break for them to go somewhere children could play safely and where they could relax.

There seemed to be two types of minder in this group. Some were mainly interested in the home and shared many characteristics with IIa mothers in 'Hillcroft'. While they appreciated a break from routine, they did not want to be rid of the children. They almost always had under-fives of their own. They felt highly responsible towards the minded children and often seemed to contrast their attitudes with those of the parents. 'Let's face it – we're not like them: If we were, we'd be out at work earning pots of money.' Such remarks were not normally expressions of hostility. There seemed to be a general acceptance of the need for some parents to work. The only real hostility was expressed towards parents (and minders) who were thought not to be caring adequately for the children. Strong feelings were expressed that children should be suitably dressed for the climate and well turned out. 'I mind what people say about the children I'm out with and if one of them looks scruffy, I know what they're going to say.'

Other minders seemed more outward looking and aware of the scope of the work. They tended to be confident and to have a good relationship with minded children and their parents. They saw childminding more as a profession, welcomed a national association, and preferred the idea of being employed by the local authority.

There was a wide variety of opinion as to how children should be brought up. Some practices did not find favour in current child care theory, but they nevertheless often coincided with parents' views. Some minders were quite strict, others much more easy going. 'Jim and I don't hold with children talking when we're talking . . . He'll soon let 'em know where they get off. That's how we brought up our kids and they've turned out OK.'

Sub-group IIb: 'High alienation' minders – non-starters or irregular users

Once again, a close parallel with 'Hillcroft' mothers was evident when individuals within this group were considered. Scores on the IMA define a continuum and as one moved along towards the highest scoring minders, it became clear that income was important for understanding these minders. Struggling to make ends meet, they would work at night in a local factory or hospital to augment the family income. Yet some would still make efforts to take the children to the centre 'because they like it so much'. It was hardly surprising that they often looked pale and tired. Most of the children, however, seemed lively enough.

Just as in 'Hillcroft', minders in this group characteristically seemed to blow hot and cold. Coming to the centres, looking after the children, going shopping, getting meals, could all be very much of a hit and miss affair. Much depended on the weather, whether one had overslept. 'It's a good idea to go down there [the centre] really — there's lots for the kids to do; they're forever on about when can they go again.' But minders in this sub-group, for all their good intentions, did not get to the centres regularly: 'I just couldn't face getting them all out today . . . I'll pop in next time . . . next time . . .'

Sub-group IIIa: 'Low alienation' minders – the initiative takers

This was a very small group of minders who, before the projects began, made use of local playgroups, nursery schools, or mother and toddler groups. Like other minders in the (a) sub-groups, they were pre-occupied by the children's welfare. Their chief distinguishing feature seemed to be that from experience, usually with their own children, they had come to value the opportunities afforded by playgroups. Sometimes it was the parents who were convinced and who asked the minders to take their children. More frequently it seemed to be the minder who persuaded parents that a playgroup was worth paying for or who found the money herself. These minders seemed more generally aware of services within the community; they were significantly more likely to be among those minders who considered it part of a minder's job to take the children in their care to the clinic regularly: 'I see it this way' said one, 'with their mum at work all day, who's going to take them if I don't? She doesn't make anything of it.'

Sub-group IIIb: 'Interventionist' minders

Minders in this very small group comprised those with the highest IMA scores. They are comparable with 'interventionist' mothers in 'Hillcroft' because their relationship with social workers or childminder workers was rather that of 'client' than 'colleague'. Not only would the local authority not refer mothers to them, but social workers actively discouraged them from minding. Consequently, like minders in Ib, they found their children independently. Where, for a variety of reasons, the law could not be invoked to stop them minding, children were with parental permission, taken to the centres without the minders. Problems facing these minders were as varied as in any group of mothers under stress without adequate resources to cope. They do not need further description.

These typologies demonstrate that there is a recognizable constellation of real life characteristics which define membership of the six sub-groups. They suggest that the IMA is providing relevant information for this kind of study.

THE PREDICTIVE VALUE OF THE IMA

In both 'Kingswell' and 'Higham', for example, the IMA was predictive of spasmodic, irregular, and non-users with negative attitudes to child care.

Results indicated similar patterns to those in the 'Hillcroft' study. Minders who used the centres in both areas were predominantly friendly and outgoing, they felt they could rely on the support of their family or friends. Their relationship with the minded children reflected positive attitudes to child care. They had low IMA scores.

In contrast, those who came to the centres infrequently or not at all were significantly more likely, especially in 'Higham', to be less well disposed towards their neighbours, less well integrated in the community, and to enjoy a less satisfying relationship with the children in their care. They tended, with few exceptions, to have high IMA scores.

TABLE 10 *Proportion of minders in 'Kingswell' and 'Higham' with low, average, and high scores on variables which comprise the Index of Maternal Alienation (IMA)*
(LA = low alienation; HA = high alienation)

variable	Kingswell no.	%	Higham no.	%	score
1. attitude to neighbours	23	(60)	18	(56)	1 (LA)
	4	(10)	5	(16)	2
	11	(30)	9	(28)	3 (HA)
total	38	(100)	32	(100)	
2. attitude to messy play	17	(45)	14	(44)	1 (LA)
	6	(24)	10	(31)	2
	12	(31)	8	(25)	3 (HA)
total	38	(100)	32	(100)	

TABLE 10—*cont.*

variable	Kingswell no.	%	Higham no.	%	score
3. time available for relaxed play	19	(50)	19	(58)	1 (LA)
	6	(16)	7	(22)	2
	13	(34)	6	(20)	3 (HA)
total	38	(100)	32	(100)	
4. degree of child centredness	15	(39)	14	(44)	1 (LA)
	11	(30)	11	(34)	2
	12	(31)	7	(20)	3 (HA)
total	38	(100)	32	(100)	
5. contact with extended family	15	(39)	26	(81)	1 (LA)
	5	(14)	2	(6)	2
	18	(31)	7	(22)	3 (HA)
total	38	(100)	32	(100)	
6. mother—child relationship (assessment)	24	(63)	21	(66)	1 (LA)
	4	(11)	8	(25)	2
	10	(26)	3	(9)	3 (HA)
total	38	(100)	32	(100)	

These findings did not, of course, establish any direct link between the IMA and non-use of facilities in general. It was simply that in two small samples, other than 'Hillcroft', high scores on the IMA were associated with negative response to provision. Nevertheless, results were sufficiently consistent to suggest that the IMA might be developed for use on a diagnostic, advisory, or predictive basis (see *Table 10*).

THE IMA AS AN INDEX OF CHANGE

Classification of minders into sub-groups on the basis of IMA scores also provided a rough and ready indication that some important changes took place over a comparatively short period of time.

Re-assessed after twelve months, the IMA scores were taken as a reflection of change in attitudes and in the quality of care. Strikingly, changes which took place were in a positive direction. They mainly concerned minders in Group II — those who made regular or spasmodic use of the centres. These changes resulted in an increased proportion of minders in the positive sub-group and an overall increase in the number of minders with low IMA scores. Such decreases were mainly due to changed attitudes to 'messy play' and to aspects of the minder–child relationship. This assessment included use of language and some of the problems associated with child-minding.

i. Messy play

When they first came to the centres, the majority of minders were highly suspicious and wary of play that involved painting, water, or sand. Those minders whose objections were strongest (approximately 25 per cent), seemed to go through three stages of attitude change. First there was total rejection, usually highly vocal, of all 'messy' play, coupled with a determination to keep their children away from such activities.

Two factors were thought to herald the second stage of guarded interest, verging on acceptance. These were other children's absorption and evident pleasure in such play, and discussion with the project workers and other minders. Once it was demonstrated how aprons and sleeve-savers kept clothes clean and a plastic sheet protected vulnerable surfaces, attitudes became less hard. A final stage, when messy play was incorporated into activities minders organized at home, they seemed encouraged by the opportunity for minders themselves to experiment with different media. They began by helping mix paints and prepare dough for the children's play at the centre. Some had never had such experience, even as children, and so had been unaware of the pleasure and profit that could be derived from it.

ii. The minder–child relationship

a. *language*

Perhaps one of the main functions of the centres was to foster communication. At first, some minders did not realize the importance of their role in children's language development, especially where very young children were concerned. Everybody who attended the centres regularly showed some signs of greater awareness of how they could help by listening and talking to the minded children. Fifteen minders manifested very changed attitudes. Whereas they had ignored a child trying to talk to them, or ostentatiously or with embarrassment thrust a proffered painting into the nearest waste-paper basket, they now began to take an interest and to respond warmly.

b. *problems inherent in childminding*

All the children were, in the nature of the relationship, divided between two homes and two 'care-takers', their mothers and the childminders. This, not unnaturally, led to a variety of problems. What do you do with a very aggressive child, or with children who do not get on well together? How do you cope with a deprived child? With a child from another culture? Do you treat minded children differently, or the same as your own? Such problems were fundamental to many tensions which had been observed in minder's families and between parents and minders.

Use of the IMA scores as a baseline suggested progressive improvement in the way minders coped with such problems. Informal discussions gave all the minders who attended the centres an opportunity to express their opinions, to listen to others, and to use each other and the project workers as touchstones. Certain topics pre-occupied them at succeeding stages and marked development.

It was notable, for example, that initial concerns turned not on the children and their needs, but on minder's relationships with parents and with the local authority.

Where a mother was in financial difficulties, it was sometimes hard for a minder to know how much to charge. There were mothers who left without notice and without paying. Others came with children who were too ill to leave, but they rushed away without saying anything was wrong. There were practical problems of children left with insufficient or dirty clothing; children not collected at the agreed time and those few children whom the minder suspected were being physically ill-treated at home. Quite apart from worry over the child, her own position was very vulnerable.

Minders together identified problems and, with the support of Social Services, set about standardizing practice. After some months, an indication that these problems were being successfully tackled was that minders, as a group, showed a growing pre-occupation with child-oriented problems. This represented a second stage in development. All the minders were thought to benefit from the discussions, but again about 25 per cent showed marked changes in attitude. They seemed to the project workers better able to cope with disturbed children; they were more consistent in their discipline and showed greater understanding of immigrant children and their parents. Minders recounted their own changing attitudes and development: 'What I've learned now is that you can't change parents; they're not like you, otherwise they'd be at home looking after their children. So you make the best of it, you don't try and change things for them [the minded children] because they've got to live in those surroundings'; and another: 'When I started, with my own children I mean, I had no idea about talking to them. I hardly ever played with them − I get a real kick out of it now'; and another, 'It's a new world, isn't it? You know, I go home and *think* about the children now. That's something new.'

There were two further and more objective indications of changing attitudes. Almost a quarter of the minders, from being intensely antagonistic towards the idea of formal training, actually enrolled in and completed a course. The reason for this change of mind seemed to lie in recognition that their experience as mothers did not extend to all the areas of child care needed to cope with looking after other people's children. There was also an increase from nine per cent, in the first three months of the projects, to 56 per cent twelve months later, in the number of minders using playgroups and mother-and-toddler groups as well as the centres. It looked as though they became convinced of the benefit of such provision for the children, and were then prepared to seek it out.

iii. Isolation

As the general scores on the IMA showed, those minders who were most likely to use the centres were also among the most friendly and outgoing in the sample. They were likely to be those least cut off from family and the wider community. In 'Kingswell', however, 13 per cent of minders who attended regularly had been among those who complained most of the loneliness.

In both projects, those minders who came forward to use provision presented a very different picture after eighteen months. Instead of a fragmented assortment of individuals largely unaware of each other's existence, they formed two easily identifiable groups. These generated self-help and the ability to express a coherent viewpoint.

A GENERAL VIEW OF THE STATISTICALLY-BASED EVIDENCE

By definition, the IMA is limited to a few variables which originated in a sample different in some obvious respects from 'Kingswell' and 'Higham'. Consequently one wanted to know how other characteristics, perhaps unique to the groups of childminders, were related to response to the centres.

A first, most important step was to put the IMA in the context of the whole, and to obtain a global view. A general mapping exercise gave individual items on the IMA an equal chance with all the other items in the schedule of clustering together to form a meaningful frame of reference. It was of considerable interest that a similar underlying structure to that in 'Hillcroft' emerged in both 'Higham' and 'Kingswell'. Within it, the IMA formed a distinct and statistically justified frame of reference common to all three studies.

It seemed that three other underlying determinants in 'Hillcroft' were relevant for understanding the dynamics of 'Kingswell' and 'Higham'. These concerned family size and composition, attitudes to 'authority', and a coping—non coping dimension.

Table 11 provides an overall view of the statistically-based evidence including the IMA. It highlights similarities and differences between 'Hillcroft', 'Kingswell', and 'Higham' by listing for each centre the main characteristics associated with it. There are three sections. Section 1 lists those characteristics associated with utilization in both childminding samples; 2. lists characteristics that clustered with utilization in 'Higham'; and 3. brings together characteristics that were unique to 'Kingswell'. Variables in each section are listed in order of importance.

TABLE 11 *Characteristics associated with use of facilities in 'Hillcroft', 'Higham', and 'Kingswell'*

Section 1 – *Characteristics associated with 'Higham' and 'Kingswell'*
1. minder friendly and outgoing (IMA)
2. minder prefers payment by Social Services (HC)
3. minder has understanding of messy play (IMA)
4. minder not known to leave children alone in the house
5. minder has some paper qualifications

TABLE 11—*cont*

Section 2 – *Characteristics associated with 'Higham' only*
1.   husband takes active part in childminding
2.   minder has close contact with extended family (IMA)
3.   minder child-centred (IMA)
4.   minder has outside experience
5.   minder has no money worries
6.   minder values the work she does
7.   children seem happy and well cared for
8.   minder welcoming to visitors

Section 3 – *Characteristics associated with 'Kingswell' only*
1.   time available each day for relaxed play (IMA)
2.   minder has children of her own under five
3.   minder has money worries

Key: (IMA) = Item on the Index of Maternal Alienation
     (HC) = Variable associated with use of provision in 'Hillcroft'

Some aspects of this table are particularly interesting as it shows what variables remained when all the inessential ones had been pared away.

It is noteworthy that in spite of obvious local differences, items on the IMA emerge as of major importance in relation to use of services in all three samples – social integration, and positive attitudes to child care. Attitude to authority, which in 'Hillcroft' looked as though it might be relevant, also turns out to be significant in the childminder samples. What is more, even those variables that could only apply in 'Kingswell' and 'Higham' could also be interpreted as aspects of child care or of attitude to authority.

The only exception is 'having money worries'. This is interesting because it was positively associated with use of the centre in 'Higham' and negatively so in 'Kingswell'. One explanation for this could be that the average age of minders in 'Kingswell' was lower than in 'Higham'. Consequently, minders' own families included children of school age who would tend to be a greater drain on family resources. In 'Higham', however, families were nearer completion; teenage children were more likely to be working and contributing to the family income.

Nevertheless, it was rather odd that having money worries should be so strongly associated with coming to the centre in 'Kingswell'. It looked as though the centre was particularly successful in attracting the less well-to-do. Whichever way one looked at it, money was not an inhibiting factor.

The general picture is clear. The absence of certain variables in *Table 11* suggests that some explanations for non-use of provision were less relevant than had commonly been assumed. At the same time attention is focused unequivocally on the central importance of others.

Explanations for non-use of facilities that could be discounted

Among the explanations for poor response which could be largely discounted were inconvenient siting of provision, expense and, surprisingly, 'practical difficulties'. It was remarkable that those minders who initially voiced such problems often became regular attenders. It was the strength of their conviction that the centres offered something worthwhile for the children that seemed to tip the balance. This view was also borne out by analysis of attitudes of minders who had other jobs, but who nevertheless made use of some form of provision.

Other circumstances which had been thought likely to inhibit use of the centres — language barriers, cultural differences, and colour prejudice — also failed to show any significant effect. This is not to say that problems with individuals did not arise, but they were of a minor nature and did not amount to a trend.

Explanations of some importance

Family composition, particularly the stage of family development, had some bearing on the use of centres. Minders with children under five of their own, for example, were not only more likely to use the centres, but they were also significantly more likely to spend time playing with the children, to have child centred attitudes and to enjoy friendly relations with parents of minded children. There was perhaps an element of greater awareness of the benefits offered by the centres and of the problems of parents with young children.

Yet a minder's age and the stage of family development were not in themselves sufficient to explain use or non-use of the centres. Husband's attitudes to childminding may be a decisive influence, but there was insufficiently comprehensive information to do more than suggest it as an area for further study. Contrary to expectation, however, women who had shift-worker husbands were amongst those most likely to use the centres. It happened that those husbands shared their wives' interest in children; there was a high correlation (.7) between husbands who were shift workers and those who helped with the children.

Explanations of major importance

What remained were three characteristics that appeared to be of major importance in explaining non-utilization of provision. Findings in both childminder studies as well as 'Hillcroft', suggested that among the people who did not respond — the isolated, those suspicious of 'authority' — with the exception of one small sub-group (Ia), those with more negative attitudes to child care were over-represented. A disproportionate number were also those not already using other services, like health clinics. It was also found that they were most likely to be living in cramped conditions, without outside playspace for the children. In short, they were those minders whom it was most hoped would make use of the centres.

Such findings underline the Law of Inverse Care and simply bear out what many working in the field feel they know already.

POSTSCRIPT

There were, however, some indications of ways forward which might repay experiment. They emphasize the importance of underlying attitudes, of styles of approach, and the differing roles of the statutory and voluntary sectors.

There has already been some suggestion that in 'Kingswell' something different was happening. Project workers succeeded in attracting and maintaining the interest of some of the most alienated minders. Among those who became actively involved were some who, initially, seemed the least confident, the least child-centred, and the most isolated. Whereas, in 'Higham', regular use was closely associated with a minder's confidence and positive perception of herself and her role.

Some observations suggested that the nature of the link with the local authority might provide a clue to one reason for the contrast. The centre in 'Kingswell' received a great deal of support from the local authority, but it was not identified with it. Project workers had no responsibility for registration. Their relationship with minders was more readily seen as unthreatening. They were able to concentrate on building minders' self-confidence and independence without overt criticism.

The centre in 'Higham', in the course of its development, became more closely identified with officialdom. With the object of raising standards, Social Services became more strict over the whole process of registration. The centre was presented by childminding visiting officers as a place where minders in the course of registration were expected to attend, and from which those who did not reach the required standards would be barred. A marked trend for new minders to bring four or five children with them to the centres did not persist; the number with each minder dropped to two or three.

The crucial question, however, was, how far did this reflect a genuine reduction in overminding and a rise in standards? Was it that those minders who had more children than they were supposed to, chose not to come anymore? The latter was certainly the view of some minders who used the centre. It also found some support in the striking pattern that emerged when attendances were plotted for each minder in the order in which she first came to the centre. The initial nucleus continued to come, but from a point coincidental to the change in policy, comparative newcomers simply dropped away. Minders who did not wish to be employed by Social Services were disproportionately represented amongst them, as well as minders who had normally brought more than three children.

The inference is that in building up a core of dependable childminders with recognized standards, a minority of women may be discouraged from using services, but not necessarily discouraged from taking in children. Manifestly, a few childminders who go over the prescribed limit can represent a significant number of children.

DISCUSSION

Clearly these studies raise more questions than they provide answers. They can, however, contribute to the general debate and pinpoint areas for further study and experiment.

At the outset it is important to emphasize that the samples comprised all the registered minders in each area. The studies therefore give a composite picture of legitimate home day care on offer. Minders were favoured only by comparison with support accorded their counterparts in some other boroughs. Viewed objectively, there was still considerable instability in the amount of oversight, guidance, and support the local authorities were able to give.

The discussion that follows is concerned with three issues which seem, from these and other studies, to be of crucial importance.

1. **Given support and supervision, is it possible to improve the overall quality of childminding? Can it play a generally recognized and positive role in child care services?**

Many childminders offer working mothers facilities which they cannot find anywhere else. They offer the children warmth, stability, stimulation — all that a day nursery offers — and more. For children who are overwhelmed by large groups, for parents who prefer the non-institutional character of home care, who want to influence the care their child receives, and who are prepared to search out the right childminder for them, childminding has much to commend it.

Yet it is common knowledge that this is not a universal description. Findings from these and other studies suggest discrepancies in the service and, at least hitherto, powerful disincentives to use. At least three viewpoints have to be considered: that of minders and their families, of parents and children, of social services, and the public conscience. From the minder's angle, the chief drawbacks seemed to be lack of security, long hours, inadequate pay, problems over holidays, and friction with parents. Social Service difficulties stemmed from lack of resources and the nature of the law on childminding, and lack of 'training' for childminders. Registration failed to provide practical and moral support for minders or a guarantee of standards for parents. For children and parents, problems related to the quality of care; to the possibility of children being pushed around from one minder to another, or to spending the days with little to do and perhaps in an environment very different from their own home. Parents might not even be able to communicate with minders because of language difficulties.

Can such difficulties be resolved or are they inherent in childminding? In some respects, these studies offer a hopeful prognosis. It will be summed up under the headings mentioned above.

conditions of work (minder's viewpoint)

In 'Kingswell' and 'Higham' improvements in minders' conditions of work, their pay, and consequently their morale, were manifest within the comparatively short period of eighteen months. Some of these improvements were facilitated by the centres, which provided a forum for discussion of problems; local authority childminder workers used their expertise to find solutions. Towards the end of the period, minders were beginning to build on this foundation by helping each other. This was not a uniquely local phenomenon. There were similar developments elsewhere. The BBC programme for childminders 'Other People's Children' provided considerable impetus and led to the setting up of a National Childminding Association. Subsequently, this Association has brought many childminders together to press for better working conditions and recognized status. Together with some local authorities, it has been instrumental in regularizing pay, obtaining insurance and other benefits. It has been among the most important influences in achieving a more generally accepted and standardized interpretation of the *Nurseries and Childminders Act*.

Much remains to be achieved, but there is ample evidence that where positive attitudes prevail, substantial progress can be made in improving conditions of work.

resources, the law, and 'training' (Social Services viewpoint)

These were clearly beyond the scope of the studies to assess; the following comments are a purely personal appraisal.

Difficulties seem most intractable in these areas. Social Services may have the will and the expertise to play a key part in developing childminding as a satisfactory form of day care. They are hampered by lack of resources, by ineffectual laws, and by confusion over what is expected of childminders.

The bases of a good service are recruitment and registration. They demand from childminder workers a knowledge, not only of statutory requirements, but of child development and the role of play, of individual and group dynamics. They call for skills of a high order to encourage those mothers who have much to offer, to counsel applicants who should be prevented from minding, and to deal with problems arising from diverse backgrounds.

Where registration is carried out by qualified and sensitive people, procedures are expedited, minders find practical and moral support, and the service is likely to be enhanced by a stable core of minders. If, however, registration and support is a matter of low priority, the very foundation of a satisfactory service is called in question. A career structure, with appropriate preparation for childminder workers, would enhance their status and, by extension, that of childminding.

Turning to legislation and training, real progress is unlikely until much of the existing confusion about child care clears. This will be discussed under the heading 'What can reasonably be expected of childminders?'.

quality of care (parents' and childrens' viewpoint)

These studies suggest that the vast majority of minders were caring for other people's children as competently as they had done or were doing for their own children. The areas where they were most likely to fall short as childminders were (a) where minded children presented problems over and above those that might be within the minder's experience in her own family, and (b) areas in which they could not be expected to have expertise, such as play provision and in language development.

Again, the outlook is hopeful that, given appropriate and sustained support, some significant changes are possible in these respects. Those minders in 'Kingswell' and 'Higham' who came regularly to the centres demonstrated greater understanding of the role they could play. Mushrooming courses for childminders up and down the country also testify to wider awareness of, and interest in, the many aspects of their work.

There were other factors which had more generally beneficial effects on the quality of care. Most important were increased supervision and support from social services. Coupled with care in placing children with suitable minders, these contributed to improved morale and dramatically reduced the movement of children from one minder to another. Such measures substantially scaled down difficulties that stemmed from diverse culture and language. Changed attitudes to courses and use of external resources suggested progress was possible.

In this connection, one has only to chart the development of the playgroup movement to see that when ordinary mothers grasp that specialized knowledge has something of value for them and the children they care for, they are perfectly capable of translating it into practice and adapting it to suit their needs.

This does not make them 'experts' or displace the specialist. It helps to widen horizons and extend mothers' enjoyment and satisfaction in child care, which brings us to the next consideration.

2. What can reasonably be expected of a childminder?

Society is caught up in a maelstrom of change. Opinions tend to polarize. The childminder epitomizes the old order of the traditional nuclear family. She is juxtaposed, by the very nature of her work, with a new world of one-parent families, of shared parenting, of families in which both parents work outside the home – people whose values and life-styles may be very different from her own.

New values in society are also reflected in much of the argument for professional standards, a career structure, and adequate rewards for childminders. Pre-occupation with material rewards and a 'what's in it for me?' attitude conflict with old values of traditional family life in which 'We help each other'.

Sharply contrasting views exist as to the extent of family and state responsibility for child care. Their very existence, compared with the more uniform attitudes that prevailed in the early part of the century, make for confusion and tension. Some confusion has to be accepted as a stage in the evolution of new norms. We have to live with it without creating unnecessary guilt and unhappiness. This suggests the need for freedom of choice for parents and childminders alike to adopt the type of child care that seems right to them, without undue social or economic pressures.

The dichotomy apparent in society at large is evident in microcosm amongst childminders. Findings in 'Kingswell' and 'Higham' suggested two types of competent childminder. Some respond to the notion of professional status. They may already be 'qualified' or they may be prepared to equip themselves accordingly. Others, at the moment perhaps the majority, are not cast in this mould. They are home oriented, without professional or career aspirations. It is unrealistic and may cause quite unnecessary strain to try to transform them into professional child-care workers.

If these two distinctions are accepted, then the objectives and content of many training courses might be clarified. Some courses will be designed for the more 'professional' minder who will be prepared, either in her own home or as a peripatetic worker, to cope with particular problems and to act as an adviser. Such a minder would probably prefer to be employed by the local authority, within a career structure. There might well be parts of the present childminder worker's job which could be undertaken by her, thereby releasing more time for those with special skills to exercise them.

Less career-oriented minders would also need some preparation to develop skills beyond those needed in bringing up their own families. Here, flexibility of approach is vital. Formal and informal courses, salaried schemes, television and radio programmes, home visiting, links with resource centres, playgroup day centres, and nursery schools, are all relevant. Some are supportive, some complementary, others educative.

Fundamental to this dual concept is the complementary nature of the roles, and of fluidity between them. As minders' own children grow up, as social customs change, so desires and needs alter. One role is not 'better' than the other; they each have a contribution to make. It is possible, for example, that for a small but important proportion of parents, a too professional approach is offputting. Such parents more readily accept neighbourly common sense than 'expert' advice. This brings us to the final issue.

3. A major challenge is how to make registration a guarantee of competence and, at the same time, to exert a positive influence over mothers who do not reach the required standards

Most of the suggestions for dealing with these issues concentrate on the first problem and ignore the second. The National Union of Public Employees, for example, has campaigned for a policy of direct employment of minders by the local authority, together with pick-up services and changes in legislation. Such a move has been described 'the only way to improve the quality of minding, since it gives the local authority the right to hire and fire' (Tizard, 1978).

In the light of the IMA analysis in 'Kingswell' and 'Higham', approximately two thirds of minders would be hired and one third fired. This should result in discouraging less competent minders and (assuming legislative changes were effective) control of illegal minding. It would be of value to more competent minders, to those with statutory responsibilities, and to parents who need to feel confident in the service.

Such a policy, however, leaves out of account what happens to minders who are fired — all of those in the (b) groups — as well as those few competent minders (Ia) who may not wish to become employees. A damaging gap could be created in the support network, with repercussions for the children of the minders concerned.

Yet the primary responsibility of social services must be to see that registration is a guarantee of competence. In fulfilling this obligation, they run the risk of losing sight of minders, parents, and children who sink below the horizon of the statutory body.

While it would be foolish to suggest that non-statutory workers can automatically reach the most alienated mothers — who might be among those 'fired' — the respective roles of the statutory and voluntary workers could profitably be explored. These will be discussed in Chapter 10.

SUMMARY

The Index of Maternal Alienation proved predictive of minders who did not use the centres. As in 'Hillcroft', such mothers were isolated and, with the exception of one small sub-group, those with more negative attitudes to child care. They also tended to be suspicious of 'authority'.

Minders who made use of the facilities tended to be characteristically friendly, outgoing, and child-centred. They also favoured being employed by social services.

Quality of care was associated with having a child of one's own under five and with marital support.

The IMA suggested six typologies of response to provision which might prove useful in deciding strategies of intervention. It also gave some indication of changes that took place among minders and could be developed as an index of change.

The studies offer a hopeful view of childminding. They draw attention to the need for policies that not only raise standards but also take into account their effect on children and mothers who are likely to be placed outside the supporting network of social services.

PART FOUR

CONCLUSIONS AND DISCUSSION

CHAPTER NINE
Policy and practice

In contrast to surveys based on nationwide random samples, it is not possible to generalize from small-scale studies such as these. Nevertheless, they add to the growing body of knowledge of parental attitudes and responses to pre-schooling and other services, which in turn feed debate and the further testing of ideas, contributing to policy change and development. They illustrate, for example, how diverse and changing local needs can be and emphasize that, in pre-school provision as in so much other social provision, local characteristics and local needs should define local solutions.

One outcome of concentrating on microcosms of mothers within defined areas has been to point to the possibility of at least two ways in which local and national assessment of need may go astray. Councillors and administrators who allocate funding, and professionals who give their time and expertise, are naturally gratified when response to facilities seems to justify outlay. It is an uncomfortable fact that they may not always have succeeded in reaching those families they most wish to attract. Where premises are small and cannot cope with numbers wishing to attend, a false impression that 'everyone wants provision' can disguise the true situation. Even where there are enough places for all, children coming in from outside the immediate district can mask the fact that a sizeable minority of local families may not be coming forward.

Another particulaly disturbing fact which emerged was that official lists from education offices, Social Services, and health authorities proved inaccurate — some of them seriously so. Where services are understaffed and communities mobile or where re-organization is taking place, this is understandable; but overall, experience counsels against total reliance on such information. Had it not been possible to carry out preliminary surveys which pinpointed where families with under fives were living, and then to reach all mothers and registered childminders with children eligible to use the provision, and had response rates considered respectable in sample surveys been accepted, conclusions would have been different.

Those mothers who, initially, slammed the doors in our faces or who refused or were reluctant to talk predominated amongst those who were subsequently found to be suffering from undue strain. Had they not eventually been reached, samples would have been biased in favour of the more friendly, outgoing women. Most of these came forward to use provision. Many of those who did not had the support of family and friends; they were well integrated in the community and comparatively happy and confident in keeping their under fives at home. It was the nameless faces who avoided or resented normal social contact who later said they found difficulty in coping and whose children appeared to be lacking in emotional security as well as in a stimulating environment.

It is against this background that the major findings of the studies should be judged. A statement of the main conclusions and discussion of the extent to which they contribute to our understanding will be followed by consideration of some fundamental issues. The major recurring themes will then be drawn together and a final section will be concerned with practical suggestions.

1. APPROXIMATELY ONE THIRD OF FAMILIES IN TWO OUT OF THREE STUDIES DID NOT MAKE REGULAR USE OF PRE-SCHOOL PROVISION FOR THEIR CHILDREN, EVEN THOUGH IT WAS NEAR THEIR HOME AND A PLACE WAS ASSURED FOR THEIR CHILD

In view of local demand for playgroup provision voiced by the Tenants' Association and assurance of support for it, to find nearly one third of mothers in 'Hillcroft' were disinclined to make use of it, was surprising; it was reminiscent of the proportion of non-takers in the Lambeth study described in Chapter 1, where nearly one third of mothers living in a highly deprived area also did not use a playgroup. In that particular study, however, there were obvious differences in that many had previously expressed their intention of doing so. There were also other factors such as poor housing, low incomes, large families, and high-rise flats, coupled with the cost, which could be put forward as obvious reasons for non-attendance. In 'Hillcroft', these possibilities were, to some extent, controlled, or were irrelevant, and so other explanations are needed for the unexpectedly large proportion of mothers who did not come forward to use facilities.

The most obvious explanation was the positive feeling expressed by many mothers that they wanted to be at home with their children. That this is not a local and unique phenomenon is supported by the findings in a major study in 1976/7 by Priority (the voluntary agency concerned with work with the under fives, funded by the Manpower Services Commission Job Creation Programme) of 1000 families in four contrasting areas of Liverpool. Only one mother in five was found to have a full or part-time job. One of the main reasons for this, proffered by one third of mothers, was that they preferred to be at home with their children (van der Eyken, 1978a).

Although the childminder projects were not strictly speaking comparable, issues relating to the proportion of people who actually used facilities are common to all the studies. It is therefore relevant that a similar proportion of non-user families (31 per cent) occurred in the 'Higham' childminding project. Response was better in 'Kingswell' — 18 per cent of those eligible to use the centre did not do so. In spite of the striking similarity of the proportion of mothers/childminders in 'Hillcroft' and 'Higham' who did not use the new provision, it does not follow, as will be more fully discussed later, that the same reasons account for positive response or the lack of it. It is worth noting, however, that a substantial proportion of mothers chose to stay at home and become childminders because they liked being with young children, and found the work satisfying.

In sum the relatively high proportion of families who rejected formal pre-school provision for their children in these and other studies suggests that, although there may be general approval of the availability of such provision, amounting to almost universal demand, such 'demand' may not result in almost universal take-up if the provision existed.

This is not to query the need for comprehensive pre-school facilities which offer all parents real choice and an equal opportunity in availing themselves of what is on offer. It is, however, to question whether surveys of 'demand' are comparable with surveys of 'take up'.

2. USUAL EXPLANATIONS (SUCH AS INACCESSIBILITY OF PROVISION AND BEING RELATIVELY POOR) WERE NOT SUFFICIENT TO EXPLAIN WHY SOME MOTHERS WHO MIGHT BE THOUGHT WOULD BENEFIT, TURNED DOWN EXTERNAL RESOURCES

Speculation as to the roots of poor response to services usually focuses on socio-economic variables, such as distance, cost, or inconvient siting. In the present studies, results suggest that the issue is not one of simple reasons leading to simple solutions.

a. Expense

There is little evidence, for example, to suggest that expense was a major inhibiting factor. It did not arise in the child-minding projects, since the centres were free. In 'Hillcroft', although some mothers had difficulty in making ends meet and appreciated Council help, which kept fees within their means, clearly most were willing and able to pay. Indeed, the least well-off were among those who made most regular use of the play-group and childminder centres. Financial stringency was not a characteristic of those who did not do so.

It must be stressed, however, that mothers in 'Hillcroft' were comparatively well-to-do. If charges are made in less favoured areas, expense could be an important consideration.

b. Convenient location

This would seem to have been the enabling factor, initially, for almost half the mothers in 'Hillcroft', but considerations other than distance were also operating among those who dropped away and among mothers who were also using provision outside the area.

Similarly, in 'Kingswell' and 'Higham', convenient siting of the centres was generally appreciated by minders. But where a centre offered what minders wanted, both for themselves and for the children in their care, it became abundantly clear that some were prepared to make considerable efforts to get there.

What we do not know is whether regular transport would really have been a decisive factor for some minders who did not attend. However, in a study of fifty-six poor families known to social services, Wilson and Herbert (1978) report that although collected by mini-bus, only thirty-one children attended a playgroup regularly. Other inhibiting factors must have played a part in this.

While it is clear that convenient location of premises plays a crucial role for many mothers, ease of access, by itself, does not ensure positive response to provision by those it is most hoped to attract.

c. Inappropriate provision

One possible reason for non take-up of places by mothers who were not going out to work, could have been that the type of provision failed to meet their real needs. Did they also wish to go out to work and therefore require different forms of care? The answer, in general terms, was 'no'. Contrary to the currently popular picture of mothers who want or need to go out to work, the majority of mothers in 'Hillcroft' professed themselves content to stay at home while their children were under school age; some of them probably found greater satisfaction and fulfilment in the home than they had done either at school or at work. There was no indication, therefore, among mothers who did not use the playgroup of a strong desire for either nursery schooling or day care.

Undoubtedly, local circumstances influence community attitudes and priorities. The 'Hillcroft' mothers' reactions to pre-schooling and work is by no means the only possible one. It does not tally, for example, with experience at the Coram Children's Centre in London. In the particular district which it serves, quite different conditions prevail. There are many hotels which offer employment. Economic and social pressures on mothers to work, quite independent of social class, generate different responses to pre-schooling. Moreover, these may vary, not only from one district to another, but also in the same district from one time to another. Many mothers in 'Hillcroft', for example, set great store in providing lavish toys at Christmas and birthdays. As inflation erodes their material standards, inability to do this may persuade them to consider at least a part-time job.

Even if they do find themselves in that position, they may have much in common with childminders in both 'Kingswell' and 'Higham'. For the majority, childminding sprang from their desire to earn the money they needed by staying at home and looking after children − an occupation from which many derived great satisfaction.

In contrast, mothers who worked outside the home formed another important but, in 'Hillcroft', under-represented group. For them, the new provision was clearly inappropriate and no real choice was involved. Many of them were one-parent families, eligible for day care for their children. Manifestly, a playgroup that opened at restricted times and encouraged involvement was not a solution to their problems. It offered no practical alternative to their existing arrangements.

Findings emphasized that, while not incapable or intrinsically unable to provide a stable, coping unit, one-parent families nevertheless have to contend with external conditions which constitute very real handicaps. They often have to choose between two less than ideal solutions. Either they stay at home with their children, and thereby experience financial hardship, or they go out to work. If the latter, they may have enough to live on, but they are obliged to play three different roles – breadwinner, housewife, and mother. If they use pre-school provision (day care), they may feel ousted from their children's affection by those who care for them during working hours. Conversely, if mothers do not use facilities and stay at home, they may be under constant stress and worry as to how to manage. Either way, they have little time or opportunity for social niceties or relaxation.

d. Attitudes to education

There were clearly wide ranging views among both mothers and childminders about the importance of education and what it should be like. But in spite of the wide divergence of opinion, what mothers said about pre-schooling seemed to bear little relationship to what parents and minders actually did when they were offered the facility. There was little evidence, except in relation to one small sub-group which will be discussed later, that distrust of education was associated with lack of 'enthusiasm' for any form of provision.

3. LACK OF ENTHUSIASM FOR PROVISION WAS ASSOCIATED RATHER WITH ASPECTS OF FAMILY COMPOSITION AND STRUCTURE, TOGETHER WITH ANTIPATHY TOWARDS 'AUTHORITY'

Despite the bias in 'Hillcroft' against large families, the most striking characteristics of parents who rejected the possibility of pre-school provision was that they were younger than average and had several children under five.

It seemed reasonable to assume that practical problems such as getting a play-group age child ready at a set hour, and at the same time attending to the demands of a toddler and a young baby, would be a likely explanation for such mothers deciding not to go to the playgroup.

Undoubtedly, such considerations affect some mothers and childminders, particularly when 'playgroup' hours cut across babies sleeping or feeding or children who have to be fetched from school. Nevertheless, uncertainty arises from the fact that in the childminding projects, minders who had at least three children, and consequently similar practical problems, were more likely to attend than those with fewer children. Yet it was notable that minders who had at least one child of their own under five among the minded children tended to show most enthusiasm for the centres. It suggests that perhaps one explanation for positive response lay in the value attached to the provision itself and the extent to which a mother was prepared to put herself out for it. Minders with young children of their own were understandably more interested in early childhood education than many of those with older children. They were certainly more likely to spend time playing with the children, to have child-centred attitudes, and to enjoy friendly relations with parents of minded children.

This finding runs counter to the conclusions of Mayall and Petrie (1977 : 81) in their study of thirty-one minders in two London boroughs. They stress the importance of attracting people to childminding whose own children are over five years old. They suggest that 'mothers of pre-school children may have extra difficulties in relating to other people's children, with the result that both the minder's own young children and the minded children may be required to face a social and emotional situation that they are too immature and insecure to cope with'.

Findings in the present studies, however, suggest that mothers with under fives of their own often make excellent minders. Strategies other than discouraging such mothers from minding are called for to avoid difficult social and emotional situations.

Another major characteristic of mothers and childminders who did not welcome provision was a certain apprehensiveness and suspicion of 'authority'. Even among some of the older childminders, there was strong antagonism towards people in authority. This may have owed something to unpleasant memories of school, but it seemed more likely to be an expression of one of the problems of childminding — namely tension arising from statutory responsibility for oversight versus the conviction that the 'Englishman's home is his castle' and consequent resentment of intrusion. By 1980, with increasing understanding between minders and childminder workers, this attitude is less common. Nevertheless, one explanation for the comparative success in 'Kingswell' in encouraging a higher proportion of hard-to-reach minders to use the centre, was the non-authoritarian approach of the project workers.

4. THE STUDIES ISOLATED A NUMBER OF CHARACTERISTICS ASSOCIATED WITH FAMILIES WITH PARTICULARLY POSITIVE OR NEGATIVE ATTITUDES TO EARLY CHILDHOOD EDUCA- TION, REGARDLESS OF WHETHER OR NOT USE WAS MADE OF FACILITIES

In general, it appeared that the degree of awareness and enthusiasm that mothers showed for early childhood education was a reflection of the mother's own psychological situation. For one group of mothers, those who were well adjusted, whose lives seemed 'in control' and positive, there was also a positive attitude to the welfare of their children. This attitude could manifest itself in a number of different ways. Either a mother could choose to keep her children at home, and devote herself to their interests; or she could go out of her way to find some form of pre-schooling, perhaps several miles away from her home; or third, she could with enthusiasm or diffidence, support local provision. No judgement was made as to which strategy was best for the child. It may well be the case that, depending on circumstances, any one of these lines of action would prove beneficial.

Nor did those mothers who formed the second group, with less stable personal lives, suffering from feelings of isolation, depression, acute nervousness, or perhaps fear (of her husband, of social inadequacy, of neighbours or, more generally, of society) form a homogeneous group in relation to early child- hood education. Some let their children take up external provision, possibly without whole-hearted enthusiasm. Others simply stayed away or took only a passing interest in pre-schooling. Here again, there was a variety of behaviour under-pinned by negative attitudes — aggressiveness, alienation from neighbours, and lack of confidence — which militated against the development of both mother and child.

Similar groupings were discernible amongst the child-minders. Some of the more positive ones preferred not to use external provision, considering that they could provide all that the children needed in their own homes. Others welcomed the opportunity to meet others and recognized the value of play facilities for the children. More negative minders had much in common with mothers under stress in 'Hillcroft' and were likely to be irregular or non-users.

5. MOTHERS WITH THESE 'POSITIVE' AND 'NEGATIVE' ATTI-TUDES TO EARLY CHILDHOOD EDUCATION SEEMED IDENTI-FIABLE BY ONE SMALL GROUP OF VARIABLES, THE INDEX OF MATERNAL ALIENATION (IMA). THIS INDEX MIGHT BE CON-SIDERED AS THE BASIS OF A PREDICTIVE INSTRUMENT FOR IDENTIFYING FAMILIES IN SPECIAL NEED

This group of 'predictive' variables evolved from an intensive study of those mothers in 'Hillcroft' who already used provision. It was to some extent validated in the childminder studies.

Mothers were given a score on the following variables:
(1) age mother married; (2) attitude to 'messy play'; (3) attitude to neighbours; (4) contact with family and friends; (5) the time available for relaxed play with her child; (6) the degree of child centredness; (7) the nature of her relationship with her child.

It was found that those mothers with the lowest scores had found provision on their own initiative, while those with the highest scores were likely to use provision following intervention by some agency. Low and high scores similarly distinguished between mothers who became regular attenders at the play-group and those who dropped away, and between the 'positive' and 'negative' rejectors of pre-schooling.

As has already been pointed out, there were some very basic differences between 'Hillcroft' and the childminder studies. Nevertheless, it is noteworthy that in spite of being used in different contexts, these same variables, excluding 'age of marrying' were predictive of those more negative minders who, among all who could have used the centres, chose not to do so.

'Age mother married' was an important indicator of stress in 'Hillcroft' and in a similar situation would be a helpful guide to vulnerable mothers. Generally, however, it may be of secondary importance and could actually distort the Index in circumstances where it does not produce stress.

For a small group of mothers, however, a key to the heart of the matter may lie in their youth when they married. Youth, in itself, is not a cause, but where a girl has felt unhappy at school or at work and has sought identity and release through early marriage and having children, the stress that generates the need for such a way out is not necessarily reduced. Their homes and families become, in turn, sources of crisis and simply aggravate the original problem. In this sense, the size and structure of their families are an outcome of their situation rather than a cause. The immaturity and lack of preparation for marriage and motherhood of these girls could be an important contributory factor, therefore, in explaining their disenchantment and difficulties. It is a striking fact that this should apply even in cases where there was no obvious financial hardship or housing difficulty.

Some of these mothers gave the impression that while they cared just as much for their children as any other group, personal problems provided little scope for other than marginal concern for planned provision for their children. This suggests that pre-school provision, like all other external services, is used by those already in a position to take advantage of it; further, that it is avoided by those who, though they may need it most, are unable to consider it.

This is not to say that all larger families have poor mother–child relationships or that all young mothers have unhappy marriages. It is to suggest that young mothers, coping unaided with several under fives and a disappointing marriage, are unlikely to have the personal resources equal to the situation or to become involved with outside commitments like play-groups. For a mother who lacks confidence, these can be seen as a threat, however welcoming the organizers may be.

Whatever the origins of their malaise, for mothers in the more negative group, the mother–child relationship was overlaid and distorted by stress. They had little time to play with their children and tended to be unresponsive to their child's demands. Meals were often irregular, insubstantial, and unbalanced. Children were likely to be severely restricted or left to their own devices.

Similar observations have been noted in other studies in which stress has been a salient feature. Wilson and Herbert (1978), for example, have pointed out that such characteristics were to be expected in deprived environments. They isolated five categories associated with stress which affected a high proportion of the families they studied – being below the poverty line, large family size with a number of pre-school children, having an invalid child, and the physical or mental handicap of a parent.

One's natural reaction is to conclude that mothers with large families, in poor housing, on low incomes, and with the added burden of illness to contend with, must owe their unhappy state to these conditions.

Yet if the same criteria are applied to families in 'Hillcroft', 'Kingswell', and 'Higham', few qualify as being under such extreme stress; but many remarks and feelings expressed by mothers during interviews, as well as their reactions to their children, were almost identical with those of Wilson and Herbert's families living in very much more depressing and difficult surroundings. This does not imply the view that unemployment, low wages, and chronic housing shortage are not associated with stress or that some people are never satisfied. It is to point out that improvement in physical conditions is only one (very necessary) step towards reducing human unhappiness. It does not, by itself, eradicate it.

Just as poverty is a relative concept, with many facets, there are grounds for believing that disadvantage is not an absolute. Its accompanying signs of stress are generated by a wide variety of circumstances, so that it cannot be simply contained within particular areas or remain constant over long periods of time.

The extent to which damaging stress affects mothers with young children is emphasized by a number of other studies. Two are of particular relevance. A study of families with young children (Richman, 1974) found 41 per cent of women affected by 'depression, loneliness and dissatisfaction'. This finds a striking parallel in the figures of 43 per cent of mothers in 'Hillcroft' and 37 per cent and 32 per cent respectively in the two groups of childminders, showing signs of stress and depression. The Richman investigation focused on three types of local authority housing and a sample of seventy-five families, each with a three-year-old child and at least one younger child. Although a direct, casual link has yet to be established, the study suggested that mothers living in even three- or four-storey blocks similar to many in 'Hillcroft', 'Higham', and 'Kingswell' are likely to experience loneliness and depression, as well as dissatisfaction with lack of playing space for their children.

The similarity in the proportion of mothers affected in the four studies, could, of course, be mere coincidence. Since different measures were used in each study, the definition of 'depression' would need qualification. Nevertheless, reported 'depression' and loneliness characterized the mothers who, in the present studies, are seen as in the greatest need of support.

The second relevant study concerns the origins of depression in women (Brown, Bhrolcain, and Harris, 1975). This investigation concerned two samples of women aged between eighteen and sixty-five living in one former London borough. One was a group of 114 patients, undergoing either in- or out-patient treatment, for primary depression which had begun during the twelve months prior to interview. The second group was a random sample of two hundred and twenty women; each of these was screened for possible psychiatric disturbance, and specifically for depressive conditions — sleeplessness, feelings of hopelessness and worthlessness, lack of energy, and so on.

In addition to finding a link between life-events and depression and a relationship between social class and psychiatric disturbance, already well established in the literature, the investigators went on to examine background factors that could account for the greater likelihood of breakdown amongst women with young children at home. This was shown to be due, not simply to the fact of more crises occurring in the lives of working-class women, but to their greater vulnerability to disturbance when they experienced environmental stresses. This vulnerability stemmed from four main factors and it is these that have particular relevance to the present studies: the 'dramatic change' in the quality of their marriage which takes place as soon as they start having children; loss of mother by death or separation, that is loss of contact with 'extended' families leading to isolation; having three or more children under fourteen at home; and finally lack of full or part-time employment.

As we have seen, full or part-time work outside the home was considered undesirable by the majority of mothers until children reached school age. There was also a concentration of families with three or more children at home in the sub-groups of non-users 'under strain'. As to loss of mother by death or separation, the higher 'grandma' mortality rate among non-users – as compared with those who already used pre-school provision in 'Hillcroft' – was remarkable since respondents whose own mothers had died were younger than average for the sample.

The matter of the higher death rate among a sub-group of grandmothers raises issues of some interest. It is unfortunate that there was no relevant data from the childminder studies, since it could be of considerable importance to know what lies behind these manifestations. There are questions from at least three areas of study which need answering. Does the higher death rate among these 'grandmothers', for example, reflect a genuine tendency for them to die earlier? Or was it that their daughters were born to them late in life? A possible implication of the second hypothesis would be that some inherited factor, a combination of minor genetic defects, put children of older mothers at risk. An alternative explanation would lie in the socio-economic background. Other related questions would concern the series of minor ailments reported by non-coping mothers – were they factual or some form of hypochondria? What was the nature of the depression they experienced? Did it start in the post-natal period? Was it reactive or endogenous?

Clearly, these are subjects for further study, but it seems that the sub-group of mothers which could be diagnosed as showing signs of lack of confidence and undue stress in 'Hillcroft' were particularly characterized by the vulnerability factors to depression identified by Professor Brown and his team (Brown and Harris, 1978). As in the present studies, numbers were small and conclusions tentative. The investigators point out the complexity of the interrelationships of the four vulnerability factors they have isolated. Consequently, no firm conclusions can be reached, but such speculations nevertheless make better sense of the findings in the present studies than do explanations in terms of class or other commonly held assumptions.

6. THE MAJOR OUTCOME WAS TO DRAW ATTENTION AWAY FROM FAILURE TO TAKE-UP PRE-SCHOOL PLACES AS THE CENTRAL ISSUE AND TO FOCUS ON PARTICULAR SUB-GROUPS OF MOTHERS UNDER STRESS, REGARDLESS OF THEIR RESPONSE TO FACILITIES

The crucial distinction to emerge was not simply between those parents who used provision and those who did not. It was between parents who were essentially secure emotionally, economically, and socially, compared with those who tended to be similarly insecure. The former were able to make a considered judgement as to whether or not to participate in or to use services.

The latter shared certain characteristics which placed them at a disadvantage in society. They enjoyed little contact with their own families and seldom reported support from health visitors or social workers, although they had problems that manifestly militated against a happy and secure family environment. Many of these mothers were unlikely to seek or sustain the use of existing pre-school facilities, even though they were not necessarily opposed to them and both they and their children would probably benefit from them.

These families are the core of our concern and what the studies provide is a working hypothesis that they can be predicted by a small number of indicators (IMA) occurring together. Where mothers married or started their families in their teens, where they dislike the neighbourhood and have little or no contact with family and friends, and find little time for, or pleasure in, their children's company, it suggests a gap to be bridged regardless of whether or not mothers actually use pre-school provision. The Index of Maternal Alienation provides a guide to the potential receivers of pre-schooling according to the ways families respond and to some of their outstanding characteristics. This, in turn, may help towards a better understanding of parental attitudes and suggest ways of bridging the gaps.

RESULTING ISSUES

This contention highlights a number of fundamental issues. It can be argued, for example, that little credence can be placed on the results of three small studies and that the very emergence of such groups is a statistical quirk. Indeed, there are no statistical grounds for assuming that such groups of mothers exist other than in the areas studied, and certainly not in similar proportions: but both the mass of evidence in the literature, which tallies so closely in description, and the response of people working in the field suggests that these are not unique pockets of isolated, over-stressed mothers. Doubtless other traditions, backgrounds, and social pressures will offer a different mix of needs, attitudes, and responses. One has only to compare urban and rural communities to see that uniformity cannot be expected. While the proportions of each of the six sub-groups will inevitably vary between districts and within the same district from one time to another, the typologies seem to recur and offer a basic framework for planners.

What was surprising were the unexpectedly large numbers of vulnerable mothers to emerge in non-deprived communities — but even so, when seen in the context of the whole, these particular groups were small. Consequently, some may argue that where social service resources are already overstretched, it is pointless to stress the needs of minority groups which they are not in a position to meet. Why should the administration, already overburdened and financially limited, concern itself with the few who do not take advantage of what is available and who remain silent? The State, after all, strives to make external welfare and education services available on demand; it is up to the individual to choose whether or not to come forward and make use of them. This policy recognizes the tradition that the 'Englishman's home is his castle' and that any extension of services to the home, unless invited, may endanger the inalienable right to independence and privacy within the family unit.

The problem of where support ends and intrusion begins is undoubtedly a difficult one, but it in no way enables an informed administration and a caring society to shelve its responsibility for people who are unable to help themselves, especially if their situation is detrimental to their children's well-being. Many of these mothers were arguably victims of an education system that has failed to prepared them adequately either to hold down a job or for parenthood. They are often dupes of the media which paint unrealistic pictures of romantic love and marriage, of children and homemaking. Their inarticulate withdrawal and apathy does not diminish our collective social responsibility to remedy the situation.

There are two further points. Mothers who gave cause for concern tended to have larger than average families and, as a group, more negative attitudes towards child rearing. Within ten to fifteen years, these same children will be old enough to have children of their own and the whole sorry pattern may be repeated. Many such mothers were also characterized by distrust of 'authority', so would construe help from social services ('them') as unwarranted interference. Contact with social workers was thought to carry a stigma; 'education' was considered of little relevance and educational home visitors were unwelcome; community workers were associated with neighbours and associations — to be avoided. What is likely to be acceptable to most of these mothers would not involve social services in great expenditure, but it would demand careful consideration by professionals of alternative policies.

Several major themes will recur in the discussion of such alternatives. They can be summarized as follows:

1. There is no single answer to the problem of 'hard-to-reach' families

Extension of existing provision is needed to accommodate parents who are still clamouring for places in day-care centres, nursery schools, and playgroups; but neither orthodox provision nor colossal expenditure alone are likely to meet the needs of many others whose children would benefit most. In common with other studies, findings confirm the Law of Inverse Care and beg questions of any national or regional policy based on the assumption of virtually universal demand for pre-schooling. The problem is not simply a technical and administrative one of finding the 'right method' and implementing it. It is complex, involving psychological barriers and wider structural causes in the environment and society.

2. To ensure that children from some of the most vulnerable families are not at a considerable disadvantage when they start school, approaches are called for with the emphasis directed initially on the needs of the mother — who must first be helped if she is in turn to help her child

There is a danger that over emphasis on services and professionalism may erode still further parental confidence, awareness of responsibilities, and values of family life. The psychological needs of the mother suggest that self-help is to be encouraged. The most alienated mothers initially need individual help to make decisions and to sustain efforts which they are at present unable to achieve.

3. Preventive action would benefit families and be economically viable

Considerable welfare expenditure is presently necessarily devoted to crisis cases and to long-term support of people with intransigent problems – arguably, in many cases, the consequence of failure to pursue policies of prevention. Such preventive measures could include counselling in schools, inclusion of groupwork skills in teacher training, and preparation for parenthood in clinics, as well as informal support and follow-up for mothers whose needs were not met by existing provision.

4. Volunteers and para-professionals could play a crucial part in such approaches, to be organized on a 'patch' basis

The statutory service does not cater for all groups and cannot hope to reach all potential clients. Philosophical differences exist between the volunteer and the professional; thus volunteers may extend the range of work rather than simply extend the amount of work done. This implies a fundamental and difficult shift in emphasis and a basic willingness by all those involved to share their concerns. To complete the local network of resources, at least one agency needs to be responsible for each small area.

5. Co-operation across boundaries is vital

This implies the translation of theory into practice by the creation of collaborative projects funded jointly by Health, Social Services, Education, and involving Voluntary Associations. Comprehensive policies must take into account local needs and those of minority groups and the less articulate members of society. A variety of linked measures are needed. The problems of families which are our concern, for example, are not just the province of educationalists and social services; they call for concerted efforts, understanding co-operation between specialists in health education and housing, in law and administration, in economics and psychology.

6. Attention is focused firmly on the crucial nature of the mother–child relationship and on the importance of human relationships in general

Since the roots of intelligence are laid in the very early years and the mother–child relationship is the vital part, it is a real cause for concern that many young women lack the maturity, the knowledge, and resources to cope adequately with their families. Among the most unhappy mothers are those who cannot relate to their husbands, their neighbours, and their children. Much of the quality of life depends on communication and human relationships; thus whatever policies evolve, they are put into effect by, and therefore affect, people. They will stand or fall not only by the insight and the justice they embody, but by the sensitivity, understanding, and personal involvement of those who purvey them.

Discussion of more specific points will be confined to the three groups of comparatively insecure mothers. These suggestions offer a practical basis for experiment.

1. INTERVENTIONIST USERS

One vulnerable group is characterized mainly, but not exclusively, by their use of local authority day care. It includes families in crisis and many one-parent families. Their main contacts are therefore likely to be health visitors, social workers, day nursery staff, and childminders. Families in this group are readily identifiable by established criteria as qualifying for professional support. They are mostly priority cases. Many are able to articulate their needs and, above all, to accept help; they are often well informed about their welfare rights and willing to approach anyone who could be useful to them. Others, however, are less forthcoming. The studies suggested that a proportion of mothers in this group were not being helped at all by the fact that their children were receiving pre-school provision. Mothers said their own position and relationship with their child was damaged by it, but they felt trapped by circumstances. Thus it appeared that there is sometimes a gap between what the helping agency sees as the answer to a problem and a fundamentally constructive solution for the 'client'.

Local authority policy in 'Hillcroft' was clearly to enable mothers to work full time, wherever possible, by providing day care. This, as in so many social service departments, was the routine 'ideal' solution. In view of the well-documented trend towards more women working, together with the swing of social pressures towards it, such a solution seems a sensible one.

Moreover, recent research suggests that having a job protects against depression, which is known to afflict a high proportion of women at home with young children. Thus paid employment outside the home and day nursery care for children, on demand, is increasingly canvassed as the right of every mother.

Clearly adequate services are needed for the many mothers for whom a job is a satisfying and fulfilling occupation as well as an important source of income. They need to know that their children are well looked after in day centres, by relatives, child-minders, or at their place of work. In this connection, it is noteworthy that, given support, childminders in the areas studied were found to provide a valuable service − not only in the standard of care given the children but often in neighbourly support for lonely and depressed mothers. Recruitment of more good childminders has been advocated, but with scant indication of where they are to be found. The IMA model suggests Group IIA as a likely source; mothers' characteristic lack of self-confidence, however, suggests that a recruitment drive which made an appeal for help, as opposed to stressing the responsible and demanding job, would be more likely to draw a positive response. Playgroups could provide a point of contact.

Neither an adequate childminding service nor more day nurseries meet all needs however. Where mothers, particularly mothers alone, find themselves obliged to go out to work in order to make ends meet, yet would prefer to be at home with their children, stress is compounded rather than relieved by day care. The currently popular belief that work outside the home is a universal panacea is a dangerous construction to erect on one aspect of research (Brown and Harris, 1978) which also stresses, for example, the crucial importance for mental health of the marital tie or a mother's inter-personal relationship with husband or boyfriend. Distinctions need to be drawn. For some mothers, having a job outside the home is stimulating, financially rewarding, and adds to their feelings of self-esteem and satisfaction. For others, however, the only work open is repetitive and poorly paid; while it may offer escape from the isolation of the home, it does little to enhance the quality of life. It is equally fair to point out that some husbands accept 'working wives' as natural and normal; others find it difficult to adapt to changing norms. Undue social pressures for mothers to find an outside job may seriously undermine husband/wife relationships, giving rise to other damaging stresses. Quite apart from these considerations, the effects of technological advances on the type and number of jobs available, suggests that to canvas employment, as we know it, for mothers with young children, may raise expectations that cannot, for long, be met.

The answer to the problem is not a simple one of extending facilities. Such a service, external and an alternative to the home does nothing for mothers for whom no job is available or who wish to retain their autonomy but lack resources. Extension of toy library facilities, an outward reach from existing nursery school and playgroup would be constructive moves. Mother and Toddler clubs, informal day centres like the Open Pre-school experiment in Sweden, could all help to make the bringing up of small children a social experience instead of a lonely and often stressful one. 'Floating' childminders who would go to mothers' homes in an emergency and care for a child if the mother were ill or for the sick child of a working mother would also alleviate some causes of stress (Barnomsorgsgruppen 1976).

More radical policies would include a wage for mothers who wish to stay at home — this would certainly ease the burden and at the same time would confer much needed status on mothering. Such financial help would enable many women to exercise real choice during the pre-school years. Reform of taxes which discriminate against mothers who do not go out to work, adequate child benefits, and availability of more part-time jobs would all help in the same direction.

Yet in the present economic climate, these can only be long-term goals. It is unrealistic to suppose they will be implemented to the benefit of this generation of mothers and children. Nevertheless, improvements could be achieved without great financial expenditure by re-allocation and harnessing of available resources and a critical re-appraisal of some practice.

Few social service departments, for example, consider themselves well enough staffed to offer time and skilled counselling to the many enquirers for day care. Yet by the time many mothers seeking pre-school facilities for their children get to the office, they are often tense and desperate. They may need time to talk through their needs, even to clarify them for themselves. In practice, such time-consuming procedures are seldom followed; an enquirer either qualifies for a place at a day nursery or with a childminder and social work support or she is put on a waiting list or simply sent away with regrets.

Time and time again, interviews with mothers suggested that when this happens, a critical point is passed. Many mothers take a step nearer becoming a crisis case and consequently are much more difficult and expensive to help. The picture which emerges from these studies suggests that it is not just the provision or otherwise of a pre-school place that matters, but the understanding and quality of communication between people.

It was also clear that the majority of mothers had very little idea of the different types of pre-schooling; it was easy to assume they 'wanted' one particular form when this was not the case. How many social service departments take the time to make sure that first time enquirers appreciate the difference between day nurseries, all-day playgroups, and childminders? How many involve themselves sufficiently to match children, facility, and parents? How many listen to what a mother is saying − or not saying − especially if she does not give an immediate impression of being in considerable need?

Understandably, there is reluctance to take time with people who appear to need it less than others. When there are too few qualified social workers to meet demand, preventive work is considered impossible. Yet unless more attention is paid to prevention, a cure may never be achieved.

Where there is co-operation between the statutory body and voluntary organizations, however, experiments in prevention are possible − in spite of economic stringency.

One example of the way it can work is demonstrated by a Neighbourhood Scheme in Lewisham. Playgroup supervisors and Social Service officers have for some time been concerned about young, often single, mothers living alone with little family support. It is known that many of them feel that full-time employment will be the solution to all their problems. At the same time, many of them seem to have unreasonably high expectations of their children; they certainly do not enjoy their company and see them as the cause of all their problems. Because of the shortage of day care, mothers must often wait a year or more for a day nursery place or a registered childminder. During this period, resentment of the child grows. A useful scheme to help in such cases would provide friendly visiting and personal contacts for mothers in the waiting period. Problems may be met by listening, encouraging, and demonstrating, by practical help and constructive advice offered by visitors who complement the efforts of professional, statutory, and voluntary agencies.

This Scheme is preventive and focused on particular areas. Initiated by the local branch of the Pre-school Playgroups Association, it comes about with financial help from Urban Aid and the Bunbury Trust because individuals in the voluntary and statutory agencies were aware of needs beyond the obligations of their particular roles. They were determined to seek ways in which available resources might be combined to maintain contact with families who otherwise become more and more demoralized.

Support, as opposed to service, offered by volunteers to mothers who have to contend with overwhelming problems and are simply not coping, can work. It is demonstrated by the well-established Home-Start Scheme in Leicestershire.

After a course of preparation which communicates the basic Home-Start approach, a home visitor is matched to two or three families and is sustained in her work by a close network of support and supervision. Families are referred mainly by health visitors and social workers who have neither the time nor who see their role as making real friendships. Although not the original intention, due to the method of referral, Homestart tends in practice to be interventionist rather than anticipatory or preventive. Volunteers with very varied backgrounds and experience are not in competition with professionals, however; their roles are different and complementary. Friendships which develop between Home-Start volunteers and mothers are not fleeting 'professional' relationships, but often persist after the period of initial difficulty which led to the referral. Perhaps one of the most encouraging aspects of this scheme is that some of the mothers who were at first so in need of support, benefited from it to the extent that they have themselves been able to become volunteers.

Such developments encourage the view that policies which recognize the contribution of volunteers and are attentive to cues from initial enquirers could avert some of the seemingly stop-gap, unrewarding nature of so much social work.

2. SPASMODIC USERS AND NON-STARTERS

Two points that are often made to explain why families do not use pre-school and other facilities are inconvenient siting of premises and the difficulty many families are thought to experience in paying for provision.

It is in relation to this type of statement that the next group is of particular interest. Convenient siting was clearly very important and made all the difference for about half the mothers in each project area. But oddly enough, those who initially most stressed the importance for them of close proximity of the playgroup, tended to be those who subsequently dropped away altogether or became very irregular attenders. Moreover, although they were among the least well off, they were far more likely to say they would 'prefer to pay something'.

This second vulnerable group shared characteristics with the interventionist group of comparative youth at marriage, isolation in the community, lack of family support, and lack of enjoyment in their children − but they were not in contact with social workers. They tended to have visited the clinics regularly when their children were babies, but unless they had a young baby or an ailing child, they were seldom seen by health visitors. They were, however, on the health visitor lists.

Consequently, the chief point of contact for these mothers would be nursery school or playgroup staff. Such contact may be short-lived however. For reasons which it was beyond the scope of these studies to investigate, the enthusiasm of mothers in this group soon waned. The IMA indicators can be useful here, as they may forewarn staff as to which mothers (who are not otherwise easily identifiable) are most likely to drop away. A general question about whether they have lived in the district long is usually enough to release a flood of comments about the neighbourhood, the children, and family, sufficient to begin to identify components of the IMA. Some tendencies shared by the group may offer clues as to why, for them, involvement in pre-school provision was not an experience they chose to prolong.

It was obviously not just a question of proximity to the premises; something else intervened to prevent or inhibit continued attendance. Expense could be the explanation; in spite of saying they preferred to pay for provision, mothers may have found difficulty in paying and sought some face saving device for opting out. This would be compatible with the observation that they had a strong need to impress − they were particularly prone to describe their husbands' occupation in misleadingly glowing terms, for example.

An obvious recommendation would be for pre-school provision of all kinds to be free — to get rid of the anomolous
situation whereby nursery schools are free, attendance at a day
nursery is subject to a means test, and playgroup fees cover a
wide range. Such a measure, although desirable in principle,
may however be only of partial benefit to mothers in this group.
It leaves out of account the psychological barriers which may be
operating.

As some of the anecdotal evidence in Chapter 3 suggested,
mothers who have most difficulty in paying often feel a strong
need to contribute, at least in kind. They need to feel wanted.
Even if provision is free, they still have this need and they tend to
be hypersensitive. Thus, they easily feel diminished by being
told what to do, they are embarrassed by their children's
behaviour, they feel rejected by the other mothers; they are
pulled in two directions at once — part of them wants to
participate, the other is desperately fearful and often puts on an
aggressive front.

Clearly, the continued attendance of such mothers largely
depends on the understanding and skill of playleader or nursery
staff in adopting the right approach for each individual. Much
of this skill is intuitive. Nevertheless, the need for teachers and
those coming in contact with families to be aware of the ways in
which a wide variety of mothers think and feel and to develop
skills in dealing with parents as well as children, has implications for the selection of students for training, for course
content, and for the choice of applicants for a job.

One particularly positive and hopeful experiment among
practicing teachers stemmed from the conviction that teachers
who understand and respect parents' influence in the education
of their children are likely to be better teachers. Conducted by
Dr Nehama Nir-Janiv, Director of Early Childhood Education
in Israel, it has shown how teacher attitudes can change towards
parents they formally considered had little or nothing to contribute either to their own understanding of children's needs or
to the child's education. Kindergarten teachers regularly spent
some of their free time with parents in order to learn from them
how they brought up their children and about the values they
encouraged, both explicitly and implicitly. Parents' diffidence
and incredulity gradually diminished in the face of increasingly
genuine interest; teachers' doubts that they could learn from
parents, especially disadvantaged ones, gave way to respect and

empathy. They discovered, in the course of informal discussions, that parents were 'human beings capable of thinking and expressing their thoughts' (Nir and Tick, 1973 : 88). They learned to listen and came to regard their profession as more worthwhile — yet to be more accepting of parents and para-professionals as partners in the educational process.

These discussions helped to broaden teachers' understanding of the children and their families; following new ideas and insights, their performance in the classroom showed measurable improvement. Perhaps equally important, however, was that the experience enabled some parents to see themselves, for the first time, as having a decisive role to play in bringing up their children.

One last point in connection with mothers in this second vulnerable group concerns recognition of 'at risk' children. A hypothesis for further research is that mothers in this group, that is, those who dropped away or came very irregularly, tended to be unusually ambivalent about their children. One part of them felt deeply concerned and affectionate, but at the same time, there was a vein of deep antagonism and resentment. This was perhaps reflected in the apparent indifference and seeming callousness manifested towards the children, followed by impulsive buying of large and expensive presents they often said they could ill afford; and the way lethargy and depression seemed to alternate the bouts of frenetic energy and enthusiasm.

These retrospective impressions call for further study; but if mothers in this group are subject to more than usual ups and downs, then they need especial care, understanding, and follow-up from pre-school teachers and playleaders. Once again, the importance of the quality of personal relationships is underlined.

3. NEGATIVE REJECTORS OF PROVISION

The third vulnerable group comprises hard-to-reach families of which social workers and health visitors alike were frequently unaware. Like the other mothers we have discussed, they were isolated and felt under considerable strain; but their natural reaction was to turn inwards towards the home. Such mothers want their children about them, even though, at the same time, their energies are depleted and they find difficulty in coping, sometimes to a completely incapacitating extent. When this happens, the mother–child relationship seems, at least for the time being, to be unstable and unhappy. Mothers are often overwhelmed by personal problems and alienated from 'authority' and society. They suffer a degree of strain which distorts their perceptions and can rebound on the children. A striking illustration was that even where money was 'no problem', their apathy resulted in a diet that was irregular, unbalanced, and inadequate. It was not a question of cultural differences, but rather of people who were 'too tired to bother'.

No matter how well equipped an external facility may be and how helpful the professionals within it, these mothers are unlikely to leave the safety of their own homes. Nor will they accept help easily from their neighbours. They did not use any form of pre-school provision; most were not even on the health visitors' lists. They were therefore cut off from helping agencies and, as they presented it, from the support of family and friends.

Research has established the 'disadvantaged' mother as the key figure in many of the most effective pre-school programmes – epitomized in Elizabeth Newson's dictum that 'parents are uniquely knowledgeable, if given techniques and know-how' (Pre-school Playgroup Association, Annual General Meeting, 1972); but this insight is not commonly extended, even in spirit, to some mothers for whom it could be a turning point. The Home Instruction Program for Pre-school Youngsters (HIPPY) in Israel, for example, employs community aides who visit mothers in their homes and show them how to teach their children a variety of enriching activities. This and similar highly successful schemes have been limited to small groups of carefully selected or highly motivated mothers who volunteer to take part. Those mothers who cut themselves off from the community and are struggling with more fundamental issues of their own existence, which prevent them achieving a mutually fulfilling relationship with their children, are vital steps away from wanting to take part in such programmes.

Is there any hope at all of bridging the gap? Some would answer quite categorically that the problems stem mainly from over-taxed congenitally incapable young women who lack the resources to cope adequately with their under fives. The solution, according to this oversimplified analysis, is to remove the children to a more educationally orientated environment from which they will naturally benefit, thereby freeing the mother to take a job or to enjoy some respite from looking after the children full time.

It is a mistake to think that, in their present state, mothers in this group would necessarily want or be able to hold down a job, let alone derive anything like the satisfaction achieved by so many of the articulate protagonists of working women.

This solution also leaves out of account the way mothers view the education system and, in spite of all appearances to the contrary, their strong emotional ties to their children. To expect a mother willingly to deliver her children up to a punishing system from which she has only recently 'escaped' is to invite her to embark on a course of action that will, if successful, inevitably inculcate values not shared by herself and her husband; thus family ties will be eroded rather than strengthened. If 'unsuccessful' her children stand to be as confused and discomforted by the experience as she had been and to end up with a similar lack of confidence and educational skills. Non-utilization of facilities, intuitively viewed from this angle, is not as irrational as it is sometimes made out to be.

Other 'solutions' recognize the need to build up a mother's confidence in her own abilities and to acquire, even belatedly, necessary basic skills before she can seek help or cope with bureaucracy. They also grapple with difficulties for professionals in communicating such skills. The basic problem is diagnosed as one of social distance. Accordingly, local women, often with few formal qualifications but distinguished by having overcome many of the problems thought to overwhelm those they wish to help, are recruited to form small informal groups and to encourage the development of such skills.

Such a strategy is unlikely to be successful with the mothers in this sub-group if, as these studies suggest, they are alienated not only from 'authority' but also from their neighbours – however well disposed. Moreover, local women who have themselves thrived in the system are not necessarily in a strong position to convey the 'techniques and know-how' they have learned. This type of approach assumes that mothers want to be like the 'way-showers', whereas they may have a strong antagonism towards them and what they think they stand for.

For the less vulnerable mothers described in these studies, groupwork of this kind and courses like those provided by the Open University and the Pre-school Playgroups Association make sense. They have been described as offering 'growth, development, excitement, pain, fun, enlightenment, insight – the dynamism of relationship shot through with wisdom, knowledge and a few facts' (Crowe, 1976 : 1). For the most alienated mothers, however, although designed to 'help mothers quicken their sensitivity to children's needs, abilities, developmental limitations and progress as well as to the network of community and family relationships', even 'Appetizer' courses are too threatening and remote. What is needed initially for these mothers is a one-to-one relationship, geared to individuals and circumstances, with confidentiality assured, together with genuine respect between people. They need support which will enhance their self respect, not erode it still further; they need to gain satisfaction from doing things for themselves, not simply to relinquish responsibility to others. Just as disadvantaged children have been found to change in classes conducted by teachers who are 'flexible, naively optimistic, enthusiastically committed and unburdened by traditional occupations and beliefs' (Shore, Milgram, and Malasky, 1971 : 449), so these mothers are more likely to respond to people who are straightforward, who do not disparage but believe in their ability to learn, who project the positive side of their negative attitudes, and who are sufficiently aware not to be manipulated. They need people who are flexible, who have a sense of humour, and are mature enough to accept the emotional drain and a lengthy commitment; people they can trust and accept.

How can such needs be met?

Response in all three study areas suggested that characteristic mistrust of 'authority' placed the professional, however caring and aware, at a disadvantage. In spite of all the pitfalls that attend work with and by volunteers, they have unique strengths and weaknesses which enable them to develop relationships with mothers of a totally different and essentially complementary nature from those of professional and client. Such relationships may help to support and mature the rapport between mother and child to a point where mothers are able to take a more positive approach to the welfare and education of their children. In this way, mothers are not separated from their children either physically or emotionally.

In this respect, work being done in Chile, where 90 per cent of children have no pre-schooling, is interesting. The work of Schlomo Magendzo (1980) recognizes barriers that exist between people who are alienated from 'authority' and 'experts', and those who wish to help them. A number of community projects have led to a model which is particularly successful in motivating parents who are suspicious of authority. Experts and volunteers alike eschew professionalism; they are 'facilitators'. The onus is on parents to take responsibility for developing their own curriculum and evaluating it. The balance of power is shifted to the community.

In a context nearer home, Samaritans have demonstrated that volunteers can work together in an effective and viable national organization. They provide a day and night resource for people at the end of their tether by 'befriending' them on a short or medium term basis to see them through a difficult period. They work with the knowledge and consent of doctors and have other professional support. The crucial distinction, however, is that whereas Samaritan clients normally take the initiative and phone in, mothers in this group are, by definition, unlikely to make the first move.

It is necessary both to find the families and to work towards acceptance before any move to help can be made. Families are unlikely to be referred to existing organizations like Home-Start which would offer exactly the non-judgemental friendships that might help. The essential link, normally the health visitor, is missing. One explanation for families slipping through the doctor – health visitor network could be that since the attachment of health visitors to individual General Practitioners, no one person is responsible for a particular 'patch'. Where families move into a new district, perhaps from an inner city area, without notifying their doctor (assuming they already have one) and do not re-register, and especially if mothers do not go to the clinic or seek out available services, no one officially knows about them.

Nevertheless, the doctor and, by extension, the health visitor were the people most highly regarded and were the ones to whom mothers would 'turn in times of trouble'. This, together with the fact that these were often mothers with several under fives, makes it all the more remarkable that few had seen a health visitor during the previous two years.

According to provisional figures for the Child Health Education Study which followed up 93 per cent of children nationwide born in one week in 1970 (Butler, 1979), there is a drop from 80 per cent of mothers attending baby clinics in the first year to

25 per cent in the third and fourth years. Mothers in the group under discussion may well be among the 20 per cent who do not attend at all.

What this suggests is that volunteers/para-professionals could work within specified small areas, making contact with all mothers of pre-school children on a door-to-door basis. This inevitably raises the question of where support ends and where intrusion begins, and whether, unless it is sought, there is any likelihood that help would be accepted. Some also consider that only a professional is sufficiently knowledgeable to run the risk of contacting 'problem' families; and further, that it is an imposition for strangers to knock on doors indiscriminately without authority.

The crux of the matter lies in the purpose of the call and in the sensitivity and skill of the visitor, together with the relationship she has with others working in the field. Observations made during the course of the studies suggested a valid short-term purpose. General ignorance as to what facilities were available in the neighbourhood and, particularly amongst this group, the ineffectiveness of both the written word and the 'grapevine' as a means of communication indicated that face-to-face contact was necessary. The gradual acceptance of the interviewers over a period of about one year as non-authoritarian, relaxed listeners, with confidentiality assured, suggested that volunteers could ensure that families knew what facilities were available and had a better understanding of what was offered. As independent disseminators of information, they would become known in the neighbourhood; and in proportion to their skill and degree of acceptance would be able to offer informal support where called for. They would aim initially to reach all mothers with pre-school children; they would 'map' the district, being especially attentive to newcomers, to irregular attenders, and to mothers in the group under discussion. It would not be part of their brief to encourage mothers to use any particular type of provision; rather to help bring them to the stage when they could make a rational, informed choice between alternatives. They would make sure that families who needed professional help had access to it; and, more importantly, that many families did not reach the state where such help was needed. They would liaise with health visitors, doctors, social workers, and teachers but would work independently and complement rather than supplement the work of the statutory body.

A fundamental requirement would be that they would accept mothers as they were (people who had not asked for help), without an immediate need to change them or criticize their attitudes. They would need to be able to cope with suspicion, rejection, and frustration. This implies considerable maturity and the need for regular meetings with informed outsiders — a small advisory group — as a safeguard against over-involvement and lack of objectivity. Their preparation and support for the job would ensure they understood its limits and when to call in a professional. It would help them support the overstrained mother, offering practical help and, at the same time, fostering the feeling of being valued and having something acceptable to offer. Volunteers' would need to be able to recognize when a 'depressed' mother needed medical help and when dietary supplements might help her cope. In short, they would be a community based resource, acting as a link for many mothers between the home and the community, helping them extend their interests as well as enjoy their families more.

The example of voluntary organizations such as Samaritans and the Pre-school Playgroups Association, as well as Home-Start and Scope, suggests that suitable recruits could be found and organized. Given appropriate preparation and support, they could help tip the balance towards more positive attitudes and a happier life for mothers and children described in these groups. Numbers involved and expenditure are unlikely to be high; but the well-being of mothers and children would represent a significant advance in family welfare.

Such measures are no substitute for earlier preventive work, however. The youth and backgrounds of parents in this group suggest the need for intervention in schools, clinics, and work places. There is hope that this would be fruitful, but more needs to be known about 'when' and 'how'. Professor Berry Brazelton, for example, speaking at the 1979 Annual Conference of the National Children's Bureau, presented new and convincing evidence. He demonstrated the effectiveness in 'netting relationships' of spending quite brief periods of time with parents of very young babies. Even ten minutes spent with them by an understanding doctor who pays attention to emotional as well as medical needs, may be more valuable than hours of 'intervention' before or after.

Much depends on how it is done. If there is to be any rapprochement between home and school for many families which are our central concern, radical changes in attitude and practice, based on respect for persons whatever their status, are necessary. This applies as much to staff in primary and secondary schools, in hospitals and clinics, as to a playgroup leader or a mother's 'befriender'.

Many mothers are almost certainly identifiable early on in their school careers. Their unhappiness is probably recognizable as increasing disinterest in work, unwillingness to concentrate, resentfulness at being told what to do. These are clear indications that things are going wrong. In contrast to comparable physical symptoms of disease, they are frequently ignored. 'Treatment' is unchanged, except for an expression of official disapproval.

At this early stage, many might benefit from discussion with persons skilled in group work or counselling or possibly from working out thoughts and feelings through drama. This is not a soft option; it is common sense to find out what is going wrong and to develop a trusting relationship between a child, who may well have no adult it feels it can talk to, the family, and a mature person.

Furthermore, if the role of the husband is really a key to helping a mother cope with the physical and mental demands of her pre-school children — as these and other studies suggest — then a major concern of schools should be to deepen understanding of personal values and relationships, as the core of preparation for parenthood.

These recommendations affirm the value and values of the family, as well as the rights of individuals to choose for themselves. They are concerned with the ways in which such rights are eroded by the unalleviated strains on young mothers and draw attention to means, compatible with the present economic climate, of improving a situation in which provision for many families with pre-school children compares unfavourably with that in the European Economic Community.

In conclusion, the message to emerge most clearly from these studies is that if we want services to be acceptable to those mothers who need them most, we have to take account of psychological factors that intervene to prevent take-up of places.

Clearly, more detailed evidence is needed, but at this point it looks as though even if financial resources were available to provide free and splendidly flexible institutionalized provision, the hoped-for goal of reaching over-stressed mothers who lack confidence would not be achieved. This is because the key features which characterize them — their isolation and alienation from 'authority' — override their ability to respond positively to external resources.

To break through barriers built up over years, perhaps where authority has been exercised without warmth or explanation, has implications for immediate pragamatic action and for long-term planning. Increased isolation and stress are, after all, symptomatic of the present age of technological advance. Moreover, dissatisfied school leavers, tomorrows parents, who lack the basic skills to compete in the search for fewer and fewer jobs as well as the emotional stability to cope with social change, are increasing in numbers. Circumstances like theirs are at the very heart of the problem.

APPENDIX 1a

A guide to the data base

The purpose of this appendix is to provide a guide to the data base, so that readers who require more detailed information will know where to find it in the thesis (Shinman, 1978).

General design considerations, instrumentation, and sources of error are discussed on pp. 78–104 ('Hillcroft') and pp. 345–60 ('Higham' and 'Kingswell'). Included in the appendices are the two interview schedules, 'Hillcroft' (containing 200 variables and the Saxby Grid) on pp. 431–73 and for the childminder studies (ninety-six variables) on pp. 516–20, as well as the Rotter I-E Locus of Control Scale (pp. 476–78).

The investigation fell into several stages:

1. Examination of the main sample ('Hillcroft', N = 77) on the basis of mothers' response to newly available pre-school facilities (pp. 179–222). Results are fully tabulated.
2. Analysis of within group differences which led to the development of the Index of Maternal Alienation (IMA) (pp. 223–84).
3. Two follow-up studies to explore further the nature and usefulness of the IMA (pp. 361–88). These monitored the use made by two groups of child-minders (1. N = 32; 2. N = 38) of provision designed to meet their needs.

Analysis in stage 1 was by Chi Square and other non-parametric statistics to establish the basic parameters for study.

Subsequently, in stages 2 and 3, factor analysis was used because, in spite of its known limitations, it seemed at these particular stages in the study, to be an appropriate and powerful tool. It made possible the reduction to manageable proportions of the necessarily large number of variables using a statistical technique, as opposed to personal hunches. It was also a means both of explaining the observed interrelationships in terms of their basic dimensions and of maximizing relationships with criterion variables, so that salient characteristics associated with these criteria were pin-pointed.

The advantages and disadvantages of these strategies, together with details of methods and results are discussed in the text in relation to the general structure of the data (pp. 285–307), to the major groups (pp. 308–22), to the six sub-groups (pp. 323–44) and to 'Higham' and 'Kingswell' (pp. 361–88). A technical account of the use of factor analysis and of the computer package used is to be found in Appendix X. Additional tables, correlation matrices, and hand rotations of factors are given in Appendix VIII.

Since the Index of Maternal Alienation is crucial to the study, its development is outlined here. Readers who require more detail are referred to Chapters V and VII of the thesis.

THE INDEX OF MATERNAL ALIENATION (IMA)

The first stage in development was a cluster analysis, undertaken by hand, in which individual families in Group III (existing users of pre-school provision) were plotted according to their responses on the whole range of ninety variables that showed significant variance. Two by three tables were drawn up to explore the relationship of one variable with another in this small sub-sample.

On inspection, seven variables were isolated as grouping five families who tended to 'clump' together. A principal components analysis of these seven variables suggested that all loaded on one factor, accounting for 83 per cent of the variance. The initial components of the factor suggested that those mothers who scored highly on such a factor were under stress or possibly suffering from some degree of alienation, both from their own family and the community at large.

Analysis showed that the seven variable score, used as a cumulative score, distributed the total sample. Using the median for Group III (12.5) as an arbitrary cutting point for the purpose of further analysis, two major sub-groups were created. Low scorers in all three groups, those who fell to the left of the median, formed one group and all high scorers (those to the right of the median) formed the second group. High scorers were defined not only by their response to the seven key variables, but where also characterized as having made use of provision following intervention of an external agency or of falling away or being spasmodic users of pre-school facilities.

There were no such 'behavioural' criteria for Group I families, but it was clear that high scoring mothers shared stress characteristics with spasmodic and interventionist users.

Subsequent analysis postulated at least four major principles of organization or determinants underlying the data. The 'alienation' factor or IMA was closely allied to one of these. It suggested that the sample could legitimately, as well as meaningfully, be divided into two groups as characterized by the Index of Maternal Alienation.

Key to scores on the Index of Maternal Alienation

1. Q. How do you feel about your neighbours?
   R. Score 1. Very friendly indeed – see them at least two or three times a week – reciprocal visiting – if appropriate, help given with baby sitting, shopping, etc. On first name terms.
   2. Felt themselves to be on 'good terms' with their neighbours – knew them by name, but not usually first names. Greeted them in the street and would be prepared to help in an emergency, but tended to 'keep themselves to themselves'.
   3. Antagonistic towards neighbours – did not know their name – did not greet them in the street, and did not wish to have anything to do with them. 'Does not mix.'

2. Q. How old were you when you married?
   A. Score 1. 22.1 +
   2. 18.1–22
   3. 16–18

3. Q. How do you feel about 'messy' play? (painting, water play, sand, dough).
   A. Score 1. Encourages regular 'messy' play in controlled circumstances – perhaps 'helping mother wash up', playing in the bath or outside in a paddling pool in the summer, having extra pastry/dough to knead and bake . . . taken as a matter of course.
   2. Allowed 'messy' play occasionally and with reluctance – because it was difficult or undesirable in the house, rather than because there was no point in it.
   3. *Either* hypersensitive to anything 'dirty' and too houseproud to allow any form of 'messy play'. 'I'm having none of that in *my* house . . .'
   Or too tired or apathetic to care what sort of play, messy or otherwise her child indulged in. 'Let him get on with it, I say, as long as he doesn't bother me.'

4. Q. How often do you see your family or close friends?
   A. Score 1. 'Daily or at least once or twice a week.' Mothers who were too far from close family for this, but who kept in touch by other means (phone, letter) and who felt they were supported through any difficulties.

2. 'Usually every two weeks or so.' 'Every few months.' 'Whenever we can.' Mother is not in frequent contact, but does not feel cut off. In an emergency, she has someone to whom she can talk and on whom she feels she can rely for help.

3. 'Very seldom' or 'not at all'. Mother feels there is no one on whom she can call for help or to whom she could talk.

5. Q. Do you have any time each day when you can play with X in a relaxed way, without having other things to think about?

A. Score 1. One hour or more daily.

2. Less than one hour.

3. Seldom any time at all.

6. Q. How does X fit into the scheme of things at home?

A. Score 1. For this mother, her child was integrated in the pattern of family life. Responses include remarks like 'He's got to take his turn', and 'He's got to learn he's not the king pin' *as well as* 'We always try and do something he'd like when dad's home'.

2. This mother was more emphatic that her first concern was her child — before herself, husband, or siblings. 'Everything I do, I do for him'; and 'X comes before everyone else'.

3. This mother put her child last. Responses which fell in this category included 'We're not going to let a kid change our lives' or 'I'm not changing my way of doing things for anyone' or 'I sometimes take him with me when I go down the town, but he's a bit of a bind really. He doesn't enjoy it and he spoils my day. Otherwise, I stay in the flat.'

7. The mother–child relationship rating

Score 1: indicated the mother who coped confidently with the interview situation. Perhaps she explained to her child that she 'wanted to talk to the lady for a while' and suggested various occupations or simply cuddled him. She would respond to his questions in a matter-of-fact way, interrupting the conversation with the interviewer when she felt her intervention was called for. When her child was 'naughty', she might slap him or 'tick him off', but she was basically in control of herself and her child. She was more likely to be collaborative ('let's show the lady your bedroom — where you play') then restrictive ('go and play in your bedroom while I'm talking; I can't do with that mess in here'). She would leave the door open so as to give free access and keep an eye on her child if he were playing in an adjoining room. This type of relationship implied an easy, fairly relaxed partnership between mother and child and was the norm for the sample.

Score 2: Mothers categorized in this way fell into two groups: subjects in both were judged 'less mature' than those described in the section above. First, there were those who appeared tense in a new situation, inclined to be over-supportive to the child; for example, giving lengthy and complicated explanations about the tape recorder which were quite beyond the understanding or interest of a three or four year old, yet insisting that he held her hand when going upstairs 'because you might fall'. Such lack of relaxation and confidence seemed to affect the child and there was a sense of strain about the relationship.

Then there was a second group who, while wanting the best for their child, appeared under-supportive and took the quickest way they could to keep the child quiet. One mother, typical in her reaction, seized a handful of iced lollies from the freezer and thrust them upon her son. 'Here you are then!' and, with a sigh, 'That'll keep him quiet'. Soon puddles of melting lollies and sticky fingers demanded her attention; she alternated offers of crisps and biscuits with scolding him for 'making a mess'.

Score 3: These mothers shared some of the characteristics of the 'bribing' mother described above, but their relationship with their child appeared less stable, even tenuous. The mother's needs were divorced from her child; it was a mother in this group, for example, who said that she couldn't be bothered to make a meal most days, even though she knew her child was hungry. Another mother, who said she was not ill, was still in her dressing gown in the afternoon slumped in front of the television with the previous day's pots and pans in the sink; she said that she didn't know where her child was — he'd been out all day, but would turn up sooner or later. Tension for her was evidently reduced if he were elsewhere ('he's not a bad boy; he's out all day — rain or shine').

Glossary of pre-school services

CHILDMINDING

Any person who looks after other people's children in her own home for payment for two hours or more during the day is required to register with the local authority as a childminder and to comply with health and safety regulations (*Health Services and Public Health Act*, 1968). Most local authorities limit a minder to three children under five, including her own. The law is difficult to enforce. Considerable variation exists between local authorities both as to standards expected from childminders and the amount of support afforded them. Childminders nevertheless provide a service for working mothers with children under five at times when no other provision is available for them. Payment is usually agreed between minder and parent, but there is no uniform pattern.

DAY NURSERY

This form of provision is usually run by the local authority Social Services Department and caters for children under five 'in special need', often from single-parent families or referred by welfare services. Parents are means tested. Premises are open all the year round from about 8am to 6pm. Most children attend full-time and are often cared for in family groups. Resources are limited, but most staff are qualified nursery nurses, with some unqualified assistants. Standards regarding accommodation, health care, and play equipment are laid down in the Ministry of Health Circular 37/68. The recommended staff : child ratio is 1 : 4.

Some day nurseries or crèches are provided by private or voluntary organizations, including employers. They may be free or heavily subsidized, but they have to be registered with the local authority.

NURSERY SCHOOL

Nursery schools are provided by local education authorities (free), or by private enterprise, to meet the educational and other needs of children between two and five years of age. There are normally two sessions each day, 9.30am–12 noon and/or 1–3.30pm. Schools are open during term time only (about forty weeks in the year). Attendance may be full or part-time. Staffing standards vary in fee-paying schools, but State nursery schools conform to generally high standards and are staffed by qualified teachers and assistants. The recommended staff : child ratio is 1 : 13. Many schools increasingly try to involve parents, but this is not a universal objective.

NURSERY CLASS

These classes are similar to nursery schools run by a local education authority, but they are attached to primary schools.

PRE-SCHOOL PLAYGROUP

Playgroups are set up outside the statutory provision and aim to give three- and four-year-old children the opportunity to mix with other children, as well as providing them with safe and satisfying play. Such groups are usually run by voluntary organizations or by the mothers themselves. Some are subsidized, some have trained supervisors, and all are registered with a local authority Social Services Department. Groups may meet for two- to three-hour sessions each day during school term time, with a regular leader and assistant(s), but most children attend part time. Fees vary considerably. The recommended staff : child ratio is 1 : 8. Many playgroups are characterized by the extent to which they involve and support parents.

In addition to these main forms of provision, there are a number of other pre-school services for under fives and their families, including the following:

ALL-DAY PLAYGROUPS

In order to meet the demand for day care, some local authorities have encouraged playgroups to lengthen their day from a two and half hour session to last from 9am to 4pm daily throughout the year.

MOTHER AND TODDLER CLUBS

These are run by and for mothers with young children mainly under the age of three. Clubs vary according to local needs and resources, but mothers typically take some responsibility in running a weekly two-hour session. They do not leave their children, even if there is a regular playleader, and consequently there is no need for registration with a local authority. Activities for the children usually include 'messy play' and mothers can sit and chat in the same room as the children. Sessional fees are normally supplemented by fund-raising activities.

ONE O'CLOCK CLUBS

These Mother and Toddler Clubs are found in London. They are free, funded by the Local Authority. Premises are set in an enclosed area in parks or housing estates. Paid staff supervise the children and provide a wide range of indoor and outdoor activities. Mothers do not take responsibility for management, but they can help during sessions if they want to. These clubs are informal and no registers are kept.

DROP-IN CENTRES

As the name implies, these are informal meeting places usually available one to three times a week, often in a church hall or unused schoolroom and sometimes shared with a playgroup. Childminders, and sometimes other mothers with young children, can 'drop in' for as long or short a time as they wish. Such centres provide a social setting for minders and a variety of play opportunities for the children, usually under the guidance of a trained playleader. Centres may be organized and funded by a voluntary association, by the local authority Social Services Department, and/or by a group of minders, or a combination of all three.

FAMILY CENTRES

Flexibility characterizes centres formed by a linked group of facilities. For example, a nursery school, a playgroup, a day nursery, and mother and toddler group are found under the same roof as medical and community resources. There are very few such centres.

References

AMBROSE, A. (ed.) (1969) *Stimulation in Early Infancy*. London and New York: Academic Press Inc.

BARNOMSORGSGRUPPEN (1976) *Forsoksvevksamhet med foraldrautbildning i Vallby, Vasteras*. Lagesrapport II. Stockholm: Departeriuntens Offsetcentral.

BEREITER, C. and ENGELMAN, S. (1966) *Teaching Disadvantaged Children in the Pre-School*. New Jersey: Prentice Hall.

BERNSTEIN, B. (1961) Social Structure, Language and Learning. *Educational Research* 3: 163–76.

_____ (1962) Linguistic Codes, Hesitation Phenomena and Intelligence. *Language and Speech*. No. 5.

_____ (1965) A Socio-linguistic Approach to Social Learning. In J. B. Gould (ed.), *Penguin Survey of the Social Sciences*. Harmondsworth: Penguin.

_____ (1970) Education Cannot Compensate for Society. In D. Rubinstein and C. Stoneman (eds), *Education for Democracy*. Harmondsworth: Penguin.

BETTELHEIM, B. (1971) *Children of the Dream*. St Albans, Herts: Paladin.

BONE, M. (1977) *Pre-School Children and the Need for Day-care*. London: HMSO.

BOWLBY, J. (1951) *Maternal Care and Mental Health*. Geneva: World Health Organisation.

BRADSHAW, J. (1972) The Concept of Social Need. *New Society*. March 30.

BRENT CAMPAIGN FOR NURSERY EDUCATION (1972) *Fair Do's for All*. Information obtainable from Mrs E. Lohr, 27, Mulgrave Rd, London NW10.

BRIMBLECOMBE, F. (1975) Bridging in Health. *Reports of Studies on Health Services for Children*. Oxford: Oxford University Press for Nuffield Hospitals Trust.

BRONFENBRENNER, U. (1972) *Two Worlds of Childhood*. London: George Allen and Unwin.

_____ (1973) *Is Early Education Effective?* Ithica: Cornell University Press.

_____ (1976) Is Early Intervention Effective? In M. Guttentage and E. L. Struenig (eds), *Handbook of Evaluation Research*. London: Sage.

BROWN, G., BHROLCHAIN, M., and HARRIS, T. (1975) Social Class and Psychiatric Disturbance Among Women in an Urban Population. *Sociology*, May.

BROWN, G. and HARRIS, T. (1978) *The Social Origins of Depression*. London: Tavistock Publications.

BULLOUGH, B. (1972) Poverty, Ethnic Identity and Preventive Health-Care. *Journal of Health and Social Behaviour* 13 (4) December.
BUTLER, N. F. (1979) Paper presented on unpublished data from 'Child Health and Education in the Seventies' study, Bristol University, Dept of Child Health, at World Organisation for Early Childhood Education Conference, Leicester Polytechnic, April 12.

CASLER, L. (1961) *Maternal Deprivation: A Critical Review of the Literature. Monograph of the Society for Research into Child Development* 26 (2).
_____ (1968) Perceptual Deprivation in Institutional Settings. In G. Newton and S. Levine (eds), *Early Experience and Behaviour*. Springfield, Illinois: C. C. Thomas.
CLARKE, A. and CLARKE, A. D. B. (1976) *Early Experience, Myth and Evidence*. London: Open Books Publishing Ltd.
COATES, K. and SILBURN, R. (1970) *Poverty: the Forgotten Englishmen*. Harmondsworth: Penguin.
COHEN, L. and BAGSHAW, D. (1973) A Comparison of the Achievements of Nursery School and Non-Nursery School Children. *Durham Research Review*. No. 30.
COHEN, M. L. (1964) Social Class and Parent–Child Relationships. In F. Riesman, J. Cohen, and A. Pearl (eds), *Mental Health of the Poor*. New York: The Free Press.
COMMITTEE ON CHILD HEALTH SERVICES (1976) *The Court Report – Fit for the Future*. London: HMSO.
COMMUNITY RELATIONS COMMISSION (1975) *Who Minds? A Study of Working Mothers and Childminding in Ethnic Minority Communities*. Reference and Technical Services Division, 15–16 Bedford Street, London WC2.
CROWE, B. (1974) *The Playgroup Movement*. London: George Allen & Unwin.
_____ (1976) *Training and Courses*. Unpublished PPA Paper.

DAVID, M. and APPELL, G. (1966) Mother–Child Relations. In J. G. Howells (ed.), *Modern Perspectives in International Child Psychiatry*. London: Oliver and Boyd.
_____ (1969) Mother–Child Interaction and its Impact on the Child. In J. A. Ambrose (ed.), *Stimulation in Early Infancy*. New York: Academic Press.
DEPARTMENT OF HEALTH AND SOCIAL SECURITY and DEPARTMENT OF EDUCATION AND SCIENCE (1976) *Low Cost Provision for the Under-Fives*. London: HMSO.

EDUCATION WHITE PAPER (1972) *A Framework for Expansion*. London: HMSO.
ELSE, M. (1969) *Pre-School Playgroups and Social Networks*. Unpublished thesis, University of Sussex.
ENAG REPORT (1972) *Working Class Mothers and Nursery Education*. Newcastle.
EQUAL OPPORTUNITIES COMMISSION (1978) *I Want to Work, But What About the Kids*. Manchester: Equal Opportunities Commission.

FERRI, E. (1976) *Growing up in a One-Parent Family*. A National Children's Bureau Report. Slough: National Foundation for Education Research.

FERRI, E. with NIBLETT, R. (1977) *Disadvantaged Families and Play-groups*. A National Children's Bureau Report. Slough: NFER.

GENERAL ASSEMBLY OF THE UNITED NATIONS (November 20, 1979) *Declaration of the Rights of the Child*.

GITTUS, E. (1976) *Flats, Families and the Under Fives*. London: Routledge & Kegan Paul.

GRAVES, NANCY B. (1969) City, Country and Child Bearing in Three Cultures. Cited in J. Bruner, Poverty and Childhood. Paper presented at the Annual Citation Award of the Merill-Palmer Inst., Detroit, Michigan, June 9, 1970. University of Colorado, Inst. of Behavioural Sciences.

HAGGSTROM, W. (1964) The Power of the Poor. In F. Riesman, J. Cohen, and A. Pearl (eds), *Mental Health of the Poor*. New York: Free Press.

HALSEY, A. H. (ed.) (1972) *Educational Priority. Vol. I. E.P.A. Problems and Policies*. London: HMSO.

____ (1980) Education Can Compensate. *New Society*, January 24.

HANNON, P. (1978) Minders of our Future? *New Society*. May 11.

HANSARD (1978) Vol. 950 : 121. London: HMSO.

HARLOW, H. F. (1961) The Development of Affectional Patterns in Infant Monkeys. In B. M. Foss (ed.), *Determinants of Infant Behaviour*. Vol. II. London: Methuen.

HARLOW, H. F. and ZIMMERMAN, R. (1959) Affectional Responses in Infant Monkeys. *Science* 130: 432-42.

____ (1966) Maternal Influences upon Early Learning and Cognitive Environment of Urban Pre-school Children. In R. D. Hess and R. M. Bear (eds), *Early Education*. Chicago: Aldine.

HESS, R. D. and SHIPMAN, V. C. The Cognitive Environment of Pre-school Children. Chicago: Graduate School of Education, University of Chicago.

HOGGART, R. (1957) *The Uses of Literacy*. London: Chatto & Windus.

HOLMES, T. H. and RATHE, R. H. (1967) The Social Readjustment Rating Scale. *Journal of Psychosomatic Research* II: 213.

HOME-START (n.d.) c/o Leicestershire Council for Voluntary Services, 32, de Montfort St, Leicester LE1 7GD.

HUNT, A. (1968) *A Survey of Women's Employment*. London: HMSO and Government Social Survey.

JACKSON, B. and JACKSON, S. (1979) *Childminder. A Study in Action Research*. London: Routledge & Kegan Paul.

JEPHCOTT, P. (1971) Homes in High Flats. *University of Glasgow Social and Economic Studies*. Paper No. 13. Edinburgh: Oliver Boyd.

JOSEPH, A. and PARFIT, J. (1972) *Pre-School Playgroups in an Area of Special Need*. National Children's Bureau Report. Slough: NFER.

JOSEPH, K. (1972) Speech to Pre-school Playgroups Association. Annual General Meeting, June 29.

KAGAN, J. (1979) *The Growth of the Child*. Brighton: Harvester Press.

KARNES, M. B. (1968) *Final Report: Research & Development Program on Pre-school Disadvantaged Children*. Urbana, Illinois: Institute for Research of Exceptional Children.

KATZ, L. G. (1980) Mothering and Teaching: Some Significant Distinctions. In L. G. Katz, *et al.* (eds), *Current Topics in Early Childhood Education. Vol. III*. Norwood, New Jersey: Ablex.

KELLMER-PRINGLE, M. (1973) The Pre-School Comprehensive. *Where?* June : 165.

____ (1979) Putting Children First. *Concern* (33). London: National Children's Bureau.

KESSEN, W. (ed.) (1975) *Childhood in China*. New Haven: Yale University Press.

LOCAL AUTHORITY ASSOCIATIONS' STUDY (1977) *Under Fives*. London: Association of County Councils, Association of Metropolitan Authorities.

LEWIS, O. (1961) *The Children of Sanchez*. New York: Random House.

____ (1965) *La Vida: a Puerto Rican Family in the Culture of Poverty*. New York: Random House.

LOMBARD, A. (1974) *Home Instruction Program for Pre-School Youngsters* (HIPPY). School of Education, Hebrew University, Jerusalem.

LONDON COUNCIL OF SOCIAL SERVICES (1977) *Childminding in London, a Study of Support Services for Childminders*. London: LCSS.

MAGENDZO, S. (1980) *Dialogical Approach to Non-formal Pre-school Education*. Paper presented at the International Congress on Early Childhood Education, Tel Aviv, Israel.

MAIZELS, J. (1961) *Two to Five in High Flats*. London: Rowntrees Housing Centre Trust.

MARSDEN, D. (1969) *Mothers Alone*. London: Allen Lane, Penguin Press.

MAYALL, B. and PETRIE, P. (1977) *Mother, Minder and Child*. London: University Institute of Education.

MCKINLAY, J. B. and MCKINLAY, S. M. (1972) Some Social Characteristics of Lower Working Class Utilizers and Underutilizers of Maternity Care Services. *Journal of Health and Social Behaviour* 13 (4) December.

MEAD, M. (1954) Some Theoretical Considerations of the Problem of Mother, Child Separation. In *American Journal of Orthopsychiatry* XXIV July.

____ (1962) A Cultural Anthropologist's Approach to Maternal Deprivation. In *Deprivation of Maternal Care: a Re-assessment of its Effects*. Geneva: World Health Organisation.

MIDWINTER, E. (1972) *Projections. An Educational Priority Area at Work*. London: Ward Lock Educational.

MILLER, G. W. (1971) *Educational Opportunity and the Home*. Harlow: Longman.

MOSS, P., TIZARD, J., and CROOK, J. (1973) Families and their Needs. *New Society*, March 22.

MOORE, S. G. (1978) The Persistence of Pre-School Effects: A National Collaborative Study. *Young Children* 33 (3) : 65–7, March. National Ass. for the Educ. of Young Children, 1834 Connecticut Ave, N.W. Washington D.C. 20009.

NATIONAL EDUCATIONAL RESEARCH AND DEVELOP-MENT TRUST, CHILDMINDING RESEARCH AND DEVELOPMENT UNIT (1974) *Action Register, No. 2.* As at November 1, 1974. Available from 32, Trumpington St, Cambridge.

―――― (1976) *Action Register, No. 3.* As at November 1, 1975. Available as above.

NATIONAL LABOUR WOMEN'S ADVISORY COMMITTEE (1966) *Labour Women's National Survey into Care of Children.* London.

NATIONAL UNION OF TEACHERS (1974) *Provision for Pre-School Education.* London: Ward Lock Educational.

NEWSON, J. and NEWSON, E. (1968) *Four Years Old in an Urban Community.* London: George Allen & Unwin.

―――― (1976) In M. Shipman (ed.), *The Organisation and Impact of Social Research.* London: Routledge & Kegan Paul.

NIR, N. and TICK, T. (1973) *Kedmah* (Parent–Teacher Discussion Groups). Research Report No. 172. Publication No. 525. The Henrietta Zold Institute, Jerusalem.

OFFICE OF POPULATION CENSUSES AND SURVEY (1976) Day Care for Pre-School Children: Uses and Preferences. In, *Low Cost Day Provision for the Under Fives.* Sunningdale Conference Paper. London: Department of Health and Social Security.

OSBORN, A. F. (1975) *The Demand for Pre-School Provision.* Dept. of Child Health Research Unit in conjunction with Somerset PPA (unpublished).

PLOWDEN REPORT (1967) *Children and their Primary Schools.* London: Central Advisory Council for Education and HMSO.

POLLAK, M. (1972) *Today's Three Year Olds in London.* Lavenham, England: William Heinemann Spastics International Medical Publications.

POULTON, G. A. and JAMES, T. (1975) *Pre-School Learning in the Community: Strategies for Change.* London: Routledge & Kegan Paul.

PRE-SCHOOL PLAYGROUPS ASSOCIATION (1972a) *A Play-group in a High Need Area.* Unpublished Report. London: Alford House, Aveline St, London SE11 5DH.

―――― (1972b) *Analysis of Housegroups.* Unpublished Report. London.

―――― (1974) A Quarter of a Million Pre-School Children. *Facts and Figures about Playgroups.* March.

―――― (1978) *Facts and Figures about Playgroups, 1977.* London.

―――― (1979) *Facts and Figures about Playgroups, 1978.* London.

―――― (in press) *Patterns of Oversight and Support for Playgroups.* London.

RICHMAN, N. (1974) The Effects of Housing on Pre-School Children and their Mothers. *Developmental Medicine and Child Neurology.* **16**: 53–8.

ROTTER, J. (1966) Generalized Expectancies for Internal Versus External Control of Reinforcement. *Psychological Monographs* **80** (609).

RUTTER, M. (1972) *Maternal Deprivation Re-assessed*. Harmondsworth: Penguin Books.

SAXBY, P. J. (1973) *Playgroups and Parental Involvement*. Unpublished report. Moorhaven: Devon PPA

SCHOOLS COUNCIL (1972) *Study of Nursery Education* (Working Paper 41). London: Evans/Methuen Educational.

SCOPE (n.d.) The Firs, Beacon Rd, West End, Southampton.

SEEBOHM REPORT (1968) *Report of the Committee on Local Authority and Allied Personal Services*. London: HMSO.

SHINMAN, S. M. (1978) *Pre-School Facilities; Some Factors Affecting Demand and Utilization*. Ph.D. Thesis, Brunel University (S 525). British Lending Library No. D7783/78.

SHORE, M. F., MILGRAM, N. A., MALASKY, C. (1971) The Effectiveness of an Enrichment Program for Disadvantaged Young Children. *American Journal of Orthopsychiatry* **41** (3) April.

SKEELS, H. M. (1966) Adult Status of Children with contrasting Early Life Experiences: A Follow-up Study. *Child Development Monograph*. Vol. 31(3). Chicago: University of Chicago Press and Society for Research in Child Development.

SMITH, G. and JAMES, T. (1975) The Effects of Pre-School Education: Some American and British Evidence. *Oxford Review of Education* **1** (3).

SOCIAL SURVEYS (Gallup Poll) (1979) Commissioned by *Woman's Own* Magazine. February.

SOUTHWARK COMMUNITY PROJECT (1972) *Study of Save the Children Fund Playgroups in Southwark*. Unpublished.

TIZARD, B. (1975) *Early Childhood Education – A Review and Discussion of Research in Britain*. London: Social Science Research Council, Educational Research Board.

TIZARD, J. (1978) Address to the London Childminder—Workers Group. Kensington Town Hall, December 8.

TIZARD, J., MOSS, P. and PERRY, J. (1976) *All Our Children: Pre-School Services in a Changing Society*. London: Maurice Temple Smith in association with *New Society*.

TOWNSEND, P. (1979) *Poverty in the United Kingdom*. Harmondsworth: Penguin Books.

TURNER, I. (1977) *Pre-School Playgroup Research and Evaluation Project*. Report submitted to DHSS in Northern Ireland. Available on Inter-library loan from the Queens University, Belfast.

VAN DER EYKEN, W. (1978a) *Under Five in Liverpool*. An unpublished commentary on a survey of 1,000 families in four areas of the City of Liverpool undertaken by the Liverpool Institute of Higher Education, in conjection with PRIORITY, and directed by Martin Bradley.

—— (1978b) The Politics of Day Care. *Where?* (137): 102–105.

WEDGE, P, and PROSSER, H. (1973) *Born to Fail*. London: Arrow Books in association with the National Children's Bureau.

WHITE, B. L., KABAN, B., SHAPIRO, B., and ATTANUCCI, J. (1976) *Competence and Experience*. Mimeo. Graduate School of Education, Harvard University.

WHITE, B. L. and WATTS, J. C. (1973) *Experience and Environment*. Vol. 1. New Jersey: Prentice Hall.

WILLMOTT, P. and CHALLIS, L. (1977) *The Groveway Project: An Experiment in Salaried Childminding*. London: Department of the Environment.

WILSON, H. and HERBERT, G. W. (1978) *Parents and Children in the Inner City*. London: Routledge & Kegan Paul.

WOODHEAD, M. (1976) *Intervening in Disadvantage – A Challenge for Nursery Education*. Slough: NFER.

WORLD HEALTH ORGANISATION EXPERT COMMITTEE ON MENTAL HEALTH (1951) *Report on the Second Session*. Geneva: World Health Organisation.

YUDKIN, S. and HOLME, A. (1963) *Working Mothers and their Children. A Study for the Council of Children's Welfare*. London: Michael Joseph.

Name index

Subject index